# Praise for *Integrative DBT for Complex Trauma Recovery*

"Lane Pederson has created a compelling and highly practical approach to trauma treatment that bridges the gap between theory and real-world clinical care. This is a meaningful contribution to the evolving field of trauma recovery."

—**Frank Anderson, MD,** internationally renowned trauma expert and author of *Transcending Trauma and To Be Loved*

"Complex PTSD can be a very challenging condition to treat. In *Integrative DBT for Complex Trauma Recovery*, expert DBT teacher Dr. Lane Pederson builds on his extensive clinical experience and deep understanding of psychological research to integrate a practical trauma treatment approach with the solid foundation of DBT.

Through the five modules of the Dialectical Trauma Recovery Model (DTRM), Dr. Pederson provides clinicians with clear explanations, memorable teaching strategies, practical tools, and vivid clinical vignettes that bring the concepts to life. With an emphasis on real-world application, this book helps clients find the dialectical balance of acceptance and change across the emotional, cognitive, physiological, relational, and developmental dimensions of trauma.

No matter what clinical population you serve, this book offers valuable insights and practical interventions that can enhance your work. I highly recommend it for therapists seeking an organized, skills-based approach to trauma recovery."

—**Richard Sears, PsyD,** psychologist and author of *ACT with Anxiety* and *Cognitive Behavioral Therapy & Mindfulness Toolbox*

"Lane Pederson cuts through the noise in trauma treatment with a model that is both grounded and usable. *Integrative DBT for Complex Trauma Recovery* offers clinicians a clear way to understand what's happening for clients and what to do about it. The strength of this work lies in its integration. Rather than adding another competing model, Pederson brings together key ideas in a way that prioritizes client outcomes, therapeutic flexibility, and real-world effectiveness. If you are looking for a trauma approach that makes sense in the room and helps people actually get better, this book delivers."

—**Barry L. Duncan, PsyD,** CEO, Better Outcomes Now, and coauthor of *The Heart and Soul of Change*

"Pederson's model is a practical, accessible extension of DBT skills into trauma work—well-organized, ready to use from the first session, and refreshingly clear about prioritizing stabilization over exposure. An essential resource for clinicians grounding their trauma practice in skills."

—**Linda Curran, BCPC, LPC, CACD, CCDPD,** author of *101 Trauma-Informed Interventions* and *Trauma Competency*

"Few clinicians have done more to expand the practical application of DBT than Lane Pederson. As a practitioner, trainer, author, and innovator, he has consistently pushed the field forward while remaining grounded in what works for real clients. *Integrative DBT for Complex Trauma Recovery* may be his most significant contribution yet, offering clinicians a clear and actionable framework for treating complex trauma with precision, compassion, and effectiveness."

—**Mark Carlson, PsyD, LP,** cofounder, Mental Health Systems, Inc., and author of *CBT for Chronic Pain and Psychological Well-Being* and *CBT for Psychological Well-Being in Cancer*

# Integrative DBT for Complex Trauma Recovery

## A Skills-Based Guide for Treating Emotional, Cognitive, Somatic, and Relational Dysregulation

Lane Pederson, PsyD, LP, DBTC

INTEGRATIVE DBT FOR COMPLEX TRAUMA RECOVERY



Published by
PESI Publishing, Inc.
3839 White Ave
Eau Claire, WI 54703

Cover and interior design by Abby Isackson
Editing by Jenessa Jackson, PhD

ISBN 9781683739302 (print)
ISBN 9781683739319 (ePUB)
ISBN 9781683739326 (ePDF)


Printed in the United States of America.

Lane Pederson, PsyD, LP, C-DBT, is not affiliated or associated with Marsha M. Linehan, PhD, ABPP, or her organizations.

PESI Publishing
pesipublishing.com

# Dedication

For the survivors who continue moving toward healing, and for the thinkers and clinicians whose wisdom illuminated the paths ahead, one of which grew into the Dialectical Trauma Recovery Model.

# Table of Contents

# Preface

I am, and always have been, a dialectical behavior therapy (DBT) therapist. My name is Dr. Lane Pederson, and if you've come across my books, trainings, or clinical work, you probably know that my approach to DBT has always reached beyond the boundaries of the original standard model.

From the beginning, I've viewed DBT not as a fixed model but as a flexible and evolving framework that must adapt to the real-world needs of clients and treatment settings. As such, I've never subscribed to the notion that rigid treatment fidelity is *the* guiding principle in applying the approach. Indeed, I've seen how strict adherence has ossified the approach for many therapists and, unfortunately, their clients.

Instead, I practice, write about, and train others from the perspective of evidence-based practice in psychology (EBPP) as defined by the American Psychological Association (2006). EBPP represents the *dialectical* integration of research evidence with clinical expertise, guided by the culture, characteristics, and preferences of clients. In other words, it's about customizing the approach to the needs of clients. Along with customizing treatment to the client, EBPP calls for collecting clinical outcomes at the local level, also called practice-based evidence, which is the *only* indicator of clinical effectiveness.[1]

This commitment to personalization and customization aligns with the common factors of therapy, which emphasize the therapeutic relationship, client engagement, and shared understanding as central drivers of change, regardless of the specific model used. Indeed, "common" therapeutic factors can only be applied one client at a time. Further, in my experience, the boundaries between treatment frameworks often blur, revealing significant overlap in both principles and outcomes. So while DBT remains my clinical home base, I'm consistently drawn to technical assimilation and integration, guided by what works best for the client, wherever it originates.

At my clinics in Minnesota—Mental Health Systems Inc. (MHS)—we've developed DBT programming that is responsive to real-world clinical needs and tailored to diagnostic complexity, level of care, and client readiness. Historically, these programs have emphasized stage 1 of DBT: stabilization and behavioral control. Like many DBT providers who focus on acute stabilization, we did not directly address trauma, as this work has been traditionally reserved for stage 2 and conducted in individual sessions, often incorporating protocols like prolonged exposure or eye movement desensitization and reprocessing (EMDR).

Yet I noticed something important in our stage 1 work: Clients diagnosed with posttraumatic stress disorder (PTSD) who gained traction with stage 1 skills often showed significant decreases in trauma

1 Those promoting treatment fidelity and rigid manualization falsely conflate the results of randomized clinical trials (RCTs) with real-world outcomes. Research subjects, which are carefully selected, are not identical to clients with a complexity of human factors who are seen in real-world practice. Further, as the internal validity of a study increases, its external validity (generalizability) decreases. Therefore, the only way to know the clinical outcome of a case is to measure it in clinical practice.

symptoms, even without targeting those symptoms directly. This ongoing observation planted a seed that would grow in a meaningful way.

In 2023, I was awarded a Department of Justice contract to develop DBT curricula for the Federal Bureau of Prisons (BOP), including a DBT Trauma Treatment Program. The challenge was clear: The BOP has limited resources, faces high clinical acuity and need, and requires trauma interventions that are group based, have a low risk for retraumatization, and are effective within inherently invalidating and triggering environments. People in custody often live in the fire of trauma, continually surrounded by the potential for reactivation and reexposure, so the approach had to offer healing without asking them to walk through fire again and again.

To meet this challenge, I began where I always do: with the literature and clinical wisdom, all informed by client experience. I filtered the available research evidence through years of seeing how DBT skills reduced trauma symptoms even when trauma wasn't the explicit target. Then I built an evidence-based program rooted in that research and focused on what works for clients.

As I developed this trauma program for the BOP, I simultaneously launched a trauma program at my clinics following the same emerging methods. The results were remarkable in that it quickly became the fastest-growing program in our twenty-three-year history. Clients embraced it. They told us it was validating, practical, straightforward, and effective.

This new DBT approach is a targeted means of applying DBT skills to trauma work that's accessible, teachable, actionable, and grounded in the real lives of those we serve. Along the way, the mission evolved, and this manual expands that work and takes it to the next level. What began as a specific project became a larger purpose:

- To integrate and simplify trauma treatment, connecting core theoretical ideas with real-world practice
- To make the approach skills based, immediately useful, and empowering to clients
- And to develop a model that is effective, validating, and widely accessible

In this process, I began to look beyond DBT's biosocial theory and became increasingly interested in how many major trauma theories converge. Whether viewed through the lens of somatic experiencing, polyvagal theory, EMDR, attachment theory, cognitive models, or other perspectives, a core pathology remains consistent: some form or combination of *dysregulation* (emotional, cognitive, somatic, or relational) coupled with some form or combination of *invalidation* (be it from the self, others, or society itself).

To me, unifying these theories based on their commonalities is not only logical; it's clinically essential. Research is clear that effective treatment requires a shared understanding between therapist and client, namely a common language and rationale that fosters the mutual buy-in that guides action. The integrative DBT model presented herein provides this clarity, structure, and direction.

Teaching DBT skills that have been reimagined for trauma work—skills that help clients regulate themselves, manage triggers, and build lives worth living, all within a validating therapeutic environment—just makes sense. It also aligns with the least invasive treatment principle, which often mirrors client preferences: Do what works, and do no harm. This approach empowers clients and gives them agency without the significant risk of decompensating them or driving them into early dropout without clinical gains.

I have always believed that the best therapists make the complex more simple, not the other way around. When things get confusing, we return to the foundations. And we don't need to put people through unnecessary distress if there's a better way forward. We don't need to walk clients through the fire over and over when we can provide the means to extinguish it in a skills-based manner and use the warmth that remains to germinate growth. (And yes, that's a real thing: In the aftermath of a forest fire, the soil becomes rich in nutrients, the sunlight reaches new ground, and dormant seeds sprout. That's not just poetic, it's ecological science. And it's trauma recovery.)

And why DBT skills? Because they were never exclusive to DBT in the first place. They were drawn from diverse evidence-based therapies, and they translate seamlessly across treatment approaches. And in a nutshell, DBT skills offer a shared language between client and therapist to facilitate in-the-moment change and build long-term recovery. There has been no need for a new wheel, only a reimagined one.

So here it is.

The *Dialectical Trauma Recovery Model (DTRM)*, which makes trauma treatment more understandable, practical, and effective—both for clinicians and for the people who deserve to heal and live more fulfilling, satisfying lives: our clients.

—Dr. Lane Pederson

# Introduction to the Dialectical Trauma Recovery Model

*Complex trauma* refers to repeated and prolonged exposure to overwhelming, and often interpersonal, traumatic experiences where safety and escape aren't possible. This includes experiences such as abuse, neglect, captivity, and systemic oppression (Ford & Courtois, 2020; Herman, 1992). Unlike single-incident trauma, complex trauma unfolds over time. It disrupts development and identity formation, impairing an individual's ability to regulate their emotions, feel connected to their body, trust others, and make meaning of their experiences. It causes an enduring pattern of dysregulation across multiple biopsychosocial systems, frequently emerging as chronic distress, somatic symptoms, dissociation, and entrenched maladaptive beliefs about the self and the world (van der Kolk, 2014).

Research suggests that many clients seeking trauma treatment present with complex trauma histories rather than single-incident events (Ford & Courtois, 2020; Felitti et al., 1998; van der Kolk et al., 2005). These clients often display overlapping symptoms of emotional, cognitive, somatic, and relational dysregulation—symptoms that are rooted in cumulative exposure to harm, often during critical developmental periods.

For this reason, the treatment of trauma demands more than sensitivity, theoretical alignment, or reliance on borrowed therapeutic techniques. It requires a model that accounts for the complexity of trauma's impact while offering clinicians and clients a clear and structured path toward recovery. The *Dialectical Trauma Recovery Model (DTRM)* was created in direct response to the limitations of existing paradigms, particularly the fragmented application of skills, the gaps between theory and practice, and the insufficient integration of psychological, physiological, and behavioral dimensions in trauma care.

Contemporary trauma science has convincingly demonstrated that trauma is not defined solely by the precipitating event itself but by its enduring effects across systems of regulation. In particular, it is a disruption that compromises emotional stability, cognitive processing, somatic awareness, neurological organization, meaning making, memory, interpersonal functioning, and identity development (Herman, 1992; Porges, 2011; van der Kolk, 2014). Clinically, trauma is less a single wound and more a disruption of entire regulatory systems, sending ripples through domains that support functioning, resilience, and recovery. Therefore, DTRM views trauma through an integrated systems lens, recognizing that we must address multiple areas of dysregulation to restore balance and coherence.

DTRM's approach is consistent with the evolving field of trauma recovery, which increasingly emphasizes the need for integrative frameworks that bring coherence to these complex disruptions. Recent developments in trauma science call for models that unify bottom-up and top-down interventions, aligning neurobiological, cognitive, and relational mechanisms of change (Ford & Courtois, 2020; Lanius et al., 2020). Despite this growing consensus, trauma treatment remains fragmented in practice, and no single "gold standard" approach adequately addresses the full scope of trauma's effects (Cloitre et al., 2011; Wampold, 2010). Many existing treatment models focus too heavily on exposure to traumatic material, overlook stabilization and skills building, or split care across approaches that are not well integrated. While each treatment model offers valuable insights, few provide clinicians with a cohesive framework that they can apply consistently across diverse presentations of trauma.

DTRM bridges this gap by offering an integrated, phase-based trauma treatment model grounded in a unified theory of trauma, which conceptualizes trauma not as a singular disorder but as systemic disruptions across *multiple* systems of regulation, resulting in emotional, cognitive, physiological, relational, and developmental consequences. Rather than focusing on narrative exposure or reprocessing, DTRM prioritizes stabilization and functional regulation in the present moment. Grounded in DBT's dialectical philosophy, the model allows for both *acceptance* of survival-based adaptations and *change* through skill acquisition and practices that support nervous system regulation.

The model integrates the five DBT modules—dialectics, mindfulness, distress tolerance, emotion regulation, and interpersonal effectiveness—to *specifically* target regulation across mind, body, behavior, and relationships. Mindfulness skills teach clients how to anchor their awareness in the present and support regulation across all systems while also being foundational to the practice of other skills. Distress tolerance skills stabilize their nervous system and expand their capacity to remain grounded under stress. Emotion regulation skills help clients create predictability by attending to vulnerability factors, engaging in behavioral activation, and practicing consistent self-care. Interpersonal effectiveness skills reestablish safety and reciprocity following relational harm, while dialectics fosters synthesis and flexibility, helping clients hold both acceptance of what *was* and hope for what can *be*. Together, these complementary processes create safety, stabilization, and integration (Herman, 1992; International Society for the Study of Trauma and Dissociation, 2011) while minimizing the risk of retraumatization.

Yet importantly, DTRM is not merely "DBT informed," a term often used to describe partial or superficial applications of DBT principles outside their theoretical context. Nor is it simply "trauma informed," a useful orientation for safety and sensitivity but insufficient as a treatment protocol. Rather, DTRM is a comprehensive trauma recovery model with a clear theoretical foundation, actionable skills, a clinical structure, and outcome-oriented goals. In short, it represents a full-fledged theoretical orientation designed for the treatment of trauma.

## Theoretical Foundations

DTRM expands directly from Linehan's (1993a) biosocial theory, which proposes that emotional dysregulation emerges from the transactional relationship between individual vulnerabilities and invalidating environments. This framework provides an elegant starting point for understanding trauma as the reciprocal influence between *dysregulation* and *invalidation*—forces that appear across nearly all major trauma theories and treatments.

Across theoretical traditions, these twin forces consistently emerge as the core mechanisms through which trauma becomes entrenched. Whether described as shattered assumptions (Janoff-Bulman, 1992), broken attachment (Bowlby, 1988), disrupted neuroception (Porges, 2011), or thwarted integration (Herman, 1992; van der Kolk, 2014), the same dynamic repeats: Overwhelming internal experiences occur in environments that cannot recognize, contain, or repair them. Across models, these forces serve as shared denominators that explain both how trauma persists and how recovery unfolds: through reregulation and validation.

DTRM organizes these insights within a single, coherent clinical framework that is both explanatory and actionable. It builds on the biosocial theory, broadening its focus beyond emotional dysregulation into a unified theory of trauma. This unified theory views trauma as emerging from the interactions between biological vulnerabilities—both innate and caused by trauma—and invalidating environments, leading to pervasive patterns of dysregulation across multiple interrelated domains. In this way, DTRM extends far beyond DBT's original focus on emotional dysregulation, identifying eleven areas of dysregulation grouped into five systems.[2] In doing so, it illustrates how trauma disrupts regulation across the entire mind-body network.[3]

---

2 The theory also includes a supplementary twelfth domain related to therapists' own need to remain regulated, both to be effective in this work and to protect their own well-being. We will discuss this additional domain in chapter 1.

3 While DTRM defines eleven primary domains across five interdependent systems, several related forms of dysregulation—such as existential or transpersonal, moral, social/systemic, identity, attachment, temporal, and metacognitive—are also recognized within the broader trauma literature. These constructs are conceptually integrated within existing DTRM domains (e.g., meaning and belief, relational, developmental) rather than presented as stand-alone categories. A discussion of these additional forms appears in the appendix.

## The Five Systems and Eleven Domains

### I. Mind and Meaning System

These domains reflect the higher-order processes that shape perception, emotion, and interpretation. They form the mind's central regulatory network, determining how people's experiences are felt, understood, and integrated into their identity.

1. **Emotional dysregulation:** Instability, intensity, or suppression of emotions that overwhelm adaptive control
2. **Cognitive dysregulation:** Rigid, distorted, or intrusive thinking patterns that perpetuate distress, are disconnected from reality, and impair attention and concentration
3. **Meaning and belief dysregulation:** Trauma-shaped distortions in worldview, morality, and identity-based meaning making (e.g., "I'm broken," "The world is unsafe")

### II. Body-Based System

These domains represent trauma's imprint on the nervous system and body, leading to physiological states of threat, tension, and disconnection that persist long after the danger has passed.

4. **Nervous system dysregulation:** Autonomic imbalance manifesting as chronic fight, flight, freeze, or collapse (not fawn) responses[4]
5. **Somatic dysregulation:** Physical tension, pain, and body-holding patterns that embody traumatic memory and defensive states
6. **Interoceptive dysregulation:** Misreading or disconnecting from internal bodily cues such as hunger, fatigue, or safety signals

### III. Consciousness and Memory System

These domains capture how trauma fragments awareness, distorts time, and disrupts a coherent self-narrative.

7. **Dissociative dysregulation:** Detachment, depersonalization, or derealization that fragments awareness and narrows consciousness under perceived threat

---

4 The popular "four F's" framework groups fight, flight, freeze, and fawn together as if they were equivalent survival responses. In DTRM, these patterns are organized more precisely according to the systems that generate them. Fight, flight, freeze, and collapse are autonomic nervous system reflexes: rapid, involuntary survival reactions driven primarily by brainstem and subcortical circuitry. These responses mobilize or immobilize the body without conscious intention and therefore belong within the nervous system domain of the Body-Based System.

Fawn, by contrast, is not an autonomic reflex but a relational appeasement strategy shaped by attachment learning and interpersonal history. It emerges when safety depends not on physical defense but on pleasing, accommodating, or staying attuned to another person's needs. This pattern relies on the social engagement system and reflects relationally conditioned adaptations to danger. For this reason, DTRM places fawning within the relational domain of the Action and Connection System. Distinguishing these patterns allows clinicians to intervene with far greater accuracy, targeting autonomic defenses with bottom-up regulation and relational adaptations with skills that restore boundaries, assertiveness, and connection.

8. **Memory dysregulation:** Trauma-associated difficulties with recall and fragmented autobiographical memory that reinforce suffering and disrupt continuity of identity

### IV. Action and Connection System

These domains describe how dysregulation manifests behaviorally and relationally, where internal chaos becomes visible through avoidance, conflict, or withdrawal.

9. **Behavioral dysregulation:** Impulsive, avoidant, or self-defeating actions that perpetuate the trauma cycle
10. **Relational dysregulation:** Disruptions in trust, attachment, or boundaries that compromise safety, intimacy, and connection

### V. Developmental Integration System

This system reflects the lasting imprint of early trauma and cumulative adversity on identity, attachment, and self-regulation across the lifespan.

11. **Developmental dysregulation:** Arrested growth, unmet needs, and identity diffusion rooted in early trauma and relational failure

This five-system, eleven-domain framework forms the backbone of DTRM's clinical formulation process, guiding both assessment and intervention. These domains are not isolated silos but dynamically interwoven, each influencing the others. Together, they provide a multidimensional map for understanding how trauma disrupts regulation and, more importantly, how precise, domain-targeted interventions can restore integration, stability, and vitality.

In this way, DTRM serves as both a map and a method. It provides a clear structure for assessment, intervention, and outcome measurement, while still allowing clinicians to individualize treatment to each client's unique pattern of dysregulation. Importantly, DTRM does not prioritize one form of dysregulation over another. Each person's trauma response reflects a distinct configuration shaped by their personal history, developmental stage, and environment. Our task as clinicians is not to fit the client to the model but to use the model to *find* the client—identifying areas of dysregulation and guiding skills-based repair across domains.

## From Theory to Practice

DTRM follows a progressive, phase-oriented structure that supports recovery without requiring reexposure to traumatic material. Treatment begins by strengthening regulation and safety through mindfulness, grounding, and skills practice.

In particular, DTRM follows a structured, step-by-step process represented by the acronym RISE:

1. Recognize the symptoms and the associated domains of dysregulation.
2. Identify what triggered the symptoms and dysregulation.
3. Make a Skills-based response.
4. Evaluate the outcomes and adapt as needed.

This simple yet powerful structure allows for both case conceptualization and in-the-moment intervention, forming a bridge between theory and practice that yields measurable outcomes. Because RISE is recursive—meaning its steps are repeated and revisited as needed—clients engage in ongoing self-monitoring and skill use, allowing them to increase their self-efficacy over time. Clients learn not only *what* to do but *why* to do it, allowing them to transform these skills from external techniques into internalized capacities for self-regulation. Importantly, this repeatable and accessible framework puts clients at the center of their recovery. With repeated practice, they develop mastery over their symptoms and take an active role in restoring regulation across different domains affected by trauma.

As clients gain stability, the work naturally moves toward integration and meaning making by reconciling internal conflicts and strengthening self-agency through dialectical synthesis. The final emphasis is on reconnection and growth, helping clients expand flexibility, reengage in relationships, and build a coherent posttrauma identity. By focusing on regulation rather than reexposure, DTRM makes the treatment of complex trauma both safe and sustainable for those who have lived it and for those of us who guide them toward healing.

## The Evidence Base for DTRM: From Research Studies to Evidence-Based Practice

DTRM is grounded in a strong evidence base that spans from randomized controlled trials (RCTs) to practical applications in real-world settings. To understand its effectiveness, it's useful to start with RCTs that compare well-established trauma treatments, such as prolonged exposure, cognitive behavioral therapy (CBT), and cognitive processing therapy, with present-centered therapy (PCT). Interestingly, PCT was originally developed not as a bona fide treatment but as an "active control" to rigorously compare against trauma-focused interventions. Unlike waitlist or treatment-as-usual controls, PCT accounts for important therapeutic variables such as alliance, therapist engagement, structured sessions, and expectancy effects.

PCT focuses on a client's current functioning and life stressors rather than on the trauma itself. It emphasizes problem-solving and coping strategies, such as relaxation, communication skills, sleep hygiene, stress management, and general self-care. However, it is not trauma focused and does not involve direct processing of traumatic memories or targeting of trauma-related symptoms.

Despite this, PCT has demonstrated efficacy in reducing PTSD, depression, and anxiety symptoms, albeit with smaller effect sizes compared with trauma-focused treatments (Schnurr et al., 2003). A meta-analysis by Foa and colleagues (2016) confirms these findings, and two RCTs found no statistically significant differences between PCT and comparison trauma-focused therapies, suggesting that PCT may, in some cases, be equally efficacious (Classen et al., 2011; Batten & Hayes, 2005). These outcomes indicate that although PCT was designed as a control condition, it may serve as a valid treatment option, particularly for individuals unwilling or unready to engage in processing-based therapies. In such cases, PCT may facilitate higher treatment adherence and lower dropout rates.

What's particularly valuable about PCT is that it integrates common therapeutic factors with a skills-based approach, offering symptom relief without requiring clients to revisit traumatic content. DTRM builds on this principle by integrating trauma-specific DBT skills in a structured framework.

Additional support for DTRM comes from several studies demonstrating the effectiveness of DBT skills in reducing trauma symptoms—before even moving into trauma processing. These studies have reported significant reductions in PTSD symptoms, affirming that DBT can address trauma-related distress even in the absence of trauma-specific techniques (Rosenthal et al., 2008; Valentine et al., 2015; Wagner et al., 2007). Of course, DTRM extends far beyond these unrefined skills applications and offers a comprehensive framework for trauma recovery.

DTRM is also grounded in the American Psychological Association's (2006) definition of evidence-based practice in psychology (EBPP), which advocates for the integration of the best available research with clinical expertise, while honoring each client's individual characteristics, culture, and preferences. The EBPP framework encourages clinicians to tailor evidence-informed interventions to the specific needs of clients, and DTRM is uniquely well suited to this, offering a flexible set of tools that can be customized to target the unique dysregulation patterns of each individual. Moreover, many trauma survivors prefer structured, skills-based treatments that address their symptoms directly without reexposing them to trauma. DTRM's client-centered nature and adaptability to different cultural and clinical contexts align well with this preference.

Importantly, EBPP does not require that interventions be validated exclusively through RCTs. It recognizes the value of practice-based evidence, including clinician-observed outcomes and real-world symptom change. Remember, *the only way to determine whether a treatment is effective is to monitor clinical outcomes in practice.*

With DTRM, clinical outcomes can be routinely monitored using a measure like the PTSD Checklist for *DSM-5* (PCL-5; Weathers et al., 2013), which is a brief self-report measure widely used for PTSD assessment. The PCL-5 offers strong reliability and validity and is easy to administer, making it an ideal instrument for tracking progress over time. That said, there are many other viable measures that can be used in practice. A list of other measures to consider is found in the appendix.

Therefore, DTRM is not a departure from evidence-based practices. Rather, it fully embraces the research literature and extends into the principles of EBPP. In this way, DTRM offers trauma survivors a safe, flexible, and effective treatment approach that can be used as an alternative or precursor to other established trauma therapies.

## How DTRM Differs from Other Models

While DTRM draws from the conceptual, behavioral, and skills-based foundation of DBT, it isn't simply DBT repackaged for trauma. Rather, it reshapes treatment from the ground up to be explicitly trauma focused, reframing each skill through the lens of trauma recovery and using domain-based interventions to ensure precise, context-sensitive application. Skills aren't taught as stand-alone tools but as targeted responses aligned with the client's moment-to-moment experience, physiology, and history.

In this sense, DTRM is both modular and whole system: It's flexible enough to adapt to each client's needs while remaining faithful to its theoretical framework. Its strength lies in this dialectical balance—it's broadly applicable across populations yet customizable to each client's needs.

DTRM also aligns with the values of trauma-informed care—safety, collaboration, choice, trustworthiness, and empowerment—but takes these principles a step further. Whereas trauma-informed care offers a guiding philosophy, DTRM provides a structured, skills-based protocol that targets symptoms and supports lasting functional change. Trauma-informed care guides the therapeutic stance and clinical environment, while DTRM provides the blueprint for treatment.

In this book, the DTRM model is introduced in two main parts, along with a supporting appendix:

- **Section 1: The Clinician's Guide** outlines a unified theory of trauma as well as the guiding philosophies, phases of treatment, modes of delivery, and therapeutic presence for DTRM. This section does not provide a complete explanation of DBT, so I encourage you to seek out source DBT texts (e.g., Linehan, 1993a; Pederson, 2015) and trainings to ensure you have a solid foundation in the DBT framework. Importantly, clinicians need to have sufficient training and experience in DBT to successfully apply this model.
- **Section 2: The Client Curriculum** is designed for both individual and group formats and provides psychoeducation on PTSD symptoms, the five systems and eleven domains of dysregulation, and the DTRM approach. It also contains the five DBT-based skills modules (dialectics, mindfulness, distress tolerance, emotion regulation, interpersonal effectiveness) for achieving regulation and long-term healing.
- **The appendix** includes supplemental teachings, worksheets, and clinical forms.

DTRM represents a new direction in trauma treatment: a fully integrated, theory-driven, and clinically actionable model for trauma-focused clinicians who seek to deliver precise, effective, and hopeful care. It honors the depth and complexity of trauma while offering a structured, skills-based path to recovery. Through its unified theory and accompanying step-by-step process, it provides both the *map* and the *means* to help survivors move from fragmentation to integration to restore stability, connection, and wholeness.

Such an approach is especially important in the treatment of those with complex trauma histories who experience multisystem dysregulation. Let's move now to DTRM's unified theory of trauma.

SECTION I

# The Clinician's Guide

CHAPTER 1

# DTRM's Unified Theory of Trauma

As discussed earlier, DTRM addresses the often-fragmented landscape of trauma theory by proposing a unified theory of trauma that is grounded in DBT's biosocial theory (Linehan, 1993a). Unifying and expanding under DBT's biosocial theory makes inherent sense because trauma, at its core, is both a disruption of regulation across systems and an experience of deep invalidation, whether through abuse, neglect, systemic oppression, and so forth. These twin forces of dysregulation and invalidation form the foundation of DTRM's unified approach, bringing together the contributions of leading theorists within a coherent clinical framework that guides the treatment.

As we examine the five systems and eleven domains of dysregulation that result from trauma, it is important to remember that *DTRM does not elevate one form of dysregulation over the others*. Indeed, there is significant overlap within the eleven domains, and it is difficult to explore any of them without invoking connections to the others. As such, every trauma survivor experiences dysregulation in their own unique way, and it is up to you and the client to determine what forms of dysregulation they experience and how to target those areas with skills.

The different types of dysregulation resulting from trauma follow, as does a discussion on the role of invalidation.

## I. Mind and Meaning System (Feelings, Thoughts, Beliefs)

### 1. Emotional Dysregulation: The Storm System of Trauma

Trauma profoundly disrupts the nervous system's capacity to regulate affect, resulting in what can be described as a volatile and unpredictable storm system of emotion. Survivors often experience extremes: emotional flooding on one end and emotional numbness or blunting on the other. These states are not simply mood swings; they represent the collapse of the brain's normal regulatory systems under the weight of unresolved fear, threat, and shame. Emotional responses become intense, fast moving, and difficult to manage, particularly when environmental or internal cues activate trauma-related memories or perceptions of danger (Ford et al., 2005; Linehan, 1993a).

Emotional dysregulation in trauma survivors can manifest as hypersensitivity to emotional stimuli, difficulties identifying or naming emotions, and the tendency to either act impulsively on emotional urges or shut down entirely. Research confirms that emotional dysregulation is not merely a by-product of trauma but a central mechanism that predicts the severity and persistence of PTSD symptoms (Chappelle et al., 2019). In fact, the degree of emotional dysregulation has been shown to correlate more strongly with functional impairment than trauma severity itself.

For trauma survivors, emotions are often experienced as unpredictable and unsafe. Shame, fear, grief, rage, and disgust arise quickly, unpredictably, and often without a clear cause. Emotional memories, which are presumably stored in the body and outside conscious awareness, can be triggered by certain sights, smells, interpersonal interactions, or body sensations that resemble past trauma. When this occurs, survivors may be thrust into a full-blown emotional response without consciously understanding the trigger. The result is a sense of being emotionally "hijacked" and unable to think clearly or make effective choices in the moment.

### Vignettes

- Claire, a survivor of childhood sexual abuse, reports becoming "instantly enraged" over minor slights from others, only to be consumed by guilt and self-recrimination hours later.
- Marcus, a veteran with complex PTSD, describes feeling "numb and flat" during arguments with his partner. Emotions surface only hours or days later, usually in the form of unexpected panic or despair.
- Lena, a trafficking survivor, bursts into tears after laughing in group therapy. She is confused by the sudden shift and says, "I don't even know why I'm crying."

These vignettes underscore a core truth: Trauma survivors often do not experience emotions as helpful signals or informative experiences. Instead, emotions can feel dangerous, overwhelming, or entirely disconnected from context, further compounding the sense of chaos and powerlessness that trauma instills.

Neuroscience research supports these patterns. Studies have shown that individuals with PTSD exhibit increased activation in the amygdala, even in nonthreatening environments. This hyperarousal is paired with diminished activity in the prefrontal cortex, which is necessary for regulating emotion and exerting cognitive control (Shin et al., 2006). The net effect is emotional responses that are not only intense but difficult to interpret, predict, or soothe. This imbalance also explains why emotion regulation skills are often impaired in trauma survivors from an early age.

Moreover, emotional dysregulation contributes not only to internal distress but also to significant social and functional impairments. Survivors may struggle with interpersonal conflict, shame spirals, dissociation, and a chronic sense of "walking on eggshells" within themselves and around others. As

Linehan (2015) notes in her work on borderline personality disorder, which shares many features with complex PTSD, emotional dysregulation creates a feedback loop where heightened emotional arousal impairs problem-solving and communication, leading to more conflict and shame, which in turn heightens emotional arousal. This self-perpetuating cycle is often a major barrier to healing.

Importantly, studies have demonstrated that DBT-based emotion regulation strategies—such as identifying emotions, reducing vulnerabilities with PLEASED, and practicing Opposite Action—are effective for clients with trauma, especially those with emotional lability and co-occurring substance use issues (Ford et al., 2013). These interventions offer survivors a concrete way to build, or rebuild, the emotional capacities that trauma has eroded.

## 2. Cognitive Dysregulation: Weather Forecasting Stuck on High Alert

Trauma doesn't just stir up painful emotions; it fundamentally alters how we think. For many survivors, cognitive disruptions become as distressing as the emotional pain itself.[5] Clients may describe feeling foggy, confused, disconnected from reality, or unable to trust their own thoughts. These aren't isolated incidents of forgetfulness or distraction. Instead, they reflect a deeper breakdown in the brain's capacity to process, store, and retrieve information coherently.

Cognitive dysregulation is marked by intrusive thoughts, fragmented memories, dissociation, and executive dysfunction. Survivors may experience sudden mental blanks during stress, get stuck in rigid and catastrophic thinking, or find themselves ruminating on events without resolution.

Compounding this, trauma suppresses activity of the prefrontal cortex, the region of the brain that governs planning, organization, working memory, and impulse control. Survivors may find it difficult to concentrate, organize their thoughts, or follow through on even basic tasks. These impairments, collectively known as *executive dysfunction*, are especially debilitating because they interfere with daily functioning, decision-making, and self-efficacy.

### Vignettes

- Jasmin, a survivor of intimate partner violence, hears a loud bang and instantly thinks, "It's happening again," misreading the sound as danger and triggering panic even though she knows she's safe.

---

5 Cognitive dysregulation and meaning and belief dysregulation are distinct but interrelated domains. Cognitive dysregulation reflects disruptions in active thought processes, such as rumination, intrusive thoughts, difficulty concentrating, and racing or looping thoughts. Meaning and belief dysregulation, on the other hand, reflects deeper and more enduring disruptions captured in maladaptive schemas ("I am unlovable") and broad, generalized beliefs ("The world is unsafe"). In practice, cognitive dysregulation reflects moment-to-moment difficulties in thinking, while meaning and belief dysregulation reflects long-term patterns in perception shaped by past experiences. These domains often reinforce one another, requiring interventions that address both the immediacy of distorted cognition and the longer-term work related to beliefs and meaning.

- Eric, who witnessed a school shooting, finds that he "goes blank" during classroom tests despite knowing the material. His working memory collapses under pressure, feeding self-doubt and shame.
- Raul, who lives with complex PTSD, says, "I don't trust my thoughts." He reports struggling with constant mental confusion, second-guessing every decision, and abandoning tasks midway because he's convinced he's doing them wrong.

These examples highlight how the emotional chaos caused by trauma is closely linked with a survivor's cognitive processes. Survivors may question whether their thoughts are rational, whether their memories are real, or whether they're "losing their minds." In truth, their brains are doing exactly what they were wired to do in response to overwhelming threat: protect, compartmentalize, and disassociate.

Unfortunately, these protective mechanisms come with long-term costs. The negative appraisals that clients develop about themselves often solidify, becoming rigid cognitive schemas that distort perception and reinforce hopelessness. Survivors may withdraw from challenges, avoid tasks that require cognitive effort, or shut down during interpersonal conflict, not out of avoidance or laziness but because their thinking literally falters under pressure.

The good news is that trauma-informed cognitive strategies can reduce these impairments. Skills that encourage nonjudgmental awareness of thoughts (i.e., mindfulness), increase cognitive flexibility (i.e., dialectics), and strengthen executive functioning can help restore mental clarity and confidence. As Bowen and colleagues (2009) have shown, these practices reduce avoidance-based coping and strengthen regulatory processes that support clearer thinking under stress.[6]

## 3. Meaning and Belief Dysregulation: Skewed Internal Maps of Reality

Trauma's most lasting wounds often stem not only from what was done but from what the mind was forced to believe about it. Long after the event ends, survivors may suffer less from the facts of what occurred than from the meanings that took root in its aftermath. These beliefs, often global, rigid, and shame laden, become internal maps of reality, shaping how survivors understand themselves, others, and the world.

Meaning and belief dysregulation emerges when trauma-driven interpretations go unexamined or unintegrated. Under conditions of terror or helplessness, the brain not only encodes the sensory

6 It's worth noting that a major difference between traditional DBT and CBT is that DBT is emotion focused whereas CBT is thought focused on the theory level, which directly influences the interventions. DBT therapists tend to focus first on validation and emotion regulation instead of working with thinking. In fact, DBT does not embrace traditional cognitive-restructuring methods (e.g., labeling distortions, challenging them, and replacing maladaptive thoughts with more adaptive ones). That said, DBT does have several "soft" cognitive interventions, including dialectical thinking, Nonjudgmental Stance, Wise Mind, and embracing an array of mindfulness practices with thinking. DBT also employs cognitive techniques like Check the Facts and the use of Socratic questioning when clients have been sufficiently validated and emotionally regulated. More contemporary third-wave cognitive approaches have leaned more toward the DBT philosophy and approach to thinking, eroding many of the original differences (Linehan, 2015).

and emotional aspects of the experience but also sweeping conclusions such as "I'm powerless," "It was my fault," and "I'll never be safe." These beliefs are attempts to make sense of chaos when no accurate framework is available. Over time, they harden into narratives that guide perception and behavior long after the danger is gone.

Research shows that it's often the meaning we make of trauma, and not the traumatic event itself, that predicts long-term suffering. For example, Ehlers and Clark (2000) find that negative appraisals sustain a client's sense of current threat, which prevents fear from naturally resolving. These beliefs narrow perception and reduce flexibility, leading to ongoing distress and avoidance. They blur the line between past and present, not by reviving the memory itself but by replaying its interpretation in daily life: "If I relax, I'll get hurt again."

This domain closely interacts with cognitive dysregulation (as distorted thinking reinforces entrenched beliefs) and with memory dysregulation (as unresolved memories resurface and reassert old meanings). Yet meaning and belief dysregulation stands on its own, as it governs *what the mind concludes* when recalling, avoiding, or retelling trauma. It dictates how experience is framed, how emotion is justified, and how the self is evaluated.

These consequences ripple across other domains: *Emotionally* speaking, shame, fear, and grief can spike whenever trauma-related beliefs are triggered. *Somatically*, the body may replay these meanings through tension, pain, or fatigue, which are literal embodiments of "I'm not safe" or "I can't rest." *Behaviorally*, avoidance preserves the illusion of control while silently confirming the belief that danger remains. *Relationally*, survivors may find it hard to trust the care shown by others, interpreting kindness as manipulation or rejection as proof of worthlessness.

### Vignettes

- Jared, who survived a home invasion, still startles at knocking years later. "It's not the memory that gets me," he says. "It's that I still believe it was my fault for not stopping it."
- Danielle, a nurse during the COVID-19 crisis, carries the belief "I failed them," despite knowing she did all she could. The belief itself, not the memory, drives her despair.
- Leo, who endured chronic childhood abuse, explains, "What hurts isn't remembering. It's believing I'm unlovable because of it."

In the aftermath of trauma, survivors often avoid situations that could revise their long-held and outdated meanings and beliefs. Without opportunities for safe reflection and reevaluation, old beliefs operate unchecked, coloring every new situation. Recovery depends on revising these beliefs by gradually updating internal maps through validation, mindfulness, and dialectical thinking.

To do so, structured trauma therapies guide survivors in updating the beliefs that anchor their pain—toward more balanced beliefs like "I did the best I could," "It wasn't my fault," and "That was then, and this is now." Dialectical interventions support this shift by validating both the reality of suffering and the resilience that made survival possible. Healing begins not by erasing the story but by transforming its meaning.

# II. Body-Based System (Alarm, Tension, Awareness)

## 4. Nervous System Dysregulation: The Climate Control System Gone Awry

Trauma doesn't just live in the mind or body; it reshapes the body's foundational operating system, the autonomic nervous system. This system, responsible for regulating heart rate, respiration, digestion, and arousal, becomes recalibrated by trauma to remain on constant alert or collapse into shutdown, in essence distorting the internal climate control system. Nervous system dysregulation forms the neurobiological backdrop to many trauma symptoms, manifesting not just in how survivors *feel* emotionally or somatically but in how their bodies unconsciously *respond* to the world.

Stephen Porges's (2011) polyvagal theory reframes trauma as a disruption in neuroception, which is the brain's automatic, unconscious ability to detect safety and danger. Rather than accurately reading cues from the environment, the traumatized nervous system errs on the side of threat. Even in safe environments, the body may reflexively activate defensive states like fight, flight, freeze, and collapse. The nervous system is literally functioning as though danger is ever present.

In terms of autonomic arousal, trauma can lead to persistent activation of the *sympathetic nervous system* (resulting in hyperarousal, agitation, and hypervigilance) or the dorsal vagal branch of the *parasympathetic system* (manifesting as dissociation, numbness, fatigue, or emotional shutdown). Most survivors shift between both states—chronically keyed up, then emotionally flat or collapsed—with little time spent in the balanced state of ventral vagal regulation, which supports social engagement, calmness, and connection.

### Vignettes

- Elena, who experienced chronic childhood neglect, freezes when spoken to in meetings. Her mind goes blank and her body locks up, a classic dorsal vagal response to perceived threat.
- Dre, misdiagnosed with ADHD, is in constant motion. He fidgets, interrupts, and scans his environment relentlessly, even in low-stimulus settings. His sympathetic nervous system is chronically activated, despite there being no external danger.
- Carlos, a veteran, startles violently at loud noises and feels tense and watchful at family barbecues. His nervous system does not register safety, even in familiar, loving environments.

These examples illustrate how trauma transforms the nervous system into a hypersensitive alarm, primed for danger at all times. Survivors often experience this dysregulation as a sense of being "off," an inability to relax, or a feeling of confusion about physiological reactions that seem disproportionate to the situation.

Importantly, nervous system dysregulation is distinct from, but deeply intertwined with, somatic dysregulation. Somatic dysregulation refers to the *subjective experience* of the body: pain, numbness, fatigue, or other distressing sensations. Nervous system dysregulation refers to the *autonomic control systems* generating those sensations. As van der Kolk (2014) and Ogden and Fisher (2015) note, the body *feels* dysregulated because the nervous system is *driving* dysregulation by overriding cues of safety and triggering chronic arousal or collapse. In other words, somatic symptoms are often the output, while nervous system reactivity is the source code.

The implications for recovery are profound. Because these defensive states are unconscious and automatic, insight alone is rarely sufficient for healing. Survivors may cognitively *know* they are safe, yet their nervous systems continue to act as though they are not. This mismatch often results in shame and confusion, particularly when others misinterpret symptoms as weakness, overreactivity, or inattention.

As already noted, research supports the idea that nervous system healing must involve bottom-up approaches that foster neurobiological safety. Interventions that stimulate the vagus nerve—the body's primary parasympathetic highway—can help restore ventral vagal regulation and support a felt sense of safety and connection (Dana, 2018; Porges, 2017). Practices that emphasize gentle movement, breath regulation, vocalization, and safe relational connection have all shown promise in recalibrating the traumatized nervous system, and these practices can be taught and practiced via DBT skills.

## 5. Somatic Dysregulation: The Atmosphere in Which the Weather Forms

Trauma is not confined to emotion and cognition. It is also written into the body, affecting muscles, breathing, sleep, posture, and more. Survivors of trauma often live in a body that feels foreign, unpredictable, or dangerous. This somatic dysregulation, the disorganized physiological imprint of trauma, is not an accessory symptom. It is central.

As Bessel van der Kolk (2014) famously proclaims in his book of the same name, "The body keeps the score." Trauma is not only remembered through words or images but reexperienced through visceral sensations like chronic tension, pain, digestive disturbances, racing heart, and numbness. These bodily symptoms often persist long after the threat has passed, disconnected from any clear medical cause yet fully lived and deeply distressing.

Peter Levine (1997), in his work on somatic experiencing, describes trauma as "trapped survival energy" that was never discharged. The nervous system, when unable to complete its natural defensive responses of fight, flight, or freeze, remains locked in a state of unfinished activation. This unresolved arousal manifests in the form of hypervigilance, sleep disturbance, unexplained pain, and startle responses that seem out of proportion to the moment. The body remains prepared for threat even when the mind knows it is safe.

Survivors may not initially identify these physical experiences as trauma related. Sensations like stomach cramps, migraines, or muscle tightness are easily misattributed or dismissed. Yet the inability to make sense of or tolerate these symptoms often leads to increased stress, anxiety, or avoidance, which reinforces the trauma imprint rather than resolving it.

### Vignettes

- Michelle, a sexual assault survivor, experiences recurring abdominal cramps prior to therapy sessions. Medical tests show no physical abnormalities, but the somatic anticipation of emotional vulnerability in therapy is overwhelming.
- Imani, who was trafficked as a child, develops intense migraines and full-body pain around the anniversary of her escape. Despite years having passed, her body marks the date with unmistakable precision.
- Tariq, a refugee, suffers chronic pain and insomnia when news of conflict arises. Though safe, his body reexperiences the strain and danger he endured while fleeing.

These examples illustrate how trauma is not merely remembered but is lived through the body. Survivors often feel confused or betrayed by their physiological responses, unsure why their bodies are reacting with pain or panic in moments of relative calm. This internal atmosphere becomes the stage on which emotional and cognitive dysregulation unfolds, setting the flawed forecasting and weather conditions for flashbacks, hyperarousal, or shutdowns.

Research continues to validate the centrality of somatic symptoms in trauma. Neurobiological studies show that trauma-related arousal alters baseline levels of muscle tension, respiration, and heart rate variability (Blechert et al., 2007). These physiological changes not only reflect stress; they *perpetuate* it. Because somatic symptoms are so central to trauma, it is not surprising that body-based awareness and regulation strategies can improve outcomes for individuals with PTSD and complex trauma. For example, studies have shown that treatment approaches that emphasize interoception, body tracking, and mindful somatic presence can reduce trauma-related pain, tension, and dissociative symptoms (Ogden & Fisher, 2015; Payne et al., 2015).

These findings underscore what trauma-informed practitioners have long known: Top-down cognitive insight alone is insufficient for recovery. Healing also requires bottom-up regulation, working through the body to calm the brain and restore a sense of safety. Fortunately, DBT has an array of skills to address body-based work.

## 6. Interoceptive Dysregulation: A Scrambled or Offline Radar System

Trauma often forces survivors to leave their bodies, not just metaphorically but neurologically. One of the lesser-known consequences of trauma is interoceptive dysregulation, a disruption in the ability to accurately perceive and interpret internal bodily signals such as hunger, thirst, heartbeat, breath, pain, or fatigue. This internal awareness, known as interoception, is foundational to emotion regulation, self-care, and the ability to respond effectively to physical and emotional needs.

For many trauma survivors, this internal "radar system" becomes either muted or overactive. Some may feel perpetually confused about what their body is telling them. Others may interpret benign sensations as dangerous, like reading a fluttering heartbeat as a heart attack. These disruptions do not occur randomly; they are the result of chronic physiological and neurological adaptations that develop in response to overwhelming or unsafe experiences.

Interoceptive dysregulation is closely connected to, yet distinct from, nervous system dysregulation. The nervous system governs automatic states like fight, flight, and freeze, whereas interoception governs the *conscious perception* of those internal states. In trauma survivors, these two systems often fall out of sync. The body may enter a state of hyperarousal or shutdown (due to autonomic nervous system activity), yet the survivor may either feel overwhelmed by internal signals or completely numb to them. Research confirms this relationship: Individuals with PTSD and related disorders exhibit both heightened physiological arousal *and* reduced interoceptive accuracy, leading to symptoms like panic, somatization (e.g., chronic headaches, stomach pain, gastrointestinal problems, muscle tension, unexplained fatigue, dizziness, and numbness or tingling that have no medical explanation), and emotional disconnection (Price & Hooven, 2018).

### Vignettes

- Natalie, who is recovering from sexual trauma, is unable to distinguish hunger from nausea. She often eats compulsively without recognizing what her body is asking for, then feels confused and distressed afterward.
- Tom, a firefighter and trauma survivor, reports intense chest tightness before every therapy group. Although he fears fainting or having a heart attack, his vital signs remain normal. He experiences panic not just emotionally but somatically, without a clear understanding of the source.
- Grace, who endured chronic early neglect, consistently ignores signs of exhaustion until she collapses. "I forget I have a body," she says, which is a profound reflection of interoceptive disconnection.

These experiences are common. Survivors who have learned to dissociate or override bodily signals as a survival strategy often find that they no longer trust or even *notice* those signals. What begins as an adaptive response to pain—numbing, bracing, or disconnecting—can become a chronic inability to respond to basic needs. This in turn increases the risk for self-neglect, disordered eating, and emotional dysregulation, since internal sensations are the building blocks of self-awareness.

Fortunately, body-based mindfulness practices, including breath tracking, somatic labeling, and body scans, have been shown to significantly improve emotion regulation, distress tolerance, and trauma symptoms by enhancing interoceptive awareness (Mehling et al., 2011). These findings support the clinical observation that top-down insight is insufficient when survivors are cut off from the bottom-up information of the body. Recovery depends not only on what we know but on what we can *feel* and interpret with safety and accuracy.

Interoceptive dysregulation is thus a crucial piece of the trauma puzzle. Without access to reliable internal cues, survivors may struggle to regulate their emotions, trust their instincts, or know when to rest, eat, speak up, or seek help. Rebuilding this connection is not just about learning to feel again; it's about relearning how to live inside their bodies with clarity and care.

## III. Consciousness and Memory System (Dissociation, Recall)

### 7. Dissociative Dysregulation: Power Outages During Clear Weather

Dissociation is one of trauma's most paradoxical effects. It's a brilliant survival strategy in the moment of overwhelm that becomes deeply maladaptive when it persists. Through dissociation, the brain attempts to protect itself by cutting off awareness of emotions, thoughts, sensations, and even identity. What begins as a shield against terror can eventually fragment the continuity of experience by disrupting memory, time perception, and bodily presence in ways that severely interfere with daily life.

Dissociative dysregulation occurs when this disconnection becomes habitual. Survivors may find themselves "losing time," feeling detached from their bodies, or experiencing the world through a foggy or distorted lens. They may describe events happening "as if in a dream" or refer to themselves in the third person. These disruptions affect not only experience but functioning, as attention falters, relationships become strained, and the self begins to feel unstable or unreal.

Although dissociation intersects with cognitive dysregulation, the two are not synonymous. Cognitive dysregulation involves distortions in thought (e.g., intrusive beliefs, executive dysfunction), while dissociation reflects a discontinuity of consciousness itself. A survivor experiencing cognitive dysregulation may think, "I can't focus," or "I don't know what I believe," whereas one experiencing dissociation may say, "I wasn't there," "Time just disappeared," or "That wasn't me."

Dissociation also overlaps with somatic and interoceptive dysregulation. Survivors in dissociative states often report feeling numb, unaware of physical pain or fatigue, or entirely disconnected from their body. However, while somatic and interoceptive dysregulation involve misinterpreting or missing internal cues, dissociation involves a profound severing from those cues altogether, representing a detachment from embodiment itself. As Ogden and Fisher (2015) describe, dissociation impairs our capacity to feel the body as our own or to locate ourselves in the here and now.

In terms of nervous system dysregulation, dissociation is commonly associated with parasympathetic dorsal vagal shutdown, which is a physiological state of collapse, numbness, and withdrawal. But again, it's not identical. Someone may experience nervous system collapse without the perceptual distortions of dissociation. Dissociation specifically involves an alteration in consciousness that can involve depersonalization, derealization, or identity fragmentation, often arising from severe or prolonged trauma.

### Vignettes

- Kelsey, who was sexually abused in childhood, often "blanks out" during therapy sessions and later cannot recall what was discussed. Time feels fragmented, as if she stepped out of the room mentally.
- Bruce, a trauma survivor, hears his own voice—as though it is coming from outside his body—when recounting painful memories. He says he feels like a spectator in his own life.
- Maya, who experienced chronic emotional neglect, frequently "zones out" on the drive home from work, arriving without memory of the route she took or how she stayed safe.

These vignettes illustrate how dissociation isn't simply distraction or forgetfulness; it's a trauma-driven distortion of presence and continuity. Survivors often feel ashamed or confused by these experiences, questioning their sanity or competence. Yet these states are not signs of weakness or pathology; they are the mind's best attempt to survive overwhelming stress, particularly when there was no escape or support.

Studies have shown that dissociation is especially prevalent in individuals with histories of chronic childhood abuse and disrupted attachment, where the developmental task of integrating the self, memory, and emotion was severely impaired (Dorahy et al., 2014). Neurobiologically, dissociation is linked to altered connectivity between brain regions responsible for consciousness, emotion, and bodily awareness.

Treatment interventions that emphasize present-moment embodiment, sensory integration, and relational safety have been shown to reduce dissociative symptoms. As Steele and colleagues (2017) and Ogden and Fisher (2015) describe, phase-based and sensorimotor therapies allow survivors to rebuild a coherent sense of self in time and space, not by demanding they "stay present" but by cultivating the capacity to safely *return* to presence when dissociation occurs. DBT has skills that speak to these interventions.

## 8. Memory Dysregulation: Skewed and Incomplete Archives

Trauma disrupts the brain's ability to record, store, and retrieve experiences in a coherent way. Under threat, normal memory systems fragment, and what should become a past event remains alive, felt, and intrusive. Survivors may recall flashes of detail but lack context or feel blank when asked to describe what happened. Time becomes distorted: The past feels unfinished, and the present uncertain.

In this domain, memory is not merely remembered, it is *relived.* Sensory fragments, waves of emotions, and bodily sensations return without conscious invitation. The hippocampus, which normally situates memory in time, loses coordination with the amygdala, leading to intrusive recollections or complete amnesia for key moments. Survivors often describe being "ambushed by memories" or "forgetting everything until something small brings it all back."

When memory is dysregulated, clients are unable to integrate their experiences in a coherent way. They may overencode their experiences (leading them to become hyperaccessible and vivid) or underencode them (leading them to become absent or unreachable). Both extremes maintain instability. Too much memory leads to flooding, too little leads to confusion, and oscillating between the two reinforces mistrust in their own mind. Survivors may question what is real, fear that remembering will destroy them, or feel guilty for not remembering enough.

### Vignettes

- Sofia, who was assaulted as a teenager, remembers the pattern on the carpet during her assault but not how she got home. The fragments loop like film clips without sound.
- DeShawn, a combat veteran, goes blank when asked about a deployment. Hours later, the smell of diesel and heat unleashes images so vivid he ducks for cover.
- Amira, who survived a devastating earthquake, forgets birthdays and errands yet reexperiences every tremor in her sleep, with her body recalling what her mind cannot.

Memory dysregulation interlocks with dissociation and with meaning and belief dysregulation, but it remains distinct. It concerns how information is stored and accessed, not what conclusions are drawn from it. Restoring coherence requires pairing safety with recall to link sensory fragments to language and time so that what was implicit becomes explicit and can finally stay in the past where it belongs.

These patterns are not flaws in character or willpower. They are trauma responses embedded in the nervous system showing evidence of the mind's ongoing struggle to integrate experiences that were once overwhelming or life-threatening.

Research has shown that these disruptions stem from trauma-related changes in key brain regions. The hippocampus, which organizes experiences in time and context, often shows reduced volume and altered functioning in those with PTSD. This dysfunction contributes to the persistence of intrusive memories, flashbacks, and fragmented autobiographical recall, all hallmark signs that the past continues to intrude on the present (Brewin et al., 2010).

Therapeutic work focuses on gentle titration of present-moment experience using grounding, mindfulness of the five senses, and paced awareness paired with regulating skills. Because DTRM is not an exposure-based therapy, titration refers to helping survivors notice emotions, sensations, and memory fragments only at a level that feels manageable, using skills to stay anchored rather than relive the trauma. Through this regulated awareness, fragmented memories begin to take shape and sequence. As survivors name, contextualize, and organize their experiences, memory gradually shifts from unprocessed shock to an integrated story. The mind no longer reexperiences the event; it remembers it. Integration transforms memory from an open wound into part of a coherent life history.[7]

# IV. Action and Connection System (Behaviors, Relationships)

## 9. Behavioral Dysregulation: Emergency Response Systems Gone Awry

Trauma doesn't just live in emotions, thoughts, or the body—it often shows up in behavior. When the internal system is overwhelmed, disorganized, or in pain, survivors may act in ways that seem impulsive, risky, or self-defeating. These behaviors are rarely random. They are learned and repeated attempts to escape, control, or soothe unbearable distress, often formed in environments where healthier options were unavailable.

Behavioral dysregulation refers to trauma-related patterns of action that arise in response to emotional or physiological overwhelm. These may include self-harm, aggression, substance use, compulsive behaviors, or withdrawal. While they often cause long-term harm, these behaviors originally developed as short-term strategies to numb pain, discharge arousal, or assert control in a world that felt uncontrollable.

### Vignettes

- Jenna, a college student with a history of sexual trauma, binge drinks every night before bed to stop what she calls "that anxious buzzing" in her body.

---

7 Although DTRM does not use formal exposure as a mechanism of change, all trauma therapies involve brief, natural moments of contact with emotions, sensations, or trauma-linked material. In DTRM, titration simply means noticing these experiences at tolerable intensities so that regulation, coherence, and choice become possible.

- Ron, who is currently incarcerated for violent offenses, flies into explosive rages over perceived slights. He grew up in a home marked by emotional neglect and punitive discipline.
- Ari, a highly functional administrative assistant, quietly cuts her thighs before work meetings. "It brings me back to my body," she explains. "It makes everything else go quiet."

These behaviors may seem contradictory. Some discharge emotion (e.g., aggression, impulsivity), while others numb or dissociate from it (e.g., substance use, self-injury). Yet what unifies them is their function: They are efforts to regulate internal chaos when more adaptive tools are absent or inaccessible.

Behavioral dysregulation does not arise in a vacuum. It is deeply connected to other trauma-related domains. For example, emotional dysregulation often fuels urges to self-soothe or escape through substances, sex, or self-injury. Cognitive dysregulation can lead to black-and-white thinking ("I've already failed, so I might as well . . .") or ineffective beliefs ("No one cares unless I act out"). Somatic and interoceptive dysregulation make it hard to read internal signals, so survivors may seek intense stimulation or dissociate just to feel something or nothing. And when the nervous system is in a chronic state of sympathetic activation or dorsal vagal shutdown, behavior often reflects the body's fight, flight, freeze, or collapse response playing out in real time.

Importantly, many of these behaviors have a developmental origin, particularly for children who grew up in environments where they weren't taught how to name emotions, tolerate distress, or seek support. Behaviors that were once adaptive in chaotic or abusive environments may become automatic habits in adulthood, even when those conditions no longer exist. For example, a child living in an abusive household may have learned that reacting with anger and aggression was the only way to defend themselves and protect themselves from further harm. That same pattern of explosive anger, which once served as a self-protective strategy, may now lead to isolation, legal consequences, or shame in adulthood. Similarly, numbing strategies, like binge eating or drug use, may provide temporary relief but ultimately erode health, stability, and self-trust.

The link between trauma and high-risk behaviors is well established, particularly with regard to self-harm, substance abuse, compulsivity, and unsafe sexual behavior (Najavits, 2002). Survivors are especially prone to impulsive or destructive behaviors in the absence of supportive, validating, and skills-oriented interventions. Fortunately, treatment models like DTRM offer empirically supported tools that directly target these behaviors, building on the same DBT principles that have been shown to reduce suicidal behavior, self-injury, and substance use in trauma survivors (Harned et al., 2012). One key component is a Behavior and Solution Analysis, which helps clients map out the links between triggering events, internal states, urges, actions, and consequences. From there, they can learn to interrupt these chains with distress tolerance and emotion regulation skills, replacing impulsive or avoidant behavior with intentional, effective responses.

While behavioral dysregulation is often the most visible aspect of trauma, it is also among the most changeable because *behavior is skills based.* With the right support and tools, clients can build new patterns of responding that don't abandon them in moments of distress but move them toward stability, agency, and self-respect.

## 10. Relational Dysregulation: Unstable and Unpredictable Weather Networks

Trauma rarely happens in isolation, and its aftermath is just as relational. For many survivors, the deepest wounds come not only from what was done but from who did it, who wasn't there, or who couldn't be trusted. When trauma involves betrayal, abandonment, or relational harm, it alters not just how survivors feel about themselves but how they relate to others. These disruptions often continue long after the trauma ends, shaping patterns of attachment, trust, intimacy, and conflict.

Relational dysregulation refers to trauma-driven difficulties in establishing and maintaining safe, stable, and reciprocal interpersonal connections. Survivors may oscillate between clinging and withdrawal, lash out when they feel threatened, or shut down entirely in moments that require vulnerability. Relationships can feel both intensely desired and deeply unsafe.

### Vignettes

- Mia, who survived early sexual abuse, struggles to maintain close friendships. She alternates between oversharing and ghosting, saying, "I never know whether people are going to hurt me or leave me."
- Troy, who was raised in a violent household, reacts with hostility to even mild feedback from coworkers. "I don't mean to blow up," he says. "But it always feels like an attack."
- Jasmine, a trauma survivor in a long-term relationship, dissociates during arguments with her partner and later can't recall what was said. "I just disappear when it gets tense," she says. "It's like I'm watching it happen from outside myself."

These patterns don't arise from poor communication skills alone—they are protective responses deeply rooted in earlier survival needs. As Bowlby's (1988) attachment theory explains, children learn to regulate distress, interpret social cues, and form internal models of the self and others through early caregiving relationships. When those relationships are frightening, chaotic, or neglectful, the resulting attachment patterns tend to be insecure, avoidant, or disorganized. (The ideas around this are continued in the section on developmental dysregulation.)

Furthermore, relational dysregulation often coexists with other trauma-related domains of dysregulation. For example, emotional dysregulation emerges as shame, fear, and rage in response to perceived threats or disconnection. Meaning and belief dysregulation filters interpersonal interactions through rigid, trauma-shaped beliefs like "I'm unlovable," "People can't be trusted," or "If I show weakness, I'll be hurt." Nervous system dysregulation amplifies this response by sending the body into a state of fight, flight, freeze, or collapse in response to benign interpersonal cues. Even interoceptive and dissociative dysregulation play a role, as survivors may not register relational stress building in their bodies or may disconnect entirely during conflict or intimacy.

Relational trauma often creates what Janina Fisher (2017) calls a "split in experience": Part of the self yearns for connection, while another part remains on high alert for betrayal. This inner conflict may manifest outwardly as inconsistency, reactivity, avoidance, or sabotage of closeness. Survivors may become isolated, not because they don't want relationships but because they've never known safety within them.

The research is clear that trauma exposure increases the likelihood of interpersonal violence, boundary difficulties, relational avoidance, and social withdrawal (Cloitre et al., 2011; Herman, 1992). Survivors often report patterns of repetition by choosing partners or friends who reenact familiar dynamics of neglect, chaos, or control. At the same time, relational healing is a powerful force in trauma recovery. Therapies that emphasize validation, interpersonal effectiveness, and safe co-regulation, such as DTRM, help clients rebuild connection on new terms.

In DTRM, relationship skills are not treated as generic communication tools. They are understood as corrective experiences in order to practice boundaries, assert needs, repair ruptures, and tolerate intimacy in real time. Over time, survivors dialectically learn that they can be connected *and* safe, vulnerable *and* strong, assertive *and* kind.

# V. Developmental Integration System (Early Wiring, Safety Learning)

## 11. Developmental Dysregulation: A Stalled Storm System

To understand how trauma fragments emotional, cognitive, and physiological functioning, we can look to where the capacity for regulation comes from. Self-regulation—the ability to manage emotion, attention, bodily states, and relationships—is not an innate skill. It's learned through early developmental experiences, particularly through repeated, attuned, and co-regulated interactions with caregivers. When these foundational interactions are absent, inconsistent, frightening, or invalidating, the blueprint for regulation becomes distorted from the beginning.

Attachment theory, introduced earlier, asserts that children learn to manage stress and form a stable sense of self through secure relationships. When attachment is disrupted through neglect, abuse, enmeshment, or abandonment, children adapt in order to survive, but those adaptations often compromise long-term regulation. Allan Schore's (2001) neurodevelopmental research expands this understanding, showing how chronic relational stress impacts brain architecture, particularly the development of the prefrontal cortex, limbic system, and autonomic nervous system. These disruptions are not just psychological; they are neurobiological.

Further, Bruce Perry's neurosequential model (Perry & Szalavitz, 2017) emphasizes that the earlier and more chronic the adversity, the more deeply it imprints the brainstem and midbrain, the very areas responsible for arousal, motor activity, and basic survival. In this way, trauma during sensitive developmental windows wires the nervous system toward reactivity, disconnection, or collapse long before the child has language or conscious memory to make sense of what's happening.

These early injuries shape the architecture for all future forms of dysregulation. Emotional experiences become overwhelming because the child never learns how to name, express, or soothe them. Thoughts become chaotic or self-condemning because they grow in the soil of fear, shame, or confusion. The body becomes either hyperaware or numb because it was forced to endure repeated threat without relief. In short, developmental trauma is not one domain of dysregulation, nor does it negate other domains of dysregulation. Rather, it explains them and is the foundation from which all others arise. It tells the story of how trauma gets wired, not just as moments of harm but as sustained interruptions in development.

This is why emotional dysregulation often appears as a core trauma symptom. Without consistent emotional mirroring or containment from caregivers, survivors may learn to fear their own emotions or never fully recognize them. Meaning and belief dysregulation takes root when children internalize invalidating narratives ("You're too sensitive," "That didn't happen") or are left to interpret chaos without help. Somatic and interoceptive dysregulation develop when distress in the body is ignored, punished, or misunderstood, leading to chronic confusion about internal states. The nervous system itself adapts to threat by remaining chronically activated or shutdown, forming patterns of hypervigilance or freeze, or alternating between the two. Dissociation becomes a developmental necessity when no safe attachment is available to help a child remain in their body during fear, pain, or shame.

### Vignettes

- Isabelle was raised by an emotionally absent parent and grew up walking on eggshells. Now in adulthood, she has no language for her feelings and breaks into panic during conflict, unsure whether she's angry, sad, or wrong.
- Marcus, who was exposed to physical abuse from a young age, becomes hyperfocused at work but blank and disengaged at home. He reports a lifelong sense of feeling "not real."
- Renee was neglected in early childhood and now experiences deep fatigue but doesn't recognize hunger, thirst, or stress until her body gives out. She often says, "I didn't know I needed anything."

These aren't isolated problems. They are systemic effects of early relational failure. Survivors may carry these patterns into adolescence and adulthood, confused by their own reactions and unable to name the origin of their pain. They may function well in some environments and collapse in others. Often, they believe the problem is with them rather than recognizing that their nervous systems and cognitive frameworks were shaped by experiences that left them without the tools to regulate.

Understanding trauma through this developmental lens allows us to approach dysregulation with greater empathy, precision, and patience. It reminds us to focus not just on symptom reduction but on mindful skill acquisition, attunement, and corrective experiences that repair disrupted developmental pathways. In addition, DTRM does not assume that all clients begin with the same regulatory capacities. Instead, it recognizes that some individuals may need to build core regulatory functions from the ground up—starting by establishing a sense of safety, then building the capacity for regulation, and only then moving toward integration and coherence.

By understanding dysregulation this way, we can help clients reclaim the regulatory pathways that trauma interrupted and that never had the chance to fully form. DBT skills go far in developing effective behaviors that clients didn't have the opportunity to form early on.

## 12. Vicarious Traumatization Dysregulation: When Therapist Exposure to Weather Takes Its Toll

Trauma doesn't only affect those who survive it firsthand, which is why DTRM presents a supplementary twelfth domain of dysregulation related to therapists and other professionals.[8] For therapists, case managers, medical staff, and other frontline helping professionals, bearing witness to trauma on a regular basis carries its own cost. Over time, the cumulative effect of hearing, holding, and responding to trauma narratives can reshape our internal world. This process, known as vicarious traumatization, is not a sign of weakness or overidentification. Instead, it's a natural occupational hazard of empathic engagement with human suffering.

Vicarious traumatization refers to the internal transformation that occurs when providers are repeatedly exposed to the traumatic experiences of others. While related to burnout and compassion fatigue, it is distinct in that it involves changes to the provider's worldview, emotion regulation capacities, memory, and body, such as increased muscle tension, disrupted sleep, heightened startle responses, gastrointestinal distress, chronic fatigue, or shifts in breathing and heart rate patterns, thereby mirroring many of the same dysregulation patterns seen in trauma survivors themselves.

---

8 Clinicians are also susceptible to multidomain dysregulation, particularly when exposed to chronic trauma narratives and high emotional demands. The DTRM model conceptualizes vicarious trauma as activation across the same five systems and eleven domains that govern client functioning. To support awareness and regulation, providers can use the *Therapist Dysregulation Self-Assessment* in the appendix to identify early signs of imbalance across emotional, cognitive, meaning and belief, nervous system, somatic, interoceptive, dissociative, memory, behavioral, relational, and developmental domains, and to apply interventions to restore balance.

### Vignettes

- Alex, a trauma therapist, begins having nightmares about their clients' abuse histories. Between sessions, they find themselves procrastinating on emails and avoiding chart notes.
- Mika, a corrections officer, starts experiencing bodily tension and increased irritability. He finds that certain inmate conversations bring up reactions he "can't shake."
- Jamie, a social services case manager, notices she's emotionally flat at home. "I have nothing left to give," she says. "Even my partner feels like too much."

We often carry this impact silently. We may feel guilty for our exhaustion, ashamed of our numbness, or fearful that acknowledging our own trauma exposure means we are no longer fit to help others. But research consistently shows that vicarious trauma is widespread and predictable, particularly among those working with high-intensity, high-complexity trauma (Pearlman & Saakvitne, 1995). It is a relational transmission of distress that is subtle, cumulative, and deeply embodied.

Vicarious trauma does not just affect our mood or motivation; it causes changes in our neurophysiology. Like the clients we serve, we may develop hyperaroused nervous systems, dissociative tendencies, or altered emotional processing. We may become overly reactive to trauma cues or, conversely, emotionally disengaged. Our bodies may respond with tension, fatigue, pain, or disrupted sleep. Our minds may fill with intrusive images, intrusive thoughts, or self-doubt. These are not "secondary" symptoms—they are primary dysregulations emerging from chronic empathic strain.

In this way, vicarious trauma parallels many of the same domains seen in direct trauma survivors:

- Emotional dysregulation can appear as irritability, numbing, or tearfulness.
- Cognitive dysregulation may manifest in cynicism, intrusive thoughts, or impaired concentration.
- Somatic and interoceptive dysregulation can show up in pain, fatigue, or disconnection from the body.
- Behavioral dysregulation can take the form of overworking, avoidance, or unhealthy coping.
- And, perhaps most importantly, relational dysregulation can result in withdrawal from loved ones, compassion fatigue with clients, or difficulty setting boundaries, undermining both personal well-being and professional effectiveness.

What protects against this erosion is not toughness or emotional distancing. It is ongoing regulation by engaging in the same skills we offer clients: dialectics, mindfulness, distress tolerance, emotion regulation, and interpersonal effectiveness. Additionally, DBT specifically calls for consultation, where therapists meet *to support each other* in this difficult work in addition to discussing the clinical course of clients' treatment. The protective value of supervision, peer consultation, self-care, and mindfulness in reducing vicarious trauma cannot be overstated—all of which are captured in the DBT approach (Saakvitne et al., 2011).

Therapist regulation is not a luxury; it's the essential foundation of ethical trauma work. Our nervous system is a regulating force in the therapy room. A dysregulated clinician who is anxious, shutdown, or flooded can unintentionally coactivate client distress. By contrast, a grounded, present clinician can serve as a co-regulator, offering safety not just through their words but through their tone, posture, rhythm, and attunement.

This is why DBT's philosophies and skills are not simply self-care platitudes—they are clinical imperatives. Just as trauma survivors must learn to tolerate their own emotions and sensations without shutting down or acting out, so must those who walk with them.

In trauma work, the healer is not separate from the wound. They are shaped by it and must be continually tended by the same tools they seek to teach. As the saying goes, "We cannot pour from an empty cup." But more than that, we must remember that at least early in this treatment, we are the cup.

CHAPTER 2

# DTRM'S Guiding Philosophies

Trauma disrupts the integration of systems that are meant to function in synchrony—fragmenting emotional, cognitive, somatic, and relational capacities, among others. While these disruptions can be complex, they follow identifiable patterns rooted in two core mechanisms: dysregulation and invalidation.

Recall from the previous chapter that trauma reduces our capacity to regulate across multiple areas of functioning, creating ripple effects in emotional, cognitive, somatic, and relational domains. Invalidation compounds this dysregulation, acting as a relational salt thrown into an existing traumatic wound, deepening it through neglect, betrayal, and systemic oppression. In this way, invalidation sustains trauma symptoms, fuels dysregulation, and obstructs healing (Herman, 1992; Linehan, 1993b).

## Invalidation: The Fuel That Intensifies Dysregulation

Invalidation is more than a momentary dismissal of emotion or experience. It is a relational and systemic process that distorts reality, severs trust in the self, and compounds the core injury of trauma. Across the trauma literature and clinical theory, invalidation emerges as a pervasive and insidious force not only in the formation of traumatic wounds but in the mechanisms that maintain and worsen them.

Invalidation refers to the denial, minimization, distortion, or disregard of a person's internal experience, be it their emotions, perceptions, memories, or body-based cues. Invalidation can be subtle or overt, momentary or chronic, personal or systemic. It sends the message: "Your feelings are wrong. Your body is lying. Your truth is not real." Over time, these messages become internalized, forming the basis for self-invalidation, where the survivor begins to disbelieve or dismiss their own experience.

In Linehan's biosocial theory (1993a), the underpinning of DBT, invalidation is identified as a central etiological factor in the development of emotional dysregulation, borderline personality disorder, and other pathology. She defines invalidation not simply as emotional neglect but as any pattern in which a child's emotional responses are treated as inappropriate, exaggerated, or unworthy of attention. This includes gaslighting, shaming, inconsistent reinforcement, or punitive responses to distress.

When it comes to trauma, invalidation is woven into the event itself, especially with regard to interpersonal and developmental trauma. For instance, in attachment trauma, caregivers who respond to a child's fear or need with rejection, punishment, or disinterest not only fail to protect the child but also invalidate the child's biological and emotional signals, which undermines their ability to develop self-trust and the capacity for regulation (Bowlby, 1988; Schore, 2001).

In sexual abuse, survivors are frequently coerced or shamed into silence, directly invalidated by perpetrators or disbelieved by others. This layered betrayal often causes more enduring damage than the abuse itself (Courtois & Ford, 2009). As van der Kolk (2014) emphasizes, trauma is shaped not only by what happened but also by whether anyone was there to provide safety, attunement, and witnessing.

Even in cases of combat trauma, medical trauma, or natural disasters, survivors often experience invalidation in the form of societal minimization ("It wasn't that bad") or forced normalization ("Others have it worse"). This contributes to delayed disclosure, avoidance, and chronic shame.

From a developmental lens, invalidation interrupts a child's ability to form a sense of identity, engage in emotional learning, and integrate their experiences on a cognitive level. As Perry and Szalavitz (2017) note, children develop their regulatory systems through consistent attunement and mirrored affect. When their distress is ignored or punished, they learn that their internal experiences are untrustworthy or even dangerous, resulting in emotional dysregulation, dissociation, and an overreliance on external cues to determine what is "real."

This sets the stage for chronic self-invalidation. Individuals learn to suppress their own discomfort, gaslight themselves out of anger or grief, or habitually override somatic cues. In internal family systems (IFS; Schwartz, 2001), these parts of the individual become exiled, viewed as shameful, needy, or irrational, perpetuating internal fragmentation and further invalidation. Note that even though IFS is not highlighted in this manual, I would consider that much of IFS could be "technically assimilated"[9] into DTRM, especially when applied in individual therapy as opposed to a group process.

Invalidation also affects how trauma is encoded and interpreted cognitively. According to Ehlers and Clark's (2000) cognitive model of PTSD, trauma survivors often develop maladaptive appraisals of the trauma—"I'm weak," "I deserved it," "It didn't really happen"—that maintain their sense of current threat. These appraisals are often born of invalidating environments that refuse to name what happened or that dismiss the survivor's distress. As Judith Herman (1992) notes, trauma survivors are doubly harmed: first by the traumatic event itself and again by the denial or silence that follows.

This invalidation leads survivors to avoid uncomfortable internal experiences, suppress unwanted thoughts, and internalize shame, all of which disrupt their ability to integrate their memories and create a coherent narrative. In fact, research suggests that dissociative amnesia and fragmented recall may not

9 Norcross and Goldfried (2005) describe *technical assimilation* as a form of psychotherapy integration where the therapist selectively uses methods from other approaches to enhance therapeutic outcomes while maintaining their core theoretical allegiance. This process prioritizes customizing the approach to the client over theoretical and technical purity.

only result from the trauma itself but from prolonged exposure to environments that disbelieve or punish emotional expression (Dorahy et al., 2014).

## Systemic and Cultural Invalidation

Trauma does not occur in a vacuum. Instead, it unfolds within systems of power, culture, and belief. Invalidation operates at these broader levels as well. Examples include the following:

- **Medical invalidation** occurs when trauma-related physical symptoms are dismissed, misattributed, or minimized, often resulting in neglect, misdiagnosis, or harmful treatment. A person's symptoms may be labeled as exaggerated, psychosomatic, or imagined. For example, a trauma survivor with chronic pain might be repeatedly told by health-care providers that "it's just anxiety" and sent away without assessment or appropriate care.
- **Racial, cultural, and gender-based invalidation** devalues or pathologizes a person's emotional expression, pain, or cultural experiences based on their race, ethnicity, gender, sexual orientation, or cultural background. This includes stereotyping, minimizing, or implying overreaction. For instance, a Black woman reporting safety concerns might be dismissed as "aggressive" or "too sensitive," or a transgender person expressing fear after a threatening encounter may be told, "That's just part of being confused about your identity."
- **Institutional invalidation** occurs when organizations such as schools, courts, workplaces, or religious communities systematically dismiss, silence, or punish individuals who report abuse or seek trauma-related accommodations. For example, a student who reports harassment may be accused of "making trouble" and face retaliation rather than protection, or an employee disclosing workplace trauma may be met with skepticism and penalized for "not being a team player."

These systemic forms of invalidation magnify trauma, especially for survivors whose identities are already marginalized. As van der Kolk (2014) notes, healing requires not just internal processing but also social acknowledgment and a restoration of dignity.

Even within therapeutic and caregiving systems, invalidation can persist. Clinicians may unknowingly dismiss trauma responses as "manipulative," "noncompliant," or "attention seeking." Without a trauma-informed lens, we can inadvertently replicate the original wound, especially in settings that prioritize control over compassion. This makes therapist validation not merely supportive but foundational to treatment. In fact, astute therapists (e.g., Duncan et al., 1992) have wisely asserted that validation is instrumental to building the therapeutic alliance, which is the essential vehicle for change.

## Healing Through Validation: Providing Safe Haven from the Storm

If trauma is a storm and invalidation the lack of safe shelter, then validation becomes the safe haven that protects. It restores self-trust, enables emotional naming, and creates the conditions for regulation and integration. Linehan (1993b) places validation as a central pillar of DBT, recognizing that many clients have never had their pain reflected back with clarity and respect. She emphasizes that validation is not agreement. Instead, it is the act of seeing, naming, and staying with a person's experience.

Healing environments must validate:

- The reality of the trauma
- The survivor's emotional, cognitive, somatic, and other responses
- The meaning and impact of what happened
- The adaptive function of their behaviors
- Their capacity to heal without erasing their pain

Through this lens, validation is not just a clinical tool—it's a moral stance. It is the opposite of gaslighting. It is bearing witness with humility, consistency, and care.

DTRM builds on this with a regulation-first, validation-anchored approach. Treatment is carefully sequenced: Stabilization and skill building come before (or sometimes instead of) exposure and process-based treatments,[10] and disconnection is met with attuned presence. DTRM draws from DBT's evidence-based strategies and adapts them to domains often unrecognized and neglected by traditional models.

DTRM organizes trauma's diverse impacts within a coherent clinical framework to restore regulation, dignity, and trust in the self. Where trauma fragments, DTRM integrates. Where invalidation distorts, DTRM validates. And where treatment often overwhelms, DTRM offers clarity, sequence, and hope.

This leads us to the next core concept at the heart of DTRM: dialectics. Where trauma drives extremes—such as flooding or numbing, closeness or avoidance, and chaos or rigidity—dialectics restores flexibility, complexity, and the ability to hold multiple truths. It is the bridge across opposites that makes growth possible.

## Dialectics: An Integrated Path to Regulation and Healing

Trauma fragments and destabilizes the systems that support regulation, safety, and identity, while invalidating the self that's been left to make sense of its aftermath. Beneath trauma's varied expressions lies the common thread: a breakdown of regulation and a rupture of self-trust.

---

10 For many clients, DTRM can replace exposure-based treatments, consistent with offering least invasive treatments. For clients who choose to engage in these treatments, DTRM offers the skills needed to stay regulated during the course of treatments that require the continual revisiting of traumatic material.

When trauma dysregulates, treatment must offer regulation. Dialectics supports this process by bridging extremes. Where trauma creates false "either/or" beliefs—such as "I'm strong or broken," "I must forgive or stay angry," or "If I feel, I'll fall apart, so I'll do whatever it takes to be numb"—dialectics offers a way forward by holding both sides. The capacity to hold the relative truth in both sides becomes the engine of integration.

Dialectics grows from the foundation of both accepting and validating pain while simultaneously teaching skills that create change. Building on this foundational dialectic, clients learn to tolerate contradiction, manage ambivalence, and access Wise Mind—that inner stance where paradox can become a catalyst for transformation.

Consider Danielle, a survivor of abuse, who says, "My mom did her best . . . I shouldn't be angry" in response to her mother's inconsistent care and attention while growing up. Her therapist responds, "Can it be true that she did her best *and* she still hurt you badly?" In that moment, Danielle begins to shift—from shame to grief, from "either/or" thinking to "both/and" thinking—bridging the gaps between these seemingly conflicting truths. This is dialectical healing in action.

## Dialectical Practice as Regulation

Dialectical work is not just a cognitive exercise; it is a regulatory process. When clients learn to hold opposing truths, they move out of rigid threat states and gain greater flexibility and balance in their emotions, thoughts, and behaviors. Over time, this supports:

- **Normalization of complexity:** "I can be healing and still hurting."
- **Softening of polarizations:** "I can be conflicted and still find clarity."
- **Empowered choice:** "I can hold multiple truths and still choose how to respond."
- **Expanded self-compassion:** "I can feel broken and still be worthy."

Core strategies in dialectics include teaching "both/and" language, naming dialectical dilemmas, exploring partial truths, and practicing middle-path thinking and behaviors. These interventions create the space trauma constricts, allowing survivors to respond with awareness rather than react from a place of rigidity. Research supports this role of dialectical thinking in trauma recovery, as cognitive flexibility is associated with improved emotion regulation, reduced reactivity, and greater resilience in survivors of trauma (Neacsiu et al., 2010)—and the healing role of behavioral flexibility through skill use is self-evident.

DTRM applies dialectics directly to the central tensions that emerge in trauma recovery. These dilemmas—such as flooding versus numbness, avoidance versus overexposure, and shame versus self-compassion—are not pathologies but adaptive contradictions. Clients are not asked to resolve these by choosing one side. Instead, they are taught to hold both with skill and clarity. The following are examples with dialectical resolutions.

| Dilemma | Dialectical Resolution | |
|---|---|---|
| | **Thought** | **Action** |
| **Flooding vs. Numbness:** "I feel nothing or everything, and neither feels safe." | "I can allow myself to feel in manageable doses, knowing I can also create space to step back when needed." | Practice mindfulness to notice emotions as waves, using grounding to tolerate intensity and Sensations (ACCEPTS) when emotions fade or go flat. |
| **Hypervigilance vs. Dissociation:** "I'm either on edge or completely shutdown." | "I can stay connected to the present without needing to be hyperalert or disconnected." | Use grounding and mindful observation to remain aware but anchored, noticing surroundings without scanning or withdrawing. |
| **Rumination vs. Impulsivity:** "I'm stuck in my head until I snap." | "I can reflect without getting lost in thought and choose intentional action over reaction." | Use Wise Mind reflection followed by a chosen skill, like a distress tolerance strategy or DEAR MAN, before acting impulsively, or to reach out for help. |
| **Avoidance vs. Overexposure:** "If I face it, I'll fall apart. If I don't, I'll never heal." | "I can face my pain one step at a time, neither hiding from it nor overwhelming myself." | Approach feared situations using pacing, practicing gradual exposure with regulation skills and planned breaks. |
| **Passivity vs. Aggression:** "I stay silent or I explode." | "I can express myself firmly and respectfully without shutting down or lashing out." | Use interpersonal effectiveness skills (e.g., GIVE, DEAR MAN) to assert needs with care and clarity. |
| **Shame vs. Self-Compassion:** "I deserve love, but I hate myself." | "I can hold both my imperfections and my worth. I am a work in progress, deserving of compassion." | Practice daily self-validation and compassion exercises while gently countering shame-based thoughts with Check the Facts and Encouragement (IMPROVE). |

Throughout DTRM, therapists continuously guide dialectical thinking and actions:

- "You're afraid, and you showed up. What skills helped you do that?"
- "You feel overwhelmed, and there are skills we know that work in these moments."
- "You grieve what was lost, and you are still growing. This is holding both Radical Acceptance and creating a more satisfying life."

These stances integrate the complexity of the client's experience while negating none of it. Remember that DTRM does not resolve dialectical dilemmas by forcing neutrality or choosing sides. Instead, it offers acceptance, validation, and the skills needed to navigate complexity with dignity so clients can move from "either/or" to "both/and" thinking, not as an abstract idea but as a lived practice.

In doing so, survivors stop fighting their own minds and bodies and begin inhabiting them with purpose, freedom, and compassion. Dialectics is not just part of the model. It is the bridge to integration and the foundation of posttraumatic growth.

Next, we look to how mindfulness is applied within DTRM.

## Mindfulness: The Essence of Presence, Regulation, and Change

In DTRM, mindfulness is not merely a skill set; it is a therapeutic philosophy and clinical posture that permeates the entire treatment process. While clients are introduced to specific practices such as breath awareness, sensory tracking, or Observing and Describing without attachment, these practices are not ends in themselves. Rather, they are doorways into a broader orientation: a nonjudgmental, grounded, and compassionate way of relating to experience that is inherently regulating and validating.

### The Collapse of Presence in Trauma

Trauma pulls survivors out of the present. It tethers the mind to the past through flashbacks and learned fear or hurls it into the future through hypervigilance and anxious anticipation. Survivors learn to disconnect from emotions, distrust thoughts, suppress sensations, and avoid the body altogether. Experience becomes unsafe, and the present moment feels intolerable.

Mindfulness directly counters this collapse, not by forcing calm but by inviting contact. It offers survivors a steady, compassionate invitation: "Be here now, not to fix or flee but to witness and respond skillfully." Through repeated practice, the present moment becomes a safe-enough place to return to, even in the presence of pain.

Mindfulness offers more than stabilization; it offers a new way of being in relationship to trauma. Where trauma says, "You must numb or be overwhelmed," mindfulness says, "You can feel safely, one breath at a time." Where trauma says, "You must stay alert or be hurt," mindfulness says, "You can notice safety in this moment."

Mindfulness, like dialectics, dismantles false dichotomies by allowing complexity to be held. It invites clients to:

- Observe without judgment
- Feel without collapse
- Act without urgency
- Be without apology

These are not just therapeutic gains; they are existential shifts. Over time, mindfulness becomes not just a coping strategy but a worldview and a way of meeting experience with openness, dignity, and agency.

## Awareness Precedes Change

DTRM rests on the premise that awareness precedes regulation, and regulation precedes integration. Many trauma models move too quickly to narrative, asking clients to process traumatic material before they have the skill sets to tolerate it. DTRM begins elsewhere, with the approach of "Can you notice what's happening now and stay with it, even a little?" In this way, mindfulness becomes the platform upon which all other interventions stand:

- Without awareness of emotional cues, there can be no effective communication or boundary-setting.
- Without awareness of cognitive content, there can be no dialectical reframe or reality testing.
- Without awareness of a body sensation, there can be no somatic grounding.
- Without awareness of a rising urge, there can be no impulse regulation or more effective behavioral choice.

Mindfulness, then, is not a phase of treatment; it is its backbone. It is the foundation of regulation across every system disrupted by trauma, serving as both a stabilizing practice and a unifying process that restores awareness, safety, and choice where trauma has imposed disconnection, chaos, and automaticity. Through mindfulness, clients learn to Observe their inner experience rather than be ruled by it, bridging mind, body, memory, behavior, and development into a coherent whole. The following illustrates how mindfulness supports recovery across the five systems of DTRM's unified theory.

### I. Mind and Meaning System: Restoring Emotional and Cognitive Balance

In the Mind and Meaning System, mindfulness interrupts the fusion between emotion, thought, and belief that trauma often creates.

With regard to *emotional dysregulation*, mindfulness allows clients to name feelings as waves that rise, crest, and fall rather than as permanent or dangerous states. This practice cultivates tolerance for intensity and creates space for adaptive responses rather than avoidance or overwhelm.

Mindfulness also disrupts *cognitive dysregulation* by helping clients build metacognition—the ability to notice thoughts as mental events rather than objective truths. This shift loosens the grip of trauma-based appraisals (e.g., "I'm in danger," "I'm worthless") and replaces judgment with curiosity. Additionally, mindfulness allows clients to "take hold of their mind" and learn to redirect attention and sustain concentration according to their wants and needs, being responsive rather than reactive.

Finally, with regard to *meaning and belief dysregulation*, mindfulness offers a grounded vantage point from which clients can Observe trauma-linked beliefs without collapsing into them. Rather than treating these beliefs as literal truths or reacting automatically, mindfulness helps clients notice the interpretations they are making about themselves, others, and the world. From this steady witnessing stance, survivors can begin to question inherited meanings, scc how these beliefs were shaped by past threat rather than present reality, and gently expand in more accurate and compassionate interpretations. In this way, mindfulness becomes a bridge from rigid trauma-based meaning to a more coherent and integrated sense of self.

## II. Body-Based System: Reclaiming Safety in the Body

In the Body-Based System, mindfulness reintroduces awareness into the lived body, an experience often severed by trauma.

When there is *nervous system dysregulation*, slow, steady breathing and sustained attention engage parasympathetic regulation, quieting the fight, flight, freeze, or collapse reflex and signaling safety to the body.

To counter *somatic dysregulation*, mindful attention to posture, movement, and muscle tension helps clients inhabit their bodies safely again. The goal is not to eliminate sensation but to relate to it differently in order to experience pain, fatigue, or activation as information rather than threat.

Finally, mindfulness addresses *interoceptive dysregulation* by defining the ability to sense and interpret internal cues such as hunger, fullness, fatigue, or emotional activation. Over time, survivors rebuild trust in their body's signals, transforming confusion and detachment into accurate self-attunement.

Each of these practices supports bottom-up regulation, where safety begins not with words but with felt experience.

## III. Consciousness and Memory System: Reconnecting the Fragments of Awareness

In the Consciousness and Memory System, mindfulness reweaves continuity where trauma has fragmented time, awareness, and self.

When *dissociative dysregulation* pulls awareness away from the present, mindfulness serves as an anchor by using the breath, sensory grounding, or simple observation to reestablish orientation in the here and now.

With regard to *memory dysregulation*, mindfulness provides a method for engaging intrusive memories safely. Instead of reliving the event, clients practice witnessing it, noticing images, sensations, or emotions while maintaining an anchor in current safety. This capacity for dual awareness—in which "part of me remembers while part of me is here now"—supports integration and reduces the emotional charge of traumatic recall.

In this way, mindfulness transforms memory from an uncontained flashback into an experience that can be remembered, reflected upon, and placed back in time.

### IV. Action and Connection System: Transforming Reactivity into Intention

Within the Action and Connection System, mindfulness converts automatic survival behaviors into deliberate, values-based choices.

When there is *behavioral dysregulation*, mindfulness introduces a pause between urge and action. Clients learn to recognize impulses as signals, not commands, creating the space to choose skills such as STOP, TIPP, or Opposite Action before reacting. This moment of awareness is where freedom begins.

To address *relational dysregulation*, mindfulness strengthens attunement, first to the self and then to others. By noticing emotional shifts, body cues, and internal judgments during interactions, clients build the capacity for grounded, boundaried connection. Mindful listening and self-validation prevent reenactments of trauma within relationships and foster empathy without overidentification.

### V. Developmental Integration System: Rebuilding the Foundations of Awareness and Connection

In the Developmental Integration System, mindfulness restores the basic capacities that trauma often interrupts early in life: sustained attention, curiosity, and attuned awareness.

To repair *developmental dysregulation*, mindfulness reintroduces what was once learned, or needed to be learned, through secure attachment: moment-to-moment noticing, naming, and soothing. Clients relearn how to stay present with themselves as caring observers rather than critics.

Over time, mindfulness cultivates self-compassion, patience, and internal stability, which form the developmental foundations for all other forms of regulation. Where trauma halted growth, mindfulness becomes the practice that restarts it.

## Integration: The Unifying Function of Mindfulness

Across all systems, mindfulness acts as both a stabilizer and an integrator, quieting the nervous system while awakening awareness, allowing the five systems and associated eleven domains to communicate once again. Moreover, it functions as a top-down and bottom-up regulatory process. Top-down, it strengthens cognitive and emotional awareness, enabling reflection, reinterpretation, and choice, and bottom-up, it recalibrates physiological states, restoring embodied safety and presence.

Through this integration, mindfulness transforms fragmentation into coherence, allowing clients to live not as reactors to the past but as participants in the present, being capable of stability, connection, and growth.

## Therapist Mindfulness: Presence as Co-Regulation

Remember, too, that in DTRM, mindfulness is not only practiced by clients; it is embodied by us as clinicians. Our mindful presence becomes part of the intervention as a co-regulating, validating, and attuned force that sets the tone for safety, openness, and pacing. This therapeutic posture includes:

- Moment-to-moment awareness of the client's window of tolerance
- Nonjudgmental curiosity toward emotional and physiological signals
- The ability to self-regulate in the face of client distress or dissociation
- A willingness to *be with* rather than *fix* emotional and other pain

When we embody mindfulness, we model what it means to stay present with discomfort, complexity, and uncertainty—skills that trauma survivors must internalize to move forward. We become not just a teacher of mindfulness but a living experience of it.

At its core, mindfulness is the discipline of compassionate attention. It is the daily practice of returning to the breath, to emotion, to thought, and to the body, not to control them but to relate to them wisely. For survivors, this practice restores what was fractured: the ability to stay with what is real, feel what is true, and most importantly, to respond from a place of self-trust.

Woven through every domain of dysregulation, mindfulness becomes the means of regulation through the radical act of noticing and staying with experience in the moment.

CHAPTER 3

# From Theory to Practice: Operationalizing DTRM

In traditional trauma treatment models, there is often a clinical temptation to "go deep" too soon, inviting clients to share trauma narratives before their minds and bodies are equipped to hold the weight of those stories. While insight, memory integration, and narrative work can be important components of long-term trauma recovery, DTRM recognizes the fundamental truth that a dysregulated client cannot process trauma safely or effectively.

This is not about avoidance—it is about sequencing. Skills are not a detour around trauma; rather, they are a safe pathway through it. Without the internal resources to manage emotional, physiological, and relational triggers, trauma processing can become retraumatizing rather than healing. Survivors may shut down, dissociate, escalate, or fall into maladaptive coping behaviors when asked to confront traumatic content prematurely. The rationale is clear: If the goal is to heal, we must first equip survivors with the tools to withstand their own internal experiences.

That is why stabilization is the priority in DTRM. Stabilization is the act of creating internal and external safety, which is not just the absence of crisis but the presence of regulation, agency, and choice.

To achieve this, DTRM draws on a diverse suite of DBT skills positioned for trauma treatment that are individually tailored to clients. As mentioned previously, we find each client in their unique profile of dysregulation and customize the skill use accordingly. While the skills that underlie the five DBT skills modules are presented in section 2, an overview of those modules follows:

- **Dialectics:** As noted, survivors often feel trapped in black-and-white thinking, feeling either in control or helpless, either a victim or a fighter, either safe or unsafe. Dialectical thinking teaches them to hold two truths at once, such as "I was hurt deeply *and* I am healing" or "I feel afraid *and* I am safe right now." Skills like Wise Mind, dialectical reframing, and Pros and Cons help break rigid beliefs and allow clients to see multiple options, thereby allowing them to also act dialectically. For example, a client might use Wise Mind to respond calmly in a triggering situation while still honoring their emotional pain. Others may practice the dialectic of acceptance and change by learning to Radically Accept their trauma history while working hard to create a better life now.

- **Mindfulness:** Trauma pulls clients out of the present, either into the past through intrusive thoughts or flashbacks or into the future through dread. Mindfulness grounds them in the here and now, with a particular mindset to either tolerate or improve the moment. Core mindfulness skills shift clients from reactivity to awareness, allowing them to access Wise Mind. For instance, a client experiencing the onset of a dissociative episode might ground through the five senses to stay anchored.[11] Another may use mindful breathing and Nonjudgmental Stance to notice intrusive thoughts without getting entangled in them. Over time, mindfulness becomes a way to regain control of attention, reconnect with the body, and learn to be skillfully responsive in the face of symptoms and dysregulation.
- **Distress tolerance:** These skills help clients survive the moment without resorting to maladaptive behaviors. Think of the array of distress tolerance skills as being replacement skills for the behaviors that represent dysfunction in that domain. Yet these skills are not only about managing distress; they are also about meeting distress with acceptance through skills like Radical Acceptance and Willingness. Many of the distress tolerance skills also speak to somatic (and other) regulation, such as Self-Soothe, TIPP, and grounding, among others.
- **Emotion regulation:**[12] Survivors learn to name and navigate feelings through a model of emotions and to lower vulnerability to intense emotions via PLEASED. They also create positive emotions with Build Positive Experiences and a sense of competence and control with Build Mastery. Further, skills like Check the Facts and Opposite Action develop regulation and choice across domains of dysregulation.
- **Interpersonal effectiveness:** Skills like FAST, GIVE, and DEAR MAN restore relational agency. These tools are especially vital for clients whose trauma includes betrayal, attachment wounds, or boundary violations. Taken together, these skills build self-respect, the ability to make and maintain healthy relationships, and the ability to set boundaries as well as advocate for wants and needs.

---

11 Although grounding is a skill found in the distress tolerance module, it is fundamentally a mindfulness skill.

12 While this module retains its original name of emotion regulation, clients and therapists will find that the component skills bring regulation far beyond emotions. As an example, engaging in self-care skills via PLEASED will bring regulation to every system and domain without exception.

## From Systems to Skills: Mapping the Terrain of Dysregulation and Healing

This skills overview explains what DTRM teaches and why stabilization comes first. The remainder of this chapter explains where to apply those skills by walking through the five systems and eleven domains of dysregulation. Think of it this way: The DBT modules and underlying skills provide the tools, while the systems-and-domains framework shows the map. In the pages that follow, each system is presented with:

- A brief explanation of how trauma disrupts that part of the mind-body network
- A paired sequence of skills-based interventions that first demonstrate bottom-up applications to restore physiological safety and then top-down applications to consolidate awareness and meaning[13]
- A short clinical vignette and a note on integration within the system

As you read, you'll see how certain skills align with specific domains. You'll also notice that certain skills like mindfulness can have almost universal applications. *That said, note that these examples represent an introduction to skills-based interventions and not the entire breadth of how skills can be applied.* As mentioned earlier, clinicians using DTRM are expected to be familiar with DBT and skills training. That said, if you need a refresher with the skills mentioned, consult section 2 or the *Master Skills List* in the appendix to increase your understanding as you work through this section. With that orientation, we now move into the first system.

## I. Mind and Meaning System

The Mind and Meaning System is the central hub of trauma-related dysregulation. Emotion, cognition, and meaning making work in constant dialogue, each influencing the other. When trauma overwhelms these domains, dysregulation spirals across systems. DTRM teaches that effective intervention most often begins from the body upward. Clients first restore physiological safety, then use awareness and meaning making to integrate and sustain regulation. In other words, bottom-up work creates readiness, and top-down work consolidates change.

### 1. Emotional Dysregulation: Integrating Feeling, Physiology, and Skill

Emotional dysregulation is one of the clearest signs of trauma. Survivors often describe living inside an unpredictable storm of feeling, with flooding on one side and numbness on the other. These shifts reflect

13 Keep in mind that some skills are not purely bottom-up or top-down; many are actually a mix in practice. As an example, Wise Mind can combine the bottom-up act of tuning into feelings and embodied awareness with the top-down act of cognitive awareness and reasoning. It is therefore important not to allow too much rigidity in conceptualization to interfere with the actual practice. In the examples, you can sometimes see shades of top-down application in a mostly bottom-up intervention, and vice versa.

the collapse of normal regulatory systems under unresolved fear, shame, or threat (Ford et al., 2005; Linehan, 1993a). The amygdala becomes hyperactive, the prefrontal cortex underfunctions, and emotions dominate awareness without modulation (Shin et al., 2006).

### Bottom-Up Skills Application

Because emotion is largely experienced as a body-based process, regulation begins through physiology:

- The TIPP skill, which includes Temperature Change, Intense Exercise, Paced Breathing, and Progressive Muscle Relaxation, directly shifts autonomic states to reduce sympathetic activation and ground clients in the present moment.
- Self-Soothe, when paired with mindfulness, reconnects survivors to their present sensory experience and widens their window of tolerance before they engage in deeper insight work.
- The PLEASED skill proactively addresses biological vulnerabilities that underlie emotional instability through consistent sleep, balanced nutrition, and physical health.

These practices calm limbic activation and reengage parasympathetic balance, making higher-order reflection possible.

### Top-Down Skills Application

Once the body settles, top-down strategies refine emotional understanding and choice:

- Check the Facts helps clients test whether their emotions fit the current circumstances.
- Opposite Action allows clients to step out of mood-congruent behavior that keeps them stuck in painful emotions.
- Radical Acceptance of the moment allows emotions to pass through, rather than dominate, awareness.

Through this process, the prefrontal cortex reenters a state of regulation, allowing emotions to integrate with thought and action.

#### Vignette

After a triggering text from her partner, Mia feels a sense of panic rise sharply in her body. She first runs cold water over her wrists and practices Paced Breathing to slow her heart rate, which is a bottom-up strategy using the TIPP skill. When her body steadies, she uses Check the Facts to determine that the message was neutral and not a rejection, which reflects top-down thinking. The combination restores equilibrium and self-trust.

## 2. Cognitive Dysregulation: Rebuilding Coherence and Flexibility

Trauma alters how people think. Survivors often describe confusion, intrusive thoughts, disrupted attention and concentration, and a sense of mental fog. These patterns stem from disrupted hippocampal and prefrontal functioning, which fragments memory and weakens executive control (Brewin et al., 2010). The result is rigid, catastrophic, or self-blaming cognition that maintains emotional reactivity.

### Bottom-Up Skills Application

Cognitive clarity is difficult to access when the body is dysregulated. Starting with the body restores enough parasympathetic activity for reflective thought to follow:

- Progressive Muscle Relaxation within TIPP or IMPROVE can reduce muscle tension and calm the body.
- The Sensations portion of the ACCEPTS skill provides clients with a distraction and a physiological shift.
- Receiving GIVE with a gentle tone and relaxed posture engages a client from the bottom-up.

These interventions downshift arousal so the prefrontal cortex can reengage.

### Top-Down Skills Application

Once grounded, survivors can work directly with their thought patterns. Here's a sampling of skills to use:

- Dialectical reframing uses "Both/And" Thinking to help clients counter "either/or" thinking and build flexibility.
- Core mindfulness skills lead clients to Wise Mind, which balances emotion and reason.
- Pros and Cons restores deliberate decision-making for clients.

Together, skills such as these restore regulation in the cognitive domain.

### Vignette

Jasmine, a survivor of childhood abuse, obsessively thinks, "I should have stopped it." Her chest tightens and breath quickens. She first places a hand on her heart and breathes slowly to regulate her nervous system, which is a bottom-up strategy. Then she uses dialectical thinking to recognize and hold two truths: She was powerless as a child, and she has agency now. That is top-down thinking. This integration diminishes shame and restores clarity.

## 3. Meaning and Belief Dysregulation: Rewriting the Internal Narrative

Trauma does not only disrupt emotion and cognition. It also distorts the meanings people assign to their experiences. Survivors often form enduring beliefs of guilt, unworthiness, or danger, interpreting trauma as personal failure rather than violation (Ehlers & Clark, 2000; Shapiro, 2001). These meanings can anchor trauma in their identity and make recovery feel like they are betraying their own truth.

### Bottom-Up Skills Application

Clients first use physiological grounding before engaging in belief restructuring and redefining meaning:

- Mindful breathing with self-validation ("It's okay to feel this") grounds attention and soothes distress.
- Sensory grounding via the Self-Soothe skill helps the body believe the threat is over.
- Mindfulness of Current Emotion, practiced by anchoring attention in breath and sensation, steadies the body so clients can tolerate and examine the meanings that arise.

These practices create the safety necessary for examining meaning and belief.

### Top-Down Skills Application

Once embodied safety is present, survivors can address trauma-linked interpretations:

- Radical Acceptance allows for both the pain of what happened and the possibility of posttraumatic growth.
- Wise Mind supports integration of emotional and rational truths in which the "felt sense" that accompanies belief can be counterbalanced with reason.
- Check the Facts disentangles current experiences from past meanings.

These, with other skills, gradually reshape the meaning and beliefs that spring from trauma.

### Vignette

Danielle, a nurse haunted by guilt from her ICU work during the COVID-19 crisis, practices taking a grounding breath and engaging self-soothing touch (which are bottom-up tools) before engaging in reflective work. Once calm, she uses Radical Acceptance by telling herself, "I did everything I could in impossible circumstances," which is top-down thinking. This combination transforms guilt into compassion and meaning into growth.

## Integration Across the Mind and Meaning System

Emotion, cognition, and meaning operate in a dynamic loop. Physiological arousal fuels thought distortions. Distorted thoughts reinforce maladaptive beliefs. Those beliefs perpetuate emotional activation. Healing requires movement across all these interconnected pathways. By establishing safety with bottom-up regulation and then applying top-down strategies to consolidate insight and belief transformation, clients gradually internalize the ability to shift intentionally between these pathways to regain the flexibility and coherence that trauma once removed.

# II. Body-Based System

Trauma imprints itself deeply in the body. The physiological systems that ensure survival, including autonomic, somatic, and interoceptive processes, often become dysregulated long before cognition can intervene. These body-based domains form the substrate of emotional and cognitive functioning, so the body must be viewed as an active participant in healing. Regulation begins with felt experience and extends upward into awareness and meaning.

## 4. Nervous System Dysregulation: Recalibrating the Body's Climate Control

The autonomic nervous system regulates arousal, heart rate, and respiration. Trauma recalibrates this system toward chronic defense. Many survivors live in states of hyperarousal or collapse and rarely enter the balanced state of social engagement and safety (Dana, 2018; Porges, 2011). This imbalance becomes the invisible climate in which other dysregulation occurs.

### Bottom-Up Skills Application

These interventions target the autonomic nervous system directly:

- The TIPP skill shifts physiological states through Temperature Change, movement, and Paced Breathing. For example, cool water can activate the dive reflex, lower heart rate, and stimulate the vagus nerve.
- With awareness of facial tension and a tight, closed posture, a client practices adopting a Half-Smile and Willing Hands to communicate safety and calm from the bottom-up.
- Using Relaxation techniques (an IMPROVE skill), like gentle movement, stretching, or rocking, provides vestibular input that regulates the nervous system. Alternatively, vestibular and proprioceptive soothing techniques such as these fit within the touch and motion components of the Self-Soothe skill.

These practices work beneath conscious thought and, through sensation, tell the body it is safe now.

### Top-Down Skills Application

Once physiological calm is present, cognitive attention can reinforce it:

- Core mindfulness skills (Observe, Describe) allow clients to be aware of and label arousal states to connect felt experience with language.
- Radically Accepting states of hyperarousal removes the battle and invites calm.
- Dialectical self-talk, such as "My body is remembering, and I am here now," integrates body memory with conscious reassurance in the moment.

These practices help clients reinterpret bodily signals, redirect attention toward what is true in the present, and rebuild a coherent sense of safety from the inside out.

> **Vignette**
>
> Carlos, a veteran, startles at fireworks. His heart races and muscles tighten. He first focuses on slow exhalations while pressing his feet into the ground and identifying nearby sounds, which are bottom-up techniques. When steady, he names this response as his nervous system's memory and reminds himself that he is home and safe, which is top-down thinking. Repetition of this sequence gradually retrains neuroception toward safety.

## 5. Somatic Dysregulation: The Body That Remembers

Trauma lives in our musculature, breath, and posture (van der Kolk, 2014). Somatic dysregulation appears as chronic pain, tension, startle responses, and exhaustion. Survivors may feel betrayed by their body or detached from it altogether.

### Bottom-Up Skills Application

Mindfulness of body sensations cultivates awareness of muscle tension, pressure, or temperature and turns implicit somatic memory into explicit awareness that can be addressed with skills:

- Progressive Muscle Relaxation within TIPP or IMPROVE releases stored tension and often brings emotion to the surface in manageable doses.
- One-Mindfully practices that incorporate movement, such as walking, stretching, or yoga, support safe reentry into the body.[14]
- Breathing in for four counts and exhaling for eight counts (a TIPP skill) teaches clients to shift from shallow defensive respiration to full calming diaphragmatic breath.

These techniques help the body relearn what safety feels like.

---

14 Behaviors such as walking, stretching, and yoga can fit under a number of skill names such as Activities (ACCEPTS), Relaxation (IMPROVE), or Build Positive Experiences, to name a few possibilities. Of course, these activities are done mindfully.

### Top-Down Skills Application

Cognitive mindfulness gives structure to somatic exploration, helping clients make sense of bodily sensations and connect them with thoughts and meaning:

- Using the Observe and Describe skills to Nonjudgmentally label sensations turns diffuse discomfort into articulated experience. Language brings the prefrontal cortex online, organizes perception, and reduces avoidance.
- Radical Acceptance invites a Nonjudgmental Stance toward body sensations and shifts thoughts from "Something is wrong" to "This is what my body feels right now."
- Wise Mind integrates emotional and reasoned awareness, allowing the body's sensations to be acknowledged without being ruled by them. It translates somatic data into meaning, transforming reactive fear into grounded understanding.

Together, these practices restore coherence between mind and body, transforming awareness itself into a regulating force.

#### Vignette

Imani, a survivor of trafficking, experiences increased pain and tension around the anniversary of her escape. She begins by scanning her body, locating tension in her neck and shoulders. She breathes into the sensations after applying a warm compress across her shoulders—a bottom-up strategy. Then she names the sensations in her body and practices dialectical thinking: "My body remembers, *and* I can stay with it safely," which is top-down. Reactivity becomes integration.

## 6. Interoceptive Dysregulation: Reclaiming the Internal Compass

Interoception is the ability to detect and interpret internal bodily cues such as hunger, fatigue, and heart rate. Trauma disrupts this system and leads to either oversensitivity or numbness (Price & Hooven, 2018). Survivors may misread benign sensations as danger or ignore vital signals of need.

### Bottom-Up Skills Application

Reconnecting with internal body cues begins by safely reentering the sensory landscape of the body. Bottom-up practices help clients approach sensations directly, without judgment or analysis, transforming physiological avoidance into embodied curiosity:

- A mindful body scan trains direct awareness of sensory experience without labeling or interpretation, which strengthens the brain's afferent pathways so survivors *feel* sensations safely rather than conceptualizing or avoiding them.

- Mindful eating or drinking is an application of One-Mindfully that allows clients to savor temperature, texture, and taste. This reengages gustatory and visceral awareness, countering patterns of emotional numbing or disembodiment.
- Supportive touch through the Self-Soothe skill (e.g., placing a hand over the heart or abdomen) stimulates interoceptive awareness and supports parasympathetic activation.

Over time, clients begin to differentiate arousal from physical states such as hunger or exhaustion. This retrains the nervous system to recognize internal signals as information rather than threat, transforming confusion into grounded embodiment.

### Top-Down Skills Application

Once basic interoceptive safety is established, naming sensations helps integrate implicit bodily memory with explicit awareness, making it possible to think about sensations without becoming overwhelmed by them:

- Nonjudgmentally Observing and Describing internal sensations from a body scan develops awareness of subtle cues, helps clients name what the body is communicating, and integrates sensory experience with conscious understanding.
- Checking the Facts with body awareness encourages clients to get curiosity about their sensations. For instance, a client might ask, "Is this panic or fatigue? Fear or caffeine?" to clarify meaning and reduce misinterpretation.
- When body sensations cue withdrawal or avoidance, clients can practice Opposite Action by gently stretching, walking, or reaching out as a way to recalibrate both behavior and physiology.

Together, these top-down strategies organize perception and restore coherence between cognitive and sensory awareness, allowing the mind to accurately interpret what the body feels and to respond with compassion rather than fear.

#### Vignette

Grace, who endured chronic neglect during childhood, ignores symptoms of exhaustion until she collapses. With practice, she learns to set timers to pause and notice her body. When she feels heaviness behind her eyes, she takes several deep breaths, drinks water, and stretches, which are bottom-up strategies. Later, she journals to link these sensations with a need for rest rather than feeling guilty about productivity, which is top-down thinking in action. The practice rebuilds trust in her body's guidance.

## Integration Across the Body-Based System

The nervous system, somatic, and interoceptive domains function as a single interactive network. Trauma dysregulates them collectively, and healing addresses all three. Bottom-up work calms the autonomic system, releases tension, and reawakens bodily awareness. Top-down skills then integrate these experiences into coherent understanding and self-care. When clients learn to trust bodily sensations without fear, the entire regulatory hierarchy becomes more stable, and the body becomes the foundation of safety. From this base, higher-level processes emerge, including emotion regulation, cognitive clarity, and relational connection.

# III. Consciousness and Memory System

Dissociation and disrupted memory represent trauma's impact on consciousness. When the brain and body cannot tolerate overwhelming threat, they fragment awareness as a survival strategy. This is why regulation must occur across multiple layers of the self, including sensory, physiological, cognitive, and narrative areas. Healing begins through embodied presence and proceeds toward memory integration.

## 7. Dissociative Dysregulation: Restoring Presence and Continuity

Dissociation is adaptive in crisis and costly when chronic. In moments of inescapable threat, the mind disconnects from sensation, emotion, and even identity. When this disconnection becomes habitual, survivors experience lapses in time, derealization, or depersonalization (Dorahy et al., 2014). People often describe watching life from a distance or not being in their body. Attention, memory, and relational engagement are impaired.

### Bottom-Up Skills Application

Because dissociation reflects disrupted body-brain integration, treatment begins with sensory and physical grounding:

- A client sets an hourly alarm to remind themselves to practice grounding through the five senses, allowing them to anchor their attention to external stimuli and provide immediate orientation to the present.
- Using STOP in moments of derealization interrupts the automatic drift away from the body and reorients to the here and now.
- The Sensations portion of the ACCEPTS skill activates the senses in the here and now, creating a pleasant connection to the moment.

These methods signal safety to the brainstem and support integration across sensory and cognitive networks.

### Top-Down Skills Application

Once embodied presence is reestablished, cognitive awareness helps maintain it:

- Adopting a Nonjudgmental Stance (a mindfulness "How" skill) reframes dissociation as protective rather than failed coping, which reduces shame and fear.
- Clients combine Encouragement and Meaning (from IMPROVE) with Dialectics to generate compassionate self-talk ("I'm safe now," "My mind learned to protect me, and I can return when I'm ready") to cognitively anchor the experience of safety and repersonalize their narrative.
- Pros and Cons can evaluate the short- and long-term consequences of detaching versus staying present, guiding clients in making deliberate, values-based choices about whether to reengage.

Together, these practices transform dissociation from a reflex of escape into a mindful choice for presence, strengthening continuity of self and restoring trust in the capacity to stay connected.

#### Vignette

Kelsey, who was abused in childhood, often blanks out during therapy. When she feels the drift, she presses her feet into the floor, finds three colors in the room, and breathes through her nose—all bottom-up tools. Once grounded, she dialectically verbalizes, "A part of me is pulling away, *and* I am still here," which reflects top-down thinking. Over time, this practice strengthens her capacity to stay embodied during stress.

## 8. Memory Dysregulation: Integrating Fragmented Experience

Trauma disrupts how experiences are stored and retrieved. Survivors often retain vivid sensory or emotional fragments without coherent storylines. These fragments can intrude as flashbacks, nightmares, or sudden emotional surges. When memory remains unintegrated, the past intrudes upon the present and fuels ongoing dysregulation (Brewin et al., 2010; Shapiro, 2001).

### Bottom-Up Skills Application

Body-based safety paves the way for memory processing:

- Using Imagery to visualize a safe place (an IMPROVE skill) along with relaxed breathing establishes containment and signals that the present differs from the past.[15]
- Build Positive Experiences and Self-Soothe counterbalance trauma networks by creating new sensory and emotional experiences of calm and mastery.

15 Note that using Imagery has top-down elements, yet it "lands" in the body.

- Safe Posture Practice, a combination of mindfulness and Opposite Action, involves adopting a posture of openness during moments of recall. Over time, the body learns that remembering does not require retreat or shutdown.

These examples increase the likelihood that memory reconsolidation will occur in a regulated state and facilitate the shift from implicit to explicit memory.

### Top-Down Skills Application

Once physiological stability is present, top-down skills help organize and reframe memory:

- Validation strengthens coherent self-narratives by affirming that the survivor's interpretations are understandable and real.
- Wise Mind reflection synthesizes emotional truth ("It hurt") with reason-based truth ("It's over") to link the amygdala and hippocampus, thereby promoting balanced integration across emotional and narrative memory systems.
- Dialectical statements like "It's true this happened, *and* it's true that I'm safe now" transform the memory from a fixed trauma into a living narrative within a larger story of survival.

These top-down skills help consolidate traumatic material into a coherent narrative, allowing survivors to recognize the trauma as part of their past rather than permit it to dominate the present.

#### Vignette

Miguel, who survived a serious car accident, finds himself jolted by sudden flashes of fear when he feels vehicles make sudden, jerky movements. When this happens, he begins with Paced Breathing (TIPP) and a steadying hand on the center of his chest to calm the physical shock that accompanies these sensory fragments. Once his body settles, he uses Observe and Describe to identify that he is remembering aspects of the crash rather than facing present-day danger. With this clarity, he practices validation ("Anyone would react to those movements after what I lived through") followed by a Wise Mind dialectical reminder ("It happened, and I'm safe now"). As he continues using these skills, the once-disconnected sensory impressions gradually link into a coherent memory, allowing the accident to sit in the past instead of erupting unpredictably in the present.

## Integration Across the Consciousness and Memory System

Dissociation helps clients survive via disconnection, but recovery happens via reconnection. Mindful embodied presence—paying attention to sensations, posture, and breath—restores clients' ability to stay in their own body and in the present moment. Once safety is reestablished, reflection, meaning making, and narrative coherence can emerge. In DTRM, when clients space out or become flooded, grounding and breathing restore contact with the present. Then meaning-based interventions, such as validation, acceptance, and dialectical reframing, can safely integrate their fragmented experiences into a coherent story.

# IV. Action and Connection System

Behavior and relationship patterns reveal how internal dysregulation becomes visible. Trauma reorganizes not only the inner world but also the way people act, connect, and protect themselves. These two domains show the consequences of trauma in daily life, including impulsivity, avoidance, withdrawal, aggression, and difficulty maintaining trust. In DTRM, behavioral and relational repair arise from the integration of bottom-up stability with top-down intention, so clients move from automatic reaction to conscious engagement.

## 9. Behavioral Dysregulation: Transforming Action Under Threat

Behavioral dysregulation includes impulsive, avoidant, or self-defeating actions that arise when the system is overwhelmed. Trauma primes the body for survival responses such as fight, flight, freeze, or collapse, and these defensive states can persist long after the threat has ended (Najavits, 2002). People may lash out, shut down, self-harm, or seek numbness through substances. These actions are attempts to regulate unbearable distress and are not moral failures.

### Bottom-Up Skills Application

Behavioral stability and control begin with physiological stabilization:

- The TIPP skill rapidly downshifts sympathetic overdrive, especially during rage, panic, or impulsive urges.
- Use One-Mindfully and Participate to engage in mindful rhythmic regulation (i.e., steady, patterned movement through walking, rocking, drumming, or breathing to a beat) and entrain the nervous system to a predictable tempo. Over time, rhythm becomes a template for behavioral pacing and self-control, regulating behavior by giving the body a metronome for safety.
- An entire suite of skills—from PLEASED to IMPROVE to Self-Soothe and more—speak to calming the body as an alternative to acting on unhealthy urges.

These interventions use the body as a brake system and interrupt automatic defenses.

### Top-Down Skills Application

Once stabilized, cognitive and values-based skills help regain a sense of control:

- The STOP skill interrupts chains of impulsive behavior by creating a deliberate pause and allowing clients to choose a mindful next step.
- Bridge Burning represents a choice to remove the means of acting on harmful behaviors.

- Opposite Action teaches clients to intentionally move toward more effective behaviors (i.e., those that are opposite to destructive urges) when emotions are high.

Together, these skills teach clients to act from intention rather than impulse and to build safety through choice.

### Vignette

Ron, who grew up in a violent home, feels explosive anger when corrected by his supervisor. His muscles tighten, breath quickens, and vision narrows. He uses Paced Breathing and alternates between tensing and releasing his major muscle groups (TIPP) to facilitate bottom-up regulation. Once he's calmer, he creates a Pros and Cons list and recognizes that yelling may feel powerful but could cost him his job, which is top-down thinking. The urge toward reactive aggression transforms into mindful self-control.

## 10. Relational Dysregulation: Relearning Connection and Safety

Relational trauma disrupts the nervous system's ability to regulate through connection. When attachment figures are sources of fear, rejection, or inconsistency, intimacy can feel unsafe. People may oscillate between withdrawal and enmeshment and between mistrust and appeasement (Bowlby, 1988; Fisher, 2017). The body interprets relationships as potential threats and activates defenses even in moments of care.

### Bottom-Up Skills Application

Relational safety begins in the body. Long before trust forms in the mind, the nervous system scans for cues of danger or connection:

- Mindful presence in relationships teaches awareness of breath, tone, posture, and facial expression during interactions. Regulating these signals calms the nervous system through skills like Observe and Describe, Mindfulness of Current Emotion, and Opposite Action practices (such as Half-Smile and Willing Hands), which shift the body from guardedness toward openness.
- The GIVE skill can be practiced somatically through softened gaze, modulated voice, and open orientation toward the other person. These behaviors activate ventral vagal pathways that support connection.
- Proactive use of skills from the distress tolerance and emotion regulation modules allows clients to enter into relationships in a more regulated state.

When the body experiences calm, rhythm, and attunement, the mind interprets relationships more accurately, allowing openness and reciprocity to emerge.

### Top-Down Skills Application

Once clients are physiologically steadied, interpersonal frameworks can guide them in reconstructing relational meaning:

- FAST reinforces clients' self-respect and boundaries while helping them avoid patterns of appeasement that undermine their needs.
- DEAR MAN allows clients to assert their needs, set boundaries, and communicate more effectively.
- Dialectical thinking supports complexity. For example, clients can balance the need for connection with a need for space.

These top-down strategies integrate values, communication, and perspective taking, transforming relationships from reactive exchanges into balanced, intentional interactions.

> **Vignette**
>
> Mia, who fears abandonment, feels her chest tighten during an argument with her partner. She notices the tension, places a hand over her sternum, and breathes until her body relaxes, which are bottom-up tools. She then uses DEAR MAN to express her needs calmly: "I felt scared when you left the room. Can we talk before either of us walks away?" That is top-down thinking. She stays connected without losing self-respect.

## Integration Across the Action and Connection System

Behavior and relationships express the state of the internal system. When the nervous system is reactive, behavior becomes impulsive, and relationships swing between threat and withdrawal. Healing asks people to regulate action and connection. Bottom-up skills stabilize arousal and turn the body into a platform for safety. Top-down skills translate this stability into choice, communication, and trust. Over time, clients learn that they can act effectively without harmful behaviors and connect without losing themselves.

# V. Developmental Integration System

Developmental dysregulation is the soil in which other domains take root. It reflects the long-term effects of relational neglect, abuse, and inconsistent caregiving on self-regulation. Early trauma interrupts the co-regulated experiences needed for emotional stability, cognitive integration, and relational trust (Perry & Szalavitz, 2017; Schore, 2001). Survivors of developmental trauma may enter adulthood with fragile self-awareness, low distress tolerance, and limited agency. DTRM understands these as developmental gaps that can be rebuilt through bottom-up safety, top-down intentionality, and corrective relational experience.

## 11. Developmental Dysregulation: Rebuilding the Architecture of Regulation

Developmental trauma occurs when caregivers who should be regulating influences for their child become sources of fear or absence. Without consistent attunement, the child cannot learn to interpret internal cues, name emotions, or rely on others for co-regulation (Bowlby, 1988; Schore, 2001). The developing nervous system adapts to chronic threat by overactivating or shutting down, and it embeds defensive patterns in the brain. As adults, survivors may struggle to self-soothe, trust others, and sustain a coherent identity.

### Bottom-Up Skills Application

Because early trauma is encoded physiologically and relationally, stabilization begins with body and environment:

- PLEASED provides biological scaffolding—such as sleep, nutrition, movement, and reduced substance use—while reestablishing consistent self-care rhythms that were absent early in life.
- Self-Soothe reintroduces safe sensory comfort and functions as an externalized caregiver system.
- Grounding in safe relationships, through therapist modeling or group settings, allows the body to experience co-regulation with others.

Through rhythm, comfort, and co-regulation, the body learns that nurture is possible now, transforming survival patterns into a felt sense of safety and belonging.

### Top-Down Skills Application

Once stability is present, top-down skills support growth in agency, meaning, and self-definition:

- Build Mastery fosters competence through repeated successful experiences and counters learned helplessness.
- Build Positive Experiences with others strengthens pathways for joy and engagement and restores motivation and hope.
- GIVE and FAST provide frameworks for boundaries, reciprocity, and mutual respect.

These skills gradually rebuild the internal framework that early experiences failed to provide, supporting the emergence of a more stable and values-based identity.

#### Vignette

Renee, neglected in early childhood, experiences exhaustion and confusion about her needs. She sets small routines that represent bottom-up strategies, such as practicing self-care upon waking, taking a minute for mindful breathing several times a day, and identifying one pleasant sensory cue before bed. As her capacity for self-regulation grows, she uses Build Mastery to complete simple daily tasks and acknowledge each success, which is a top-down approach. Over time, she reports finally feeling like she is "raising herself." Caring for her body and making intentional choices rebuilds the foundation of self-regulation that her early life failed to provide.

## Integration Across the Developmental Integration System

Developmental dysregulation is both origin and convergence point for other domains. Emotional flooding, cognitive rigidity, somatic tension, relational fear, and dissociative detachment often trace back to missing experiences of consistent safety and connection. Healing recreates the developmental conditions for growth, including stability, curiosity, reflection, and relational trust. Bottom-up interventions provide the secure base that was missing. Top-down practices build identity, purpose, and mastery, which turn survival into living.

# RISE: A Clinical Framework for Regulation

Across all five systems and eleven domains, trauma creates fragmentation. Restoration and coherence occur through a deliberate balance of bottom-up and top-down methods. The process is not linear but spiral. Bottom-up grounding leads to top down insight, which deepens body trust, which expands emotional and cognitive flexibility. This recursive flow is the essence of whole-system regulation. Each skill becomes both pathway and proof that healing is possible. The acronym RISE operationalizes this process.

As previously mentioned, DTRM organizes recovery into four steps represented by the acronym RISE: Recognize the symptoms and dysregulation, Identify the triggers, make a Skills-based response, and Evaluate the outcomes and adapt as needed. This is the operational backbone of DTRM. It translates dysregulation into opportunity for regulation by providing a structured, repeatable, and flexible framework for both therapist and client.

This recursive method can be applied in the moment, retrospectively, or proactively—focusing on specific situations or more general symptoms and areas of dysregulation. Clinically, RISE helps clients transform reactive patterns into intentional regulation, and it gives therapists and clients a shared language and approach to structure sessions, track progress, and reinforce skill generalization.

RISE is not simply a handout or checklist that you fill out. Rather, it is a clinical process learned through modeling and guided practice. In session, you help clients:

1. **Locate and prioritize entry points:** Identify the affected symptom clusters where dysregulation is most accessible (body, thought, emotion, or behavior) and most in need of a targeted skills intervention.

2. **Name and normalize:** Reframe symptoms, dysregulation, and triggers as informative signals rather than personal failures.
3. **Select and practice skills:** Match and sequence appropriate DBT skills to the relevant systems and domains to achieve regulation.
4. **Reflect and adapt:** Reinforce learning through debriefing, curiosity, and compassion.

Throughout, you maintain a *dialectical stance*, balancing structure with flexibility, acceptance and validation with change, and safety with growth. Here are the four steps in clinical practice.

## Step 1: Recognize

Prompt your client to bring mindful attention to their current experience. For example, you might simply inquire, "Let's pause . . . what are you noticing in your body, thoughts, or emotions right now?" Recognition transforms reactivity into information. As you observe which systems and underlying domains are active (e.g., somatic tension, intrusive memory, relational withdrawal), you mirror the client's language to support accurate self-observation.

## Step 2: Identify

Once the client is aware of their experience, help them explore what triggered this shift. You might ask, "What happened just before you noticed this change?" or "Does anything about this moment remind you of something earlier?" Identifying internal and external triggers clarifies context, allowing your client to see that their dysregulation follows a meaningful pattern rather than being a random event.

## Step 3: Skills-Based Response

Guide the client to choose and apply one or more skills that fit the type and intensity of their dysregulation. Provide any needed psychoeducation and modeling in the moment. For example:

- For body-based activation, anchor in grounding, Paced Breathing or other TIPP skills, or Self-Soothe.
- For cognitive or emotional looping, use dialectical thinking alongside Wise Mind, Check the Facts, or Radical Acceptance.
- For behavioral or relational reactivity, apply Opposite Action, GIVE, or DEAR MAN.

Model a brief "pause, apply, and notice" rhythm so your client experiences regulation in real time rather than just a theoretical discussion about it.

## Step 4: Evaluate and Adapt

Close the loop through reflection, emphasizing learning over performance. Ask questions like "What changed, even slightly?" or "What might we try sooner or differently next time?" This process transforms skill use from trial and error into skillful experimentation. Clients learn that the goal is not to "get it right" but to remain engaged in the process of regulation. This reflection reinforces self-efficacy, reduces perfectionism, and reinforces the neuroplastic pathways that strengthen regulation.

The following are some ways you can integrate RISE across contexts:

- **In-session modeling:** Use RISE in session to slow reactivity and support co-regulation. You can guide clients through the steps by asking, "Let's recognize what's happening. What might have triggered that? Which skill could help us stay grounded as we talk about this?"
- **Between sessions:** Assign the *RISE Worksheet* for daily practice or in response to specific events (see chapter 7). Emphasize that its strengths lie in its ability to help clients make sense of their experiences and respond effectively through repeated skills practice.
- **Postcrisis or debriefing:** Use RISE retrospectively after an episode of dysregulation to debrief. Walk through the process with the client to discover what helped, what didn't, and what they learned from the experience.
- **Proactive preparation:** Plan ahead with RISE for anticipated challenges like anniversaries, appointments, or difficult family interactions. Clients can use their knowledge of personal triggers and dysregulation to "cope ahead." Rehearsing skills before stressful events happen sets them up for success.
- **Relational application:** When clinically indicated, teach the client's partners, friends, or family members the RISE process so they can provide support and ideally co-regulate with the client. They don't need to know the breadth of the clusters, systems, or domains—focusing on what specifically relates to their loved one is sufficient.

### Therapist Considerations

- **Pacing:** Adjust your level of inquiry to the client's window of tolerance. Avoid overprocessing too soon, which can create overwhelm. Take it one step at a time.
- **Flexibility:** Begin with the skills and areas of regulation that are most accessible. Some skills are much more straightforward to understand and use than others. As a rule, start with those skills.
- **Language:** Keep your observations neutral and descriptive, saving your interpretations for later. Remember to mirror the client's language to strengthen understanding.

- **Reinforcement:** Praise effort and process—not perfection. Shape skill use with feedback like "You noticed and used a skill. That's regulation in action."
- **Documentation:** Track observed symptom clusters, active systems and domains, and skill use for supervision and treatment planning.

Through repetition, clients internalize RISE as a self-directed process: "I can notice, I can understand, I can respond, I can learn." Over time, structured awareness and targeted skill use become spontaneous self-regulation, transforming therapy from crisis management into embodied mastery.

One final note: Clinical sequencing is essential to DTRM. Trauma disrupts multiple systems simultaneously, yet not all systems and domains require intervention at the same time. A central task is determining what to stabilize first, what to address next, and what can wait. Precision in applying skills is essential for effective treatment.

When sequencing is accurate, relatively simple interventions can produce meaningful regulation, often extending beyond the domain initially targeted. Conversely, when sequencing is off, interventions may fail or further destabilize the client. For example:

- Targeting interpersonal skills in the relational domain may increase distress if nervous system dysregulation is not addressed first.
- If a client is dissociating, skills that restore presence in the dissociative domain should precede other interventions.
- Addressing meaning and belief dysregulation is not usually effective when significant dysregulation persists in other domains, such as the emotional domain.

Mapping (discussed in chapter 7) identifies where dysregulation occurs, RISE operationalizes what we do, and sequencing determines when each step unfolds.

CHAPTER 4

# The Phases and Treatment Structure of DTRM

DTRM provides a progressive, skills-based framework for healing that approaches trauma treatment in a phase-based manner, similar to the work of Judith Herman (1992) and Marylene Cloitre and colleagues (2011), among others. Each phase targets specific domains of dysregulation and sequences treatment accordingly. While the phases are progressive, they are not strictly linear, as clients may revisit earlier phases as needed, just as a foundation occasionally requires tuckpointing. The goal is to strengthen stability so clients can begin to reconstruct their identity, develop meaning out of their experiences, and move toward a more satisfying life.

## Phase 1: Safety, Symptom Stabilization, and Regulation

### "Extinguishing the Fire"

When clients first enter treatment, they present in states of profound dysregulation. The first clinical priority is to extinguish the fire of acute symptoms by creating a therapeutic environment that promotes predictability, stabilization, and skillful regulation.

In this phase, you do not attempt to process trauma narratives or engage in meaning-making work. Instead, you orient treatment toward reducing immediate suffering, building trust in the therapeutic relationship, and equipping clients with actionable skills that provide a sense of control over their inner and outer experiences. Safety and stabilization are essential prerequisites for deeper trauma work.

DTRM conceptualizes this phase as a dynamic interplay between internal regulation and external safety. Your role is to be a co-regulator, offering consistent session structures, predictable interventions, and unwavering attunement to the client's shifting internal states. Check-ins, grounding rituals, and skills training and rehearsals serve not just as session openers but as anchors in the therapeutic process that reinforce the message: "You are safe here, and we have a plan."

Clinically, this work begins with dialectics, not simply as a theoretical stance but as a lived experience within the therapeutic relationship. You model a dialectical approach by validating the client's suffering while maintaining confidence in their capacity for change. For example, you might say, "It makes sense that you feel overwhelmed right now, *and* I believe you can get through this with support and skills." This dual stance dismantles black-and-white thinking, a hallmark of trauma responses, and lays the foundation for a more flexible, integrative approach to self and experience.

Building on this dialectical frame, you introduce mindfulness, emphasizing present-moment awareness as both a skill and a stabilizing practice. Rather than starting with abstract concepts, you teach core mindfulness skills through simple, concrete exercises, such as noticing the breath, observing sensory input, or practicing One-Mindful attention to the environment. The focus is on "What is happening right now?" rather than "Why did this happen?" Mindfulness becomes a tool for anchoring attention during dysregulating storms, grounding awareness when dissociation threatens, and cultivating Wise Mind as a refuge amid chaos.

With mindfulness in place, you move to teaching distress tolerance skills—those practical, immediate interventions that help clients survive acute moments of distress without making things worse. These skills are presented not as coping shortcuts but as lifesaving tools for crisis stabilization. These skills work in both a top-down and bottom-up manner, with the flexibility to target all eleven domains of dysfunction. Through in-session practice and real-life application, you guide clients to aggregate these skills into safety plans that they can rely on outside of session. With distress tolerance skills, you reinforce the message: "These skills are how you keep yourself safe while we build toward deeper healing."

As clients begin to experience some relief from acute symptoms, emotion regulation work is layered in to build the foundations of emotional literacy and stabilization. You introduce clients to the model of emotions, among other relevant psychoeducation, to help them practice identifying their emotional states and working to regulate them. Emotion regulation emphasizes that emotions, while intense, are manageable, serve a purpose, and can be influenced with skills like Build Mastery, Build Positive Experiences, and Opposite Action.

Finally, interpersonal effectiveness begins in this phase through the lens of the therapeutic relationship itself. You model consistent, attuned, and validating interactions while gently encouraging clients to express their needs, ask for help, and communicate openly within the safety of sessions. Small moments—like a client saying, "I don't know how to tell you I'm overwhelmed," and you responding with validation—become corrective relational experiences that start to rebuild trust in both self and others.

Note that this first phase of DTRM has strong parallels to stage 1 in traditional DBT, where therapists are encouraged to follow a clear treatment hierarchy that prioritizes interventions in this order:

1. Suicidal behavior and urges that the client is at risk of acting on

2. Self-harm or substance use behaviors and urges that the client is at risk of acting on
3. Treatment-interfering behaviors on the part of the client or the therapist
4. Other clinical issues that impact treatment

By the conclusion of this first phase, the client should be able to reliably identify and manage key domains of dysregulation with specific, practiced skills. They should also have a co-created safety plan, some capacity to remain present during distress, and a growing confidence in their ability to ask for and engage in help. Progress is marked not by symptom elimination but by a tangible shift from helplessness to active engagement in self-regulation.

### By the end of phase 1, clients should:

- Recognize when they are becoming dysregulated
- Use a variety of skills across modules with increasing effectiveness
- Demonstrate the capacity for presence in session during distress
- Have a collaboratively built safety and stabilization plan
- Be able to reflect on distress without retraumatization

As van der Kolk (2014) notes, "Trauma is not just an event that took place sometime in the past; it is also the imprint left by that experience on mind, brain, and body" (p. 21). Phase 1 work equips clients with the tools they need to interrupt that imprint in the here and now, laying the groundwork for deeper healing to come.

## Phase 2: Emotional Integration, Body Awareness, and Skillful Response

### "Rebuilding the Foundation"

With stabilization underway, clients often experience an increase in emotional, somatic, and interoceptive awareness. For many, this is initially unsettling. After years of numbing or hypervigilance, it can be dysregulating to feel emotions or sense the body. This phase focuses on helping clients safely explore their internal world and develop regulation across emotional, somatic, nervous system, and interoceptive domains.

We begin again with dialectics, which guides clients to hold space for the complexity of their experience: "You feel sad and safe. Grief and growth can happen at the same time." Dialectical thinking provides scaffolding to dismantle binary trauma narratives like "I must forgive or hate" or "Feeling means falling apart."

Through the continued practice of mindfulness, clients deepen their capacity to Observe and Describe internal states, which now include more subtle shifts in mood and sensation. They continue to build and integrate somatic mindfulness, including body scans, breath work, and gentle movement, to bridge the mind-body divide often created by trauma.

Distress tolerance skills remain essential in this phase. Here, we expand their use from acute crisis management to proactive maintenance of regulation across domains. Clients are encouraged to use skills like Self-Soothing, Radical Acceptance, and Willingness to navigate emerging experience, and skills like Urge Surfing are used to ride the ups and downs of experience without engaging in impulsive behaviors to escape or avoid what's happening in the mind and body.

With emotion regulation, the work deepens. Clients track emotion cycles, address vulnerability factors (PLEASED), and learn to apply Opposite Action. They are guided to build positive emotional experiences and establish mastery in areas of daily life. Through this, emotional reactivity becomes less terrifying and more manageable, and positive feelings become increasingly common.

Last, interpersonal effectiveness moves into actively building and maintaining healthy relationships. Clients increase their practice of DEAR MAN to make requests, say no, and set boundaries; GIVE to increase regulation in relationships; and FAST to maintain self-respect. These skills are practiced in session and assigned for real-world use. This feedback loop—moving between in-session practice and real-life application—shapes continued progress and reinforces success.

By the end of phase 2, clients should:

- Accurately name emotional states and their causes
- Demonstrate increased somatic and interoceptive awareness
- Use distress tolerance skills independently, consistently, and proactively
- Begin tolerating emotional discomfort without escape, avoidance, or impulsivity
- Develop increasing confidence in engaging in and navigating relationships

## Phase 3: Relational Healing, Identity Reconstruction, and Meaningful Living

### "Rebuilding What Trauma Broke"

As clients develop emotional stability, somatic attunement, and regulation across domains, the focus shifts toward healing within relationships and reclaiming identity beyond trauma. Many trauma survivors have learned that connection equals danger and vulnerability leads to harm, and their identity is either frozen in time or defined by what happened to them. This phase is about dismantling those narratives and offering alternatives rooted in connection, values, and purpose.

In this phase, dialectics is central to narrative work. Clients explore and revise core beliefs: "I can be strong and still need others" or "I am not broken. I was hurt." The therapeutic relationship serves as a reparative model of safety and repair. Clients learn to hold both anger and love, mistrust and openness, grief and joy.

In phase 3, clients increasingly practice mindfulness in relational contexts—by listening attentively to others, staying present during interpersonal interactions, and noticing the state of their body while in connection with others. They learn to identify when they are triggered interpersonally and apply mindfulness to respond rather than react.

Distress tolerance also becomes more targeted toward the relational domain. Much of the unresolved grief that emerges at this phase is relational in nature: grief for relationships that were lost or unsafe, for attachment needs that went unmet, or for parts of the self that had to disconnect in order to survive. Clients use Radical Acceptance to acknowledge these relational wounds without collapsing into them, and they lean on sensory-based skills, such as grounding and Self-Soothing, to steady the body during moments of vulnerability. These strategies allow clients to remain regulated while engaging in connection, making it possible to grieve what was broken while building relationships that feel safer and more reciprocal.

Emotion regulation in phase 3 focuses on increasing emotional flexibility and reshaping clients' personal narratives. They learn to identify emotions connected to their values and practice responding in ways that align with their chosen identity. For example, a client who values authenticity may allow themselves to feel sadness during a painful anniversary yet choose to use Opposite Action to reach out to a supportive friend instead of isolating. As clients engage in actions that match their values, they learn to handle the emotions that naturally arise—both positive and difficult—without becoming overwhelmed. They also deepen compassion for the parts of themselves that developed as survival strategies and begin to reinterpret their past experiences in ways that support agency, resilience, and authentic self-expression.

In interpersonal effectiveness, clients integrate all previously learned skills into their real-life relationships. They practice asking for what they need, setting boundaries, navigating conflict, and building trust in both old and new relationships. Over time, they reshape old relational patterns, such as avoidance or overaccommodation, and move toward more empowered, values-based connection.

## By the end of phase 3, clients should:

- View their trauma as part of their story but not their entire identity
- Sustain emotionally regulated states in complex relationships
- Apply interpersonal skills in a variety of real-world settings
- Describe a values-based identity that includes agency, meaning, and purpose
- Reconnect with community, creativity, or contribution in personally meaningful ways

## Flexible Phases Offer a Dynamic Map, Not a Fixed Path

While DTRM offers this structured, three-phase framework, it is essential to recognize that trauma recovery is rarely a straight line. Healing unfolds in cycles, with forward movement, pauses, and returns to earlier work as new challenges or life contexts emerge. Each phase serves as a compass rather than a rigid checkpoint, guiding both clinicians and clients toward growth while honoring the complexity of trauma's impact.

Phase 1 is necessary when the client's primary struggles center on acute dysregulation or unsafe behaviors. The work here focuses on establishing safety, stabilizing symptoms, and building core regulation skills. Even when clients show insight or readiness for deeper work, if they are unable to stay present during distress or lack basic coping strategies, phase 1 interventions remain the priority.

Phase 2 becomes the focus when the client shows increasing capacity for self-regulation and begins to access their emotions, body sensations, and interoceptive cues with manageable distress. This phase is marked by a shift from crisis survival to skillful engagement with emotions, urges, and relationships. You will know you are working in phase 2 when clients can remain present with discomfort, use skills independently, and begin to explore meaning making without being overwhelmed.

Phase 3 emerges when the client is ready to focus on healing their relationships, rebuilding their sense of identity, and living in alignment with their values. Signs include the client's ability to tolerate uncertainty in relationships, navigate intimacy, and use interpersonal skills effectively in real-world situations. Clients in this phase often articulate a desire to move beyond trauma-defined narratives and pursue connection, growth, and meaningful contribution.

At every phase, your attunement to the client's current capacity, not their perceived progress, guides intervention. For example, a client in phase 3 may still need grounding skills from phase 1 when facing a triggering relationship rupture. Conversely, a client in phase 1 may benefit from phase 3's values clarification to anchor motivation for change. The question is never "What phase are we supposed to be in?" but rather "What does this client need right now, given their dysregulation profile, goals, and context?"

DBT's five modules hold the tools that you apply flexibly across these phases. These modules are not bound to any single phase but are woven throughout treatment based on the client's presenting needs. The right skill is always the one that works, in the moment, for the person in front of you.

Ultimately, DTRM provides a scaffold, not a script. It empowers you to work with precision and adaptability, equipping clients to move from fragmentation to integration and from survival to agency. By recognizing each phase as a living, dynamic process, both you and the client stay aligned in the shared work of healing, rooted in flexibility, guided by purpose, and grounded in hope.

## Treatment Structures and Service Delivery in DTRM

Unlike exposure therapies or narrative-processing treatments, which may not be appropriate, feasible, or safe in certain clinical contexts, DTRM focuses on the direct regulation of trauma symptoms. This skills-centered model reduces risk, allowing more clients—who might not be able to tolerate other trauma-processing approaches—to benefit, all while maintaining clinical rigor in both individual and group settings. When implemented in group formats, DTRM leverages the known therapeutic benefits of group dynamics, including shared validation, mutual support, social learning, accountability, and enhanced motivation for change.

Clinicians delivering DTRM structure their services within four foundational treatment modes adapted from DBT. These modes are conceptual tools that offer a consistent, principle-driven method of treatment delivery across a range of client needs and clinical settings. They include:

1. **Individual Therapy**

   DTRM can be delivered as a fully individualized service, making it especially suitable for clients requiring one-on-one care, those with complex presentations, or in settings where group services are not available. Individual therapy sessions within DTRM focus on personalized assessment, targeted skills practice, symptom management, and the reinforcement of treatment goals. As the therapist, you work collaboratively alongside clients, using the DTRM framework to enhance mindful awareness, build coping skills, and decrease dysregulation across multiple domains.

   Your role is active and engaged—validating, guiding, and coaching clients toward effective use of skills in their daily lives. DTRM tools such as the Diary Card, *RISE Worksheet*, and Behavior and Solution Analysis help structure sessions, allowing you to monitor progress and foster client ownership of the treatment process.

   **Clinical consideration:** When clients participate in DTRM, they are advised not to engage in trauma-processing therapies such as prolonged exposure or EMDR. These interventions may be pursued once clients have established reliable symptom regulation through DTRM.

2. **Group Skills Training**

   When offered in group settings, DTRM provides a rich environment for skills acquisition and application, with the added benefits of peer support, modeling, and accountability.[16] Group skills training is structured around three distinct components:

   - **DBT skills training session:** Groups begin with a mindfulness practice to ground both therapists and clients. The session follows a structured curriculum that introduces, teaches, and practices DTRM skills. Facilitators foster active participation, encouraging questions, shared insights, and collaborative exercises.

   - **Structured check-in:** Clients use tools like the Diary Card or *RISE Worksheet* to report on their symptoms, skill use, and progress. This segment fosters accountability, encourages peer validation, and provides real-time feedback and support within the group. It also helps prioritize focus areas for the session.

16 A *DTRM Group Expectations Handout* is in the appendix.

   - **Targeted skills application:** This segment focuses on the application of DTRM skills to real-life trauma symptoms and triggers. Facilitators guide clients in practicing skills and adapting them to personal challenges using tools like RISE. Group problem-solving and collaborative learning further enhance skill integration. Topics that require individualized exploration are referred to individual therapy.

   **Clinical consideration:** DTRM group work is not a venue for trauma processing or detailed narrative sharing. The focus remains firmly on symptom management, regulation, and adaptive functioning through skills practice within a structured, supportive environment.

3. **Skills Coaching**

   Skills coaching, which is an essential adjunct in DTRM, involves a brief, structured phone call designed to support clients between sessions when real-time application of skills is needed. This coaching is structured, brief (typically under five minutes), and strictly focused on facilitating the use of DTRM skills for symptom management, regulation, and problem-solving. It is not a venue for therapy sessions, processing, or casual conversation.

   Therapists set clear guidelines for coaching, maintaining professional boundaries while offering clients timely interventions that promote skillful action and prevent escalation. Skills coaching also reinforces client autonomy and enhances the generalization of skills to everyday situations. You can find a client *Skills Coaching Worksheet* with guidelines in the appendix.

   **Clinical consideration:** Skills coaching is typically conducted during business hours and should be guided by clear policies outlined in client agreements and program expectations.

4. **Therapist Consultation**

   Ongoing therapist consultation is a critical component of high-quality DTRM delivery. Consultation teams provide a structured environment where you can reflect, engage in case discussion, and enhance your skills. The consultation process promotes treatment fidelity, mitigates therapist burnout, and fosters a shared commitment to delivering effective, compassionate care.

   Consultation emphasizes the dialectical balance between acceptance and change, mirroring the therapeutic stance modeled for clients. Regular participation in consultation supports you in navigating challenging cases, maintaining adherence to the DTRM model, and enhancing the overall quality of care within a treatment team or practice setting. You'll learn more about therapist consultation in the next chapter.

   **Clinical consideration:** Because trauma treatment places unique demands on the therapist, participation in consultation is not optional within DTRM. Working without consultation increases the risk of drift, overaccommodation, therapy-interfering interventions, and vicarious traumatization. Regular consultation keeps therapists grounded in the model, supported in their clinical decisions, and connected to a team that reinforces effective, ethical, and sustainable trauma care.

DTRM empowers you to deliver trauma-focused care with a high degree of flexibility and structure. Whether applied in individual therapy, in group programming, or through skills coaching, the model's adaptability supports client-centered care across diverse clinical environments. Each mode serves as a structured yet flexible pathway for delivering effective trauma symptom regulation, reinforcing the foundational belief that healing is most achievable when clients are equipped with skills, supported by a validating environment, and guided by informed, reflective clinicians.

Note that the treatment structures described in this chapter are presented in general terms. Because treatment settings and levels of care vary widely, the specific design of service delivery should be considered on a case-by-case basis. Relevant clinical experience in program design, along with consultation when needed, can help clinicians develop effective treatment structures and implementation strategies.

CHAPTER 5

# Therapist Use of Self and Clinical Culture

In DTRM, the therapist is not a passive facilitator or neutral technician delivering interventions from a distance. Instead, you are a central, living element of the healing process by being a regulating force, a consistent co-regulator, and an embodied model of integration. In trauma recovery, your presence becomes the therapeutic environment. Your nervous system, posture, tone, and attention shape what the client learns not only about trauma but about safety, trust, and the possibility of change.

If trauma is fundamentally a disruption in relationship, particularly relationships that were meant to protect, then healing must involve the restoration of relational safety. The client must not only hear about regulation or read about validation; they must *feel* it in your presence. They must experience what it's like to coexist with another human being who is attuned, congruent, and responsive. DTRM therefore positions therapist use of self not as a soft skill or side effect but as a central, active ingredient in treatment.

To teach regulation, you must inhabit a regulated state. To offer acceptance, you must embody nonjudgment. And to model safety, you must be safe in the room, not just behaviorally but physiologically and emotionally. This is not theoretical. It is a core intervention.

## The Therapist as a Regulated Nervous System

Before any skill is taught, before any trauma is named, the client's nervous system is already scanning the room. This unconscious assessment—often shaped by a history of betrayal or threat—is not influenced by theory or insight but by felt sense. Your facial expression, tone of voice, body posture, and breathing patterns communicate either safety or danger, presence or absence.

When you enter sessions grounded, with an awareness of your body, breath, and pacing, you begin the session as a co-regulating presence. The way you greet a client, transition into difficult material, or respond to escalation can either widen their window of tolerance or narrow it. Conversely, when you show up rushed, fragmented, or dysregulated, then clients, especially those with a history of chronic invalidation, may internalize that the therapy space itself is unsafe.

A therapist who notices tightness in their jaw or a racing heart when a client begins to spiral can respond by softening their voice, slowing their speech, and grounding through posture and breath. These microadjustments send powerful messages to the client's nervous system: "You are not too much. We can stay here together." Regulation, in this way, is not taught from the outside in; rather, it is transmitted from the inside out.

## Embodiment as Ethical Practice

Trauma often dislocates individuals from their bodily experience. Many survivors live from the neck up, disconnected from sensation, breath, or physical presence. In response, you must offer the opposite—not only an attuned mind but also an attuned body. Somatic awareness is not optional in DTRM; it is an ethical commitment.

Therapists who maintain somatic awareness throughout the day, such as feeling their shoulders creeping up during a tense session or sensing themselves leaning away in discomfort, are better positioned to self-regulate in the moment. The goal is not to be perfectly calm but to be responsive to your own somatic cues and capable of recentering. Even subtle shifts in posture, like uncrossing your arms, softening your hands, and grounding your feet, can create profound changes in the energy of the room.

Clients who say, "I feel like something's off, but I don't know what" are often responding not to words but to bodies. If your body says, "I'm bracing," or "I'm detached," the client's system will likely mirror or resist that message. But when you lead with grounded embodiment, the client is more likely to follow, consciously or not, toward safety and regulation.

## Rupture and Repair as Method

Relational rupture is inevitable in trauma work. A client's triggers will become activated, sometimes by your tone, pacing, missed cues, or the content of the session itself. What distinguishes healing relationships from harmful ones is not the absence of rupture but the presence of respectful, skillful repair.

DTRM clinicians are taught to actively monitor for signs of disconnection: moments when the client withdraws, becomes suddenly compliant, dissociates, or escalates unexpectedly. These are not moments to push forward or retreat from but to *pause within*. You might say, "I noticed something changed just now . . . can we check in on what's happening?" This gentle, nonpathologizing invitation builds trust and models curiosity over shame.

Repair is not about being right or smoothing things over. It is about restoring dignity to the client's experience. Research in attachment and affective neuroscience consistently shows that growth occurs not through perfection but through repair—through attunement after misattunement (Siegel, 2007; Tronick, 2007).

Your ability to provide this reparative experience is key, as clients emerging from invalidating systems—at home, in institutions, or in relationships—carry with them internalized models of disconnection, chaos, rigidity, or fear. To be effective, trauma treatment must not subtly replicate these dynamics through hierarchy, punitive boundaries, or cold professionalism. DTRM therapists actively model the culture they want clients to internalize.

This includes a tone of compassionate directness: being honest without being harsh. It involves a structure that is predictable but flexible, where sessions begin with mindfulness and check-in rituals but adapt to client needs. Boundaries are presented as protective, not controlling, and transparency about process is encouraged when clinically appropriate. A therapist who says, "This was a hard session, so let's focus on skills to use after" is not just teaching self-awareness but modeling how to stay regulated in relationship when things get difficult.

In group or team settings, the same principles apply. Sessions may begin with a shared breath or regulation practice. Skills are presented as human practices for everyone—not as tools reserved for clients alone. Clinical teams are encouraged to embody the dialectical values they teach: honesty and humility, clarity and warmth, structure and responsiveness.

## Consultation: Practicing Together What We Ask of Clients

Trauma work changes us. It shapes our dreams, memories, relationships, and thresholds. Whether subtle or overt, the emotional impact of bearing witness to suffering accumulates in a clinician's nervous system. This can manifest as fatigue, dread, numbness, emotional reactivity, overidentification with clients, sleep disturbances, and relational withdrawal. These are not signs of weakness but calls for care. Therefore, DTRM views reflective practice as necessary infrastructure and not simply extra credit.

Therapists are encouraged to build in daily rituals for checking in with themselves before, between, and after sessions. Questions like "Where am I today with my mind, body, and spirit?" and "What am I carrying that isn't mine?" help prevent dissociation and emotional leakage. End-of-week reflections may identify which client stories stuck, which boundaries softened, and what needs to be consciously released.

In addition to individual reflection, clinical teams should use regular, structured consultation groups to process vicarious trauma and reinforce mutual accountability. This consultation should be built into the rhythm of care and not used only in emergencies. Indeed, consultation in DTRM is not an optional add-on to clinical practice. Rather, it is a foundational method for sustaining therapeutic integrity, clinician well-being, and the very principles we aim to model for our clients. Just as clients need a regulated, attuned presence to support their recovery, therapists also need access to a similar relational space. In this sense, consultation becomes the therapist's own environment for co-regulation, reflection, and growth.

Borrowed from the structure of DBT, consultation in DTRM is a team-based commitment to mutual accountability and shared regulation. Here, clinicians can speak openly about the toll of the work and be met with support, not scrutiny. It is a community of practice where therapists assist each other in maintaining alignment with the model and, more importantly, alignment with themselves. This is not a supervisory function in the hierarchical sense but a validating, collaborative space where honesty, vulnerability, and dialectical thinking are explicitly encouraged. The consultation team exists to help therapists return to Wise Mind, to their values, and to their embodied presence, especially when this work inevitably evokes doubt, reactivity, or dysregulation.

In this model, consultation serves several interconnected purposes:

- First, it is a reflective space where therapists can process the emotional impact of clinical work. Bringing cases to consultation is not merely about solving clinical dilemmas but about naming the parts of ourselves that get pulled into the work, whether that's frustration with a stuck point, fear of causing harm, or the quiet erosion of compassion under the weight of chronic exposure to trauma. In this way, consultation becomes a mirror and a container in which therapists are seen, validated, and challenged with care.
- Second, consultation reinforces the dialectical stance that DTRM demands. The team helps each therapist hold both acceptance and change, self-compassion and accountability, personal impact and professional boundaries. When a therapist veers into rigid thinking, the group gently invites flexibility. When a therapist moves toward burnout or detachment, the group reflects it back with compassion and offers pathways back to presence. The consultation team, like the therapy team, models a relational culture where rupture, reflection, and repair are not just concepts but lived practices.
- Third, consultation serves as a safeguard against the slow creep of vicarious trauma and clinician drift. Regular consultation ensures that therapists are not operating in isolation, becoming overly identified with clients, or losing sight of the model's scaffolding. It creates a rhythm of checking in, recalibrating, and reconnecting, not just to clinical skills but to the deeper human work of trauma healing.
- Finally, consultation in DTRM is a dialectical process itself. It is a space where therapists can bring their fullest selves—confident and uncertain, clear and confused, regulated and reactive—and trust that these complexities will be met with attunement, not judgment. The very act of participating in consultation reflects a core DTRM principle that healing and good clinical practice happen in relationship.

In this way, consultation is not simply a mechanism for maintaining integrity to a treatment model. It is an active embodiment of DTRM's relational, embodied, and reflective values. It is where therapists come to practice what they teach, to hold each other in dialectical tension, and to remember that we are always both students and teachers in the work of healing.

## We Embody the Work

In trauma therapy, we do not sit behind the work: We *are* the work. Our regulation and attuned presence shape every intervention we deliver. DTRM reminds us that healing happens through relationship and that relationship begins with us.

To ask clients to regulate, we must regulate first. To ask them to reflect, we must be reflectively engaged. To ask them to show up authentically, we must model what it means to do so, even—and especially—when it's hard.

A DTRM therapist is not perfect, not above the work, and not immune to impact. But they are willing. Willing to reflect, repair, embody, and grow. They are regulated enough to hold space, flexible enough to respond wisely, and courageous enough to remain present. This is how healing becomes possible, not only for the client but for the clinician as well.

# SECTION II

# The Client Curriculum

CHAPTER 6

# What Is DTRM?

This curriculum, known as the Dialectical Trauma Recovery Model (DTRM), is a specialized, skills-based approach grounded in the principles of dialectical behavior therapy (DBT). The approach can be applied in individual therapy or group formats. How you receive this treatment is a decision between you and your treatment provider.

DBT is a behavioral, skills-based treatment that teaches you how to tolerate distress, regulate your emotions, improve your relationships, and live more mindfully in the present moment. Originally developed for individuals with complex emotional and behavioral challenges, DBT has since been adapted and validated for a wide range of clinical populations, including trauma survivors.

DTRM builds on this foundation by targeting specific forms of dysregulation, beyond emotional dysregulation, that often result from traumatic experiences. And while traditional trauma treatments may ask you to revisit painful memories or engage in exposure-based processes, DTRM takes a different path, offering a practical, less invasive, and empowering approach.

In DTRM, you learn how to manage your symptoms and triggers without needing to relive or reprocess the trauma. Instead, the focus is on learning practical skills that help you stay grounded, manage distress, and build a meaningful, satisfying life in spite of your traumatic past. This approach makes DTRM well suited for individuals seeking stabilization, relief, and improved functioning—without the risks or demands that can come with traditional trauma processing.

A key feature of DTRM is its emphasis on helping you understand your unique trauma-related patterns of dysregulation. Through ongoing assessment and collaborative reflection with your therapist, you'll learn where dysregulation shows up most strongly—be it in your emotions, thoughts, behaviors, body, or relationships. This understanding becomes the foundation for choosing and applying targeted DBT skills. Rather than a one-size-fits-all approach, DTRM tailors skills to address your most pressing symptoms, making treatment more focused and effective.

A key feature of DTRM is the acronym RISE, which is a straightforward way to make sense of often confusing symptoms and triggers so you can respond effectively with skills. The acronym outlines the model's four key steps:

1. Recognize your symptoms and areas of dysregulation.
2. Identify what triggers the symptoms and dysregulation.
3. Make a Skills-based response.
4. Evaluate the outcomes and adapt as needed.

DTRM is organized around five DBT modules, with each module covering a category of skills and accompanying goals:

| Module | Goal |
|---|---|
| Dialectics | Learn to think flexibly and make sense of conflicting thoughts or feelings |
| Mindfulness | Build present-moment awareness to better manage thoughts, emotions, body sensations, and stress |
| Distress tolerance | Manage urges, crises, and nervous system overwhelm without letting emotions or behaviors spiral out of control |
| Emotion regulation | Better understand and manage emotions to stabilize mood, behavior, bodily symptoms, and core beliefs |
| Interpersonal effectiveness | Develop skills to foster healthy relationships, set boundaries, and manage relational challenges |

Together, these modules and their component skills provide a comprehensive set of tools to target symptoms and dysregulation. You'll learn more about these modules and their accompanying skills in chapters 9–13. However, skills alone are not enough. Just like learning a new sport, instrument, or language, skills require consistent practice. Therefore, it is crucial that you practice skills on a regular basis and that you approach this process with patience, persistence, openness, and self-compassion.

## DTRM Tools

As part of using skills, DTRM uses the following tools to enhance treatment:

- A *Diary Card* to keep track of your symptoms and the skills you're using
- *Behavior and Solution Analysis* to understand problem behaviors and figure out how to handle them with skills
- An *Initial Skills Plan* to help you prepare for stressful or high-risk situations
- A *Personal Systems Map* to show how trauma affects different parts of your life so you can guide skill use with RISE

The first three tools are introduced here, while the Personal Systems Map is covered in the next chapter. If you commit to this work, you may find that you don't have to go back to the trauma to move forward. Rather, you can regulate the aftereffects of trauma and build a satisfying life, one skill at a time.

## The Diary Card

An important component of treatment is consistently tracking your emotional well-being, trauma-related symptoms, and skill use. This is done through a simple but powerful tool known as the Diary Card.

Research shows that clients who track these aspects of their treatment daily make more rapid and sustained progress than those who do not. The reason is clear: Self-monitoring increases mindful awareness, which improves decision-making and enhances the effectiveness of skill application.

The Diary Card serves several important functions:

- It helps you track your emotions, trauma symptoms, areas of dysregulation, urges to act on unhealthy behaviors, and skill use.
- It increases your awareness of patterns related to trauma, allowing for more skillful choices.
- It provides important information to tailor your therapy to your specific needs.
- It keeps you accountable to yourself and your goals for recovery.
- It reinforces progress by drawing attention to positive change.
- It allows your therapist to better understand your daily experience, making sessions more focused and effective.

You will fill out a Diary Card every day, ideally at the same time each day, to create consistency. When completing the card, you are reflecting on the past twenty-four hours. The process should only take about three to five minutes, which is a small investment of time that can lead to big returns in your progress.

The areas on the Diary Card and how to track them are included on the next pages. Note that each scale measures something different, so lower scores may reflect more stability in some areas, while higher scores reflect greater engagement in others. Let the description of each item guide how you choose your number. Also note that these areas will make more sense after you review chapter 7.

Finally, the Diary Card may seem overwhelming at first, but that reaction is common. With a week or two of practice, it often becomes much easier to use. You can also work with your therapist to scale it down at first, such as focusing on the one to three domains most affected (as determined by dysregulation mapping), and gradually building toward completing the full card over time.

Worksheet

# The Diary Card

## Front Side

### Medications (Rx)

- Whether you took your medications as prescribed (Y or N)

### Mind and Meaning System

- **Emotional dysregulation (EMO):** How intense your emotions felt, from low (0) to high (10)
- **Cognitive dysregulation (COG):** How disrupted your thought processes were, from low (0) to high (10)
- **Meaning and belief dysregulation (MB):** How much trauma-related beliefs or interpretations affected your day, from low (0) to high (10)

### Body-Based System

- **Nervous system dysregulation (NER):** How activated or shutdown your system felt, from calm (0) to highly activated or shutdown (10)
- **Somatic dysregulation (SOM):** How much body tension or discomfort you experienced, from low (0) to high (10)
- **Interoceptive dysregulation (INT):** How difficult it was to read internal signals such as hunger, fullness, or energy, from not difficult (0) to very difficult (10)
- **Sleep:** Number of hours you slept, as well as whether your sleep felt restorative (Y or N)
- **Movement (MOVE):** Whether you engaged in physical activity to support regulation (Y or N)

### Consciousness and Memory System

- **Dissociative dysregulation (DIS):** Degree to which you spaced out, disconnected, or detached, from not at all (0) to extreme (10)
- **Memory dysregulation (MEM):** How difficult it was to recall, sequence, or separate the past from the present, from not difficult (0) to very difficult (10)
- **Grounding (GRD):** Whether you used grounding to stay present (Y or N)

### Action and Connection System

- **Substance use urges (SUB):** Intensity of urges to use substances, from low (0) to high (10), as well as whether you acted on those urges (Y or N)
- **Suicidal ideation (SI):** Intensity of suicidal thoughts or urges, from low (0) to high (10), as well as whether you took any steps toward acting on those urges (Y or N)
- **Self-injurious behaviors (SIB):** Intensity of urges to self-harm, from low (0) to high (10), as well as whether you acted on those urges (Y or N)
- **Avoidance/withdrawal (AVD):** How much you avoided tasks, feelings, or people, from not at all (0) to completely (10)
- **Relational stress (REL):** How stressful your interactions or relationships felt, from not at all (0) to extremely (10)
- **Participation level (PART):** Your level of engagement in treatment and skills practice, from low (0) to high (10)

### Developmental Integration System

- **Needs met (NM):** Degree to which you met your basic needs, from not at all (0) to fully met (10)
- **Structure (STR):** Degree to which you kept to your daily routine, from not at all (0) to completely (10)
- **Self-support (SS):** Degree to which you practiced self-care or self-compassion, from not at all (0) to consistently (10)

## Back Side

- **General skill use:** Check all the skills you used on the back side of the card.

## Diary Card (Front)

| | | Mind and Meaning | | | Body-Based | | | | | Consciousness and Memory | | | Action and Connection | | | | | | Developmental Integration | | |
|---|---|---|---|---|---|---|---|---|---|---|---|---|---|---|---|---|---|---|---|---|---|
| | Rx (Y/N) | EMO (0–10) | COG (0–10) | MB (0–10) | NER (0–10) | SOM (0–10) | INT (0–10) | Sleep (Hrs, Y/N) | MOVE (Y/N) | DIS (0–10) | MEM (0–10) | GRD (Y/N) | SUB (0–10, Y/N) | SI (0–10, Y/N) | SIB (0–10, Y/N) | AVD (0–10) | REL (0–10) | PART (0–10) | NM (0–10) | STR (0–10) | SS (0–10) |
| Mon | | | | | | | | | | | | | | | | | | | | | |
| Tues | | | | | | | | | | | | | | | | | | | | | |
| Wed | | | | | | | | | | | | | | | | | | | | | |
| Thurs | | | | | | | | | | | | | | | | | | | | | |
| Fri | | | | | | | | | | | | | | | | | | | | | |
| Sat | | | | | | | | | | | | | | | | | | | | | |
| Sun | | | | | | | | | | | | | | | | | | | | | |

Rx = Medications, EMO = Emotional dysregulation, COG = Cognitive dysregulation, MB = Meaning and belief dysregulation, NER = Nervous system dysregulation, SOM = Somatic dysregulation, INT = Interoceptive dysregulation, Sleep = Sleep, MOVE = Movement, DIS = Dissociative dysregulation, MEM = Memory dysregulation, GRD = Grounding, SUB = Substance use urges, SI = Suicidal ideation, SIB = Self-injurious behaviors, AVD = Avoidance/withdrawal, REL = Relational stress, PART = Participation level, NM = Needs met, STR = Structure, SS = Self-support

## Diary Card (Back)

| | Mon | Tues | Wed | Thurs | Fri | Sat | Sun |
|---|---|---|---|---|---|---|---|
| Dialectics | | | | | | | |
| Wise Mind | | | | | | | |
| One-Mindfully | | | | | | | |
| Nonjudgmentally | | | | | | | |
| Effectively | | | | | | | |
| Teflon Mind | | | | | | | |
| ACCEPTS | | | | | | | |
| IMPROVE | | | | | | | |
| Self-Soothe | | | | | | | |
| Grounding | | | | | | | |
| Pros and Cons | | | | | | | |
| Willingness | | | | | | | |
| Bridge Burning | | | | | | | |
| Urge Surfing | | | | | | | |
| TIPP | | | | | | | |
| STOP | | | | | | | |
| Radical Acceptance | | | | | | | |
| Turning the Mind | | | | | | | |
| Mindfulness of Current Emotion | | | | | | | |
| PLEASED | | | | | | | |
| Build Mastery | | | | | | | |
| Build Positive Experiences | | | | | | | |
| Check the Facts | | | | | | | |
| Opposite Action | | | | | | | |
| FAST | | | | | | | |
| GIVE | | | | | | | |
| DEAR MAN | | | | | | | |

## Behavior and Solution Analysis

Behavior and Solution Analysis (also known as Chain Analysis) is a powerful tool to change problem behaviors, such as substance use, self-harm, and any other behaviors that interfere with your progress in therapy. It's a regular part of treatment designed to help you become more mindful of what's happening, understand your choices, and discover skillful alternatives so you can move away from behaviors that bring pain and make life harder.

Importantly, Behavior and Solution Analysis is never intended to be punishment. Instead, approach this tool with curiosity and a willingness to use your skills. With this mindset, you will get the most out of this tool and realize its benefits:

- Understand and change problem behaviors, especially those that are harmful to you or others or that interfere with treatment.
- Reveal the purpose behind these behaviors—what you're trying to gain or resolve—so you can find more skillful ways to meet those needs.
- Identify contributing factors such as vulnerabilities (e.g., poor sleep, missed medication), environmental triggers (e.g., stress, conflict), emotions, thoughts, bodily sensations, and more. Each link in the chain is an opportunity to "break the chain" with a skillful response.
- Practice accepting and tolerating distress when difficult experiences come up, rather than defaulting to escape and avoidance.

Your therapist will help guide you through this tool until you are comfortable enough to complete it on your own. The Behavior and Solution Analysis process is as follows:

1. **Identify the specific problem behavior** you want to change (e.g., avoidance, self-injury, substance use).
2. **Track the chain** by describing each step leading up to and following the behavior.
3. **Examine contributing factors** such as vulnerabilities, emotions, thoughts, bodily sensations, and environmental triggers.
4. **Clarify what the behavior was trying to accomplish.** What were you hoping to gain? What want or need were you trying to meet?
5. **Identify intervention points** where you could have made different, more skillful choices.
6. **Plan alternatives** by identifying skills and strategies you can use at each link in the chain and instead of the problem behavior.
7. **Review your analysis** with your therapist and/or group to improve understanding and refine your skill use.

A visual example of Behavior and Solution Analysis is included on the next page. If you prefer using a written form with guided questions, those worksheets are available in the appendix.

Worksheet

# Visual Behavior and Solution Analysis

Use this visual chain (and another sheet of paper if needed) to identify each step, or link, in the chain that led to and followed your problem behavior. Then problem-solve each link with your skills. Breaking just one link can prevent you from acting on the problem behavior in the future.

Problem behavior:________________________________________

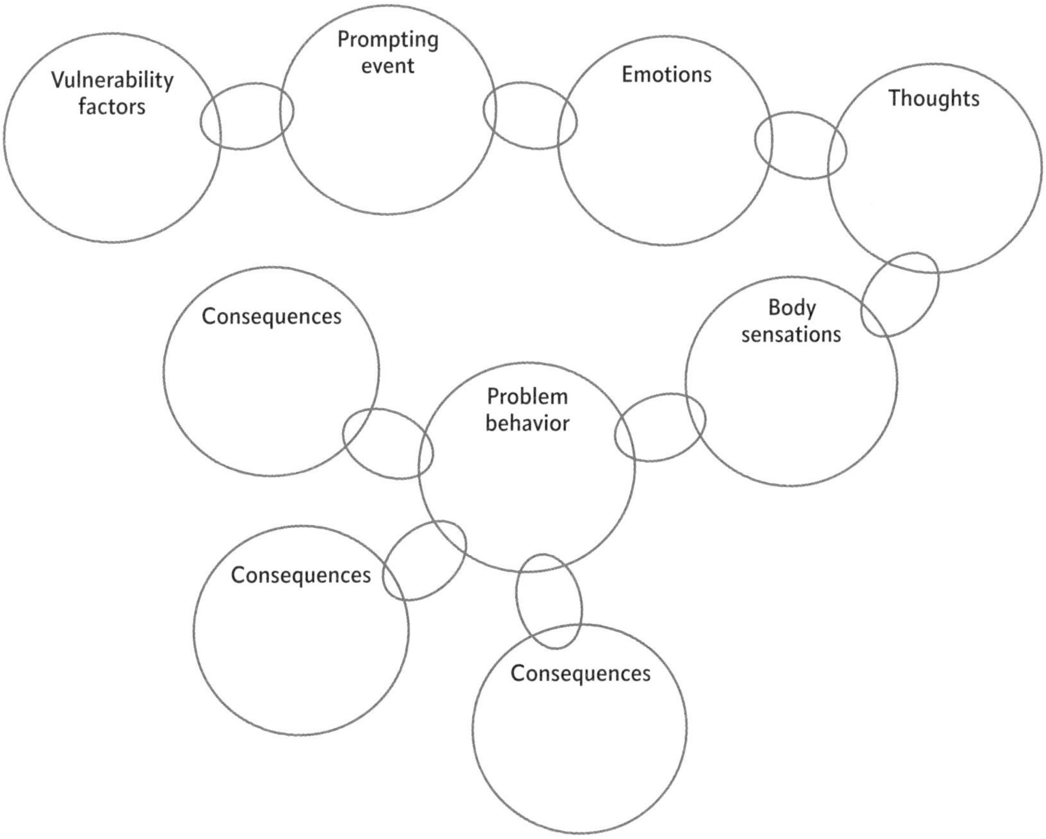


List the skills you can use at each link to "break the chain" to avoid the problem behavior, as well as skills to replace the problem behavior.

____________________________________________________

____________________________________________________

____________________________________________________

____________________________________________________

____________________________________________________

 

Worksheet

# Initial Skills Plan

As you begin your healing journey, you want to recognize the personal strengths and healthy coping strategies you already use. These strengths have helped you get through difficult times, and this Initial Skills Plan is your opportunity to reflect on what's already working. By building on these strengths and gradually adding skills, you'll create an even stronger foundation for recovery and growth.

## Step 1: Your Coping Behaviors

Think about how you currently handle difficult situations, emotions, or trauma-related stress. Everyone uses strategies, often without even realizing it. These might include:

- Physical activities like walking, exercising, or doing yoga
- Mindful moments such as deep breathing, listening to music, or being in nature
- Social support like talking to a trusted friend, mentor, or family member
- Creative outlets such as writing, drawing, or making art

Take a moment to list at least three coping behaviors you use. These can be small daily habits or larger practices like attending support groups.

1. ______________________________
2. ______________________________
3. ______________________________
4. ______________________________
5. ______________________________

## Step 2: What Works Best for You?

Reflect on which coping behaviors have been most helpful. How do you feel after using them? Maybe taking a walk clears your mind, or writing helps you express emotions. Think about the strategies that truly work for you and write a few sentences here.

______________________________

______________________________

______________________________

## Step 3: Areas You Want to Strengthen

Are there certain emotions or situations where you struggle to cope effectively? That's okay. This is a space to acknowledge where you could benefit from more support or skill building. Write down a few areas where you'd like to grow.

1. ________________________________________
2. ________________________________________
3. ________________________________________

## Step 4: Coping Behaviors You Can Use During Your Treatment

Identify coping strategies you can use to manage trauma-related stress both inside and outside the session or program.

________________________________________

________________________________________

________________________________________

## Step 5: Looking Ahead

As we move forward, we'll build on your strengths by teaching you new skills to help you manage trauma and your experience of it. You already have tools, and we'll keep adding more. When you have advanced beyond this Initial Skills Plan, you can create a more comprehensive skills plan to address behaviors such as substance use, self-injury, or any others that are difficult to change.

 

## Therapist and Client Assumptions

DTRM is built on a set of assumptions that support a nonjudgmental, skills-focused, and validating approach to trauma recovery. These guiding principles apply to both you and your therapist and are central to creating a supportive and effective therapeutic environment. Refer to these assumptions often, as they can help keep you grounded and motivated when things feel challenging:

- **You (and others) are doing your best *and* you need to do better.** Even when people act ineffectively, they're still doing their best given their history and current circumstances. At the same time, growth requires improvement. That's why we learn and practice skills.
- **Your problem behaviors are attempts to meet needs *and* DTRM offers better strategies.** Trauma can lead to behaviors that provide short-term relief but carry long-term consequences (e.g., substance use, self-harm), and treatment helps you understand these behaviors and practice more skillful alternatives.
- **You want to improve your life *and* you need new skills to do it.** Seeking treatment shows a desire for change even if you feel conflicted because of past experiences. To make that change a reality, practicing new skills is essential. DTRM provides the tools, and your practice brings them to life.
- **Skills work when you *work* the skills.** DTRM is an active, experiential treatment. Skills don't work by magic; they become effective only through consistent, repeated use. Practice builds momentum, even if progress feels slow or even nonexistent at first. Keep going.
- **Therapists balance validation *with* benevolent push for change.** Therapists focus on support and validation *and* encourage you to stretch beyond your comfort zone within your capabilities. This balance moves you from stuck patterns to growth and healing.

We hold these assumptions mindfully so we can work together effectively for lasting, meaningful change.

## Practical Tips for Using Skills Effectively

Trauma recovery involves learning how to regulate yourself using skills, and every time you use a skill, you strengthen new neural pathways that move you from survival to safety. Toward that end, follow these tips to get the most out of your skill use:

1. **Practice when calm, not just when in crisis.** When you practice in safety, your brain learns faster. The nervous system encodes regulation best when it's not in survival mode, and practicing when you are calm, as well as during distress, gradually teaches your brain and body that regulation is possible in any state.
2. **Repetition builds regulation.** Skills are like physical therapy for your mind and body. The more you repeat them, the stronger the new and regulated neural pathways become.

3. **Try a variety of skills.** The more skills you try, the more options you have, which increases your chances of success. Instead of defaulting to a few skills, continue to master new ones.
4. **Switch strategies when a skill isn't working.** Persistence is good, yet so is flexibility. If a skill is not working, stalls out, or increases distress, shift directions. Sometimes you need grounding before problem-solving, or action before reflection.
5. **Combine skills for greater impact.** You can improve your ability to regulate by using more than one skill simultaneously. For example, you might pair a body-based skill with a cognitive or relational skill to strengthen regulation from multiple directions. Or you may need to use a skill like Wise Mind or Opposite Action to access another skill.
6. **Practice with curiosity, not judgment.** Learning how to regulate yourself is a process of trial and feedback, not success and failure. Judgment narrows awareness, while curiosity expands it.
7. **Personalize skills.** You don't need to be rigid in understanding or applying skills. Adapt them as needed to your language, culture, and preferences to make them more natural and sustainable.
8. **Use skills early and often.** It's easier to prevent escalation than to recover from it. Early skill use keeps your body and mind within the window of tolerance. Your "window of tolerance" is the zone where your mind and body can handle stress without shutting down or becoming overwhelmed. Skills work best inside this window, meaning you are present enough to notice, feel, and respond.
9. **Know when you're outside your window of tolerance.** When stress pushes you *above* your window (hyperarousal) or *below* it (hypoarousal), it's harder to think or connect. If you feel "amped up," use calming, body-first skills, and if you feel "shutdown," try gentle activation like stretching, cool water, movement, or music. Both directions bring you back into your window, where healing and learning can happen.
10. **Track patterns and progress.** Awareness turns practice into data. Seeing when and where you use skills increases motivation and confidence. Use tools like the Diary Card, Behavior and Solution Analysis, and the *RISE Worksheet* to monitor patterns and progress.
11. **Expect delayed results.** Skills create incremental, not instant, change. The nervous system rewires itself slowly through consistent repetition. Be patient, stay the course, and treat yourself with compassion and encouragement.
12. **Use skills together with support.** Regulation grows faster in connection. Practicing with a therapist, group, or safe person builds co-regulation, the process through which another person's calm, attuned presence helps stabilize your nervous system, which is a relational foundation of healing.

Keep in mind that skills aren't magic; they work when you work them. The more you practice your skills, the more your system learns that calm is possible.

## Using Skills Both "Bottom-Up" and "Top-Down"

Trauma recovery requires learning to regulate from two different directions: calming the body to steady the mind and calming the mind to steady the body. These two pathways, called *bottom-up* and *top-down* regulation, work together to restore balance and regulation. Knowing which direction to start from helps you choose the most effective skills for the moment.

### Bottom-Up Regulation: Calming the Body to Settle the Mind

When trauma activates your body, it becomes nearly impossible to think clearly. Bottom-up skills use movement, breath, and sensory input to send safety signals through your nervous system. When the body settles, the mind can follow. You may need to start with bottom-up work when:

- Your heart is racing, breathing is shallow, or muscles feel tight.
- You feel shaky, spacey, or disconnected from your body.
- You can't think clearly or make decisions.

Starting bottom-up is often the most effective first step when both your mind and body are dysregulated.

### Top-Down Regulation: Calming the Mind to Steady the Body

When trauma affects your thinking and other mental processes, top-down skills activate higher brain regions that reorganize thought, support reflection, and make meaning. By using awareness and perspective, you can help calm your mind and guide your body toward safety. You may need top-down work when:

- You're caught in racing thoughts or self-criticism.
- You're replaying the past or predicting future danger.
- You feel mentally frozen yet physically still.

These skills help restore perspective, organize meaning, and anchor your body in calm understanding.

### Using Both Together

Effective healing moves in both directions. Some skills are primarily bottom-up, some are top-down, and many integrate both. As a general rule, start with the body when you're overwhelmed, and engage the mind when you're ready to reflect. Then return to the body whenever distress rises again.

Over time, this cycle of body first, then mind, and then integration creates steady regulation across your whole being. In short, sometimes you need to breathe before you can think, and sometimes you need to think before you can act. Healing means learning how to do both.

CHAPTER 7

# Understanding Trauma Symptoms and Areas of Dysregulation

DTRM begins with understanding how trauma affects your whole self: your mind, body, behaviors, relationships, and overall experience of the world. When PTSD symptoms show up, it can feel confusing, overwhelming, or even like something is wrong with you. But in truth, these symptoms and their aftereffects are often signs of your nervous system trying to protect you even when the danger is long past.

In DTRM, we teach DBT skills so you can respond to symptoms in effective, empowering ways. Yet to be successful with skills, you need to first understand how trauma presents itself in your life. To this end, this chapter walks you through the major symptoms of trauma and explains:

- What symptoms look and feel like and how they might be experienced
- How these symptoms lead to dysregulation across eleven interrelated domains, which are grouped into five systems

With practice, you'll understand how trauma affects you in unique ways, and you'll build a personalized toolbox of skills that support your progress. We'll begin with the major PTSD symptoms and then discuss the five systems that contain the eleven domains of dysregulation.

## PTSD Symptoms

PTSD can develop after you experience or witness a life-threatening or deeply distressing event. It affects the brain and body in lasting ways, often leaving people feeling stuck in survival mode long after the danger has passed. PTSD symptoms are grouped into four main clusters, each reflecting a different aspect of how trauma disrupts a person's sense of safety, stability, and well-being.[17] As you consider the

17 This section focuses on the four main clusters of PTSD symptoms and not the full diagnosis. For the complete diagnosis, consult the American Psychiatric Association's (2022) *Diagnostic and Statistical Manual of Mental Disorders, Fifth Edition, Text Revision* (*DSM-5-TR*).

clusters that follow, think about which ones best capture your experience, as that knowledge will inform your skill use:

- **Intrusive reexperiencing:** This includes unwanted and distressing memories of the trauma, flashbacks that make you feel as if the event is happening again, and nightmares. Even subtle reminders can trigger intense emotional or physical reactions.
- **Avoidance:** You may go out of your way to avoid people, places, conversations, or situations that remind you of the trauma. You may also avoid thinking or talking about what happened. While avoidance is a natural response, it often undermines more skillful ways to deal with the aftermath of trauma.
- **Negative changes in thoughts and mood:** This may involve persistent feelings of guilt, shame, or worthlessness; a loss of interest in activities; emotional numbness; and difficulty experiencing positive emotions. You may also develop distorted beliefs about yourself or the world (e.g., "I'm broken" or "The world is unsafe").
- **Heightened arousal and reactivity:** Your body and mind remain on high alert, causing you to be easily startled, feel tense or "on edge," experience irritability or angry outbursts, have difficulty sleeping, and struggle with concentration. These responses reflect a nervous system that hasn't fully returned to a state of safety.

## Domains of Dysregulation: How Trauma Affects Whole Systems

Understanding the general categories of PTSD symptoms is an important starting point, but trauma affects far more than what is captured in diagnostic checklists. Its effects ripple through multiple interconnected systems of mind, body, and relationships, often leaving survivors feeling "off" in ways that are difficult to explain.

DTRM describes these effects across five systems that contain eleven domains of dysregulation. These domains are areas where trauma disrupts your ability to stay balanced, connected, and grounded. These systems and domains have reciprocal influences, which is why trauma symptoms can feel so confusing, unpredictable, and scattered. When one system or domain becomes unbalanced, others often follow. The good news is that healing works the same way, in that *progress in one area often creates positive shifts across others.*

While these systems and domains are described separately here, remember that they operate as a living network. Your experience may involve several of these areas at once, and that's completely normal. The goal is to notice where dysregulation tends to show up so you can match it with the most effective skills to restore balance.

## I. Mind and Meaning System

1. **Emotional Dysregulation**
   After trauma, emotions can feel like tidal waves or disappear altogether. You might experience intense fear, shame, anger, or sadness that seems to come out of nowhere, or you might feel emotionally flat, disconnected, or numb. These shifts can make emotions feel unsafe or uncontrollable. Emotional dysregulation is not a flaw; it's a natural aftereffect of trauma.
2. **Cognitive Dysregulation**
   Trauma changes how you think, focus, and interpret the world. You might experience racing thoughts, mental fog, or looping self-criticism that won't turn off. It can feel hard to focus your attention and concentrate or even to trust your own mind. These thinking patterns are the brain's attempt to stay alert to danger, even when you are safe.
3. **Meaning and Belief Dysregulation**
   Trauma can distort how you make sense of yourself and your life. You might feel stuck in self-blame or hold beliefs like "I'm permanently damaged" or "It was my fault." These beliefs reflect how the mind tries to organize overwhelming experiences. They are powerful but not permanent.

## II. Body-Based System

4. **Nervous System Dysregulation**
   Your nervous system is your body's alarm system. After trauma, that alarm can become hypersensitive, keeping you in fight, flight, freeze, or collapse mode even when danger is over. You might startle easily, feel on edge, or struggle to relax and sleep. Conversely, there may be moments when you "crash out" or go into a state of collapse. These reactions are survival patterns that have become automatic and have outlived their usefulness.
5. **Somatic Dysregulation**
   Trauma lives in the body. You may notice tension, headaches, stomach issues, pain, or exhaustion without clear explanations or a medical cause. These sensations are not "all in your head." They are your body's memory of what it has endured and signs that your system is still holding survival energy.
6. **Interoceptive Dysregulation**
   Interoception is your ability to sense internal signals like hunger, thirst, or fatigue. Trauma can dull or distort this awareness, leaving you unsure what your body needs or confusing anxiety for danger. You might ignore hunger or exhaustion, overreact to small sensations, or not sense pain.

**III. Consciousness and Memory System**

7. **Dissociative Dysregulation**

   When experiences become too overwhelming, your mind may "shut off" awareness to survive. You might feel detached, lose time, or feel as if you're watching life from outside your body. Dissociation protects you in the short term but can create confusion and disconnection later.

8. **Memory Dysregulation**

   Trauma can disrupt how memories are stored and recalled. You might replay distressing memories, have flashbacks or nightmares, or notice that recall feels fragmented or "out of time," as if the past is happening now. These are signs your memory systems were overwhelmed during the trauma.

**VI. Action and Connection System**

9. **Behavioral Dysregulation**

   Behavior often reflects attempts to find balance or manage distress. You may react impulsively, isolate, or engage in behaviors that numb pain, like overeating, using substances, or self-harming. These actions temporarily reduce distress but prevent long-term healing.

10. **Relational Dysregulation**

    Relationships can feel complicated after trauma. You might crave closeness but fear it, overaccommodate to avoid rejection, or struggle with trust and communication. These patterns are understandable, as they formed to protect you. Healing happens as you learn new ways to connect safely.

**V. Developmental Integration System**

11. **Developmental Dysregulation**

    When trauma occurs early in life, it can interrupt the development of core emotional, relational, and self-regulation skills. You may feel "behind," immature, or as though certain life skills never fully formed. This is not a character flaw. Rather, it reflects how your system adapted under stress. The famous Adverse Childhood Experiences (ACE) Study found that over 60 percent of adults had at least one ACE, and one in five had three or more (Felitti et al., 1998). That means that developmental disruption is common, and it is repairable.

You might recognize yourself in several domains or notice that your challenges shift over time. This does not mean you are "broken." It means your system is responding exactly as it learned to under threat, and now, you have the opportunity to learn new ways to live.

In addition, each person has a unique profile of dysregulation. For instance, some struggle more with emotional storms, others with physical tension, and some with relational problems. DTRM allows you to accurately identify where your distress shows up and match it with specific skills for relief and regulation.

To get started, use the *Personal Systems Map* that follows to understand more about how trauma has impacted you across systems and domains. You'll use this information to put DTRM into action.

Worksheet

# Personal Systems Map: Understanding How Trauma Affects You

Trauma affects more than mood or memory. It influences how every part of your mind and body functions. It can shape how you feel, think, act, and connect, sometimes all at once. You might notice this as emotional storms, body tension, zoning out, racing thoughts, or relationship patterns that repeat no matter how hard you try to change them.

This is where understanding the clusters of PTSD symptoms as well as the five systems and eleven domains of dysregulation comes into play. Each cluster and system reflects an area where trauma can interrupt your ability to stay balanced, connected, and grounded. And no single cluster or system operates alone; they overlap, interact, and influence each other in constant motion.

Understanding where your symptoms and dysregulation show up—and what triggers them—are the first steps in identifying which skills to use to regulate yourself and feel better. Yet keep in mind that this map is not about diagnosis. Rather, it's about awareness, pattern recognition, and practical change. As you work through the map, remember that there are no right or wrong answers. Your patterns make perfect sense given what you've survived.

## Step 1

Rate how much you are affected in each PTSD cluster using a 0–5 scale, where 0 = "Not at all" and 5 = "Very much." Also list your known triggers for each affected cluster.

| Cluster | Description | Rating (0–5) |
|---|---|---|
| **Intrusive reexperiencing** | Intrusive thoughts, memories, flashbacks, and nightmares | |
| **Triggers** | | |
| **Avoidance** | Avoiding reminders of trauma (e.g., people, places, situations) | |
| **Triggers** | | |
| **Negative changes in thoughts and mood** | Intense emotions, emotional numbing, and inability to enjoy yourself, along with negative beliefs about yourself, others, and the world | |
| **Triggers** | | |
| **Heightened arousal and reactivity** | Being easily startled; feeling tense, irritable or angry; having difficulty sleeping; and having problems with concentration | |
| **Triggers** | | |

## Step 2

Rate how much you are affected in the domains in each system using a 0–5 scale, where 0 = "Not at all" and 5 = "Very much." Also list your known triggers for each affected domain.

### I. Mind and Meaning System

These domains describe how trauma shapes your emotions, thoughts, and beliefs. These are the parts of your mind that interpret experience and make sense of the world.

| Domain | Description | Rating (0–5) |
|---|---|---|
| **Emotional dysregulation** | Intense or absent emotions; rapid shifts in emotions; difficulty identifying or soothing feelings | |
| **Triggers** | | |
| **Cognitive dysregulation** | Racing thoughts, self-criticism, fog, or intrusive thinking that distort perception or affect focus | |
| **Triggers** | | |
| **Meaning and belief dysregulation** | Persistent self-blame, guilt, hopelessness, or negative worldviews shaped by trauma | |
| **Triggers** | | |

### II. Body-Based System

These domains reflect trauma's imprint on the nervous system and body. It reflects how trauma can continue to shape your body, even when the danger has passed.

| Domain | Description | Rating (0–5) |
|---|---|---|
| **Nervous system dysregulation** | Fight, flight, freeze, or collapse patterns; hypervigilance or shutdown | |
| **Triggers** | | |
| **Somatic dysregulation** | Physical tension, pain, fatigue, or bodily discomfort without a clear medical cause | |
| **Triggers** | | |
| **Interoceptive dysregulation** | Difficulty sensing internal cues like hunger, fatigue, thirst, tension, pain | |
| **Triggers** | | |

### III. Consciousness and Memory System

These domains involve how trauma alters awareness, attention, and memory. Trauma can fragment your sense of self, making the past feel unfinished and the present feel unstable.

| Domain | Description | Rating (0–5) |
|---|---|---|
| **Dissociative dysregulation** | Feeling spacey, detached, or disconnected from body or time | |
| **Triggers** | | |
| **Memory dysregulation** | Intrusive memories, flashbacks, or fragmented recall that keep the past alive in the present | |
| **Triggers** | | |

### IV. Action and Connection System

These domains describe how trauma influences what you do and how you relate to others. When internal regulation falters, it shows up in behavior and relationships.

| Domain | Description | Rating (0–5) |
|---|---|---|
| **Behavioral dysregulation** | Impulsivity, avoidance, or self-defeating behaviors used to manage distress | |
| **Triggers** | | |
| **Relational dysregulation** | Difficulty trusting, connecting, or maintaining boundaries in relationships | |
| **Triggers** | | |

### V. Developmental Integration System

This system captures how early experiences of safety or threat shaped your capacity for emotion regulation, attachment, and self-identity.

| Domain | Description | Rating (0–5) |
|---|---|---|
| **Developmental dysregulation** | Feeling "behind" emotionally or relationally; struggling with self-care, trust, or identity formation | |
| **Triggers** | | |

## Step 3

Using your ratings as a guide, circle, star, or otherwise highlight one to three clusters, systems, or domains that are most important for your healing right now. These are your starting points, meaning that it is okay and often most effective to start with only one to a few clusters and domains at a time. At the same time, you are free to use DTRM with any symptoms or areas of dysregulation that show up. The most important guide is doing what works for you.

With this information, you are now ready to learn and use the acronym RISE.

## RISE: A Four-Step Guide for Regulation and Recovery

The acronym RISE is a repeatable practice designed to help you recognize and understand your PTSD symptoms and areas of dysregulation. The more you practice noticing how trauma shows up and what triggers it, the more effective you will be in targeting skill use to restore regulation and balance. With repetition, RISE becomes your personal road map back to calm and connection. Remember that the four steps are:

1. Recognize the symptoms and associated domains of dysregulation.
2. Identify what triggered the symptoms and dysregulation.
3. Make a Skills-based response.
4. Evaluate the outcomes and adapt as needed.

Here are the steps with greater explanation.

### Step 1: Recognize the Symptoms and Dysregulation

Notice what you're experiencing right now emotionally, mentally, physically, or relationally. Ask yourself:

- What am I feeling or noticing in my body or mind?
- What PTSD symptom cluster does this align with: intrusive reexperiencing, avoidance, negative changes in thoughts or mood, or heightened arousal?
- Which systems or domains seem most affected (e.g., emotional, cognitive, somatic, relational, developmental), and what would be helpful to regulate first?

Observe and describe briefly what you're noticing. You don't need to name it perfectly. Basic awareness begins to transform confusion into clarity, and recognition itself begins to regulate your system.

### Step 2: Identify the Triggers

Once you know what's happening, look at what might have set it off. Ask yourself:

- What was happening just before I felt this way?
- Was it something external (a sound, place, tone, or situation) or internal (a thought, body sensation, or memory)?

Understanding triggers turns reactions into information. It helps you see your responses as protective rather than "wrong" and gives you power to plan ahead for next time.

## Step 3: Make a Skills-Based Response

Now it's time to respond skillfully. Choose a skill to counter what's affected and dysregulated in your system. Remember:

- **Bottom-up skills** calm the body first when your nervous system is on high alert or shutdown.
- **Top-down skills** calm the mind when thoughts, beliefs, or interpretations are driving distress.
- **You can mix and match skills**, as regulation often takes more than one skill.

You will learn these skills in chapters 9–13, which focus on the specific DBT modules upon which DTRM is based.

## Step 4: Evaluate and Adapt

After using your skills, pause to reflect and learn. Ask yourself:

- What changed, even slightly?
- Did my body feel calmer, my thoughts clearer, my emotions softer?
- What might I try differently next time?

If one skill didn't help much, that's useful data. Maybe it needs more practice, or maybe another approach fits better. The goal isn't doing it "right"; it's staying engaged and adaptable. Try small adjustments like these:

- Use the skill earlier next time.
- Combine bottom-up and top-down approaches.
- Add a relational skill for extra support.
- Practice during calm moments to prepare for distressful ones.

Each reflection strengthens your ability to recover faster and stay balanced longer.

## Practice RISE Daily

Trauma fragments regulation across your systems, and RISE brings those parts back into communication and balance. By practicing daily, you're retraining your system to respond to distress with awareness and skill rather than having automatic reactions that often make things worse.

Importantly, this method can be used in the moment, to reflect back on recent struggles, or in anticipation of known triggers, symptoms, and dysregulating experiences.

The following *RISE Worksheet* allows you to put this process into action. A brief version of the worksheet is included as well, which you can use when you are familiar enough with the process to find your recovery benefited by the streamlined version.

Worksheet

# RISE

This worksheet helps you apply RISE to recognize your symptoms and areas of dysregulation and then use your skills to restore balance.

## Step 1: Recognize the Symptoms and Associated Domains of Dysregulation

Observe what you're experiencing right now, what you've recently noticed, or what you expect to happen again.

**PTSD symptom clusters:** Start by checking the PTSD symptom clusters that best fit your experience and then briefly describe what you noticed.

- ❒ Intrusive reexperiencing (e.g., flashbacks, nightmares, intrusive thoughts)
- ❒ Avoidance (e.g., avoiding reminders, emotions, or situations)
- ❒ Negative changes in thoughts and mood (e.g., guilt, numbness, loss of interest, distorted beliefs)
- ❒ Heightened arousal and reactivity (e.g., anger outbursts, hypervigilance, easily startled, sleep disturbance)

**Description:**

____________________________________________________________

____________________________________________________________

____________________________________________________________

**Systems and domains of dysregulation:** Check the domains within each system that best capture your experience, then briefly describe what you noticed. Focus on the one to three areas you identified on the *Personal Systems Map*.

### I. Mind and Meaning System

- ❒ Emotional: Overwhelming, blunted, or unpredictable feelings (fear, shame, grief)
- ❒ Cognitive: Racing thoughts, self-blame, rigid or catastrophic thinking
- ❒ Meaning and belief: Negative or distorted meanings about self, others, or safety ("It's my fault," "The world isn't safe")

 

**Description:**

____________________________________________

____________________________________________

____________________________________________

## II. Body-Based System

- ❒ Nervous system: Hyperarousal, racing heart, agitation, or feeling frozen or collapsed
- ❒ Somatic: Tension, pain, headaches, nausea, or fatigue
- ❒ Interoceptive: Difficulty sensing or interpreting body cues (hunger, fatigue, safety signals)

**Description:**

____________________________________________

____________________________________________

____________________________________________

## III. Consciousness and Memory System

- ❒ Dissociative: Spacing out, feeling detached, losing time, or feeling unreal
- ❒ Memory: Intrusive images, flashbacks, fragmented recall, or gaps in memory

**Description:**

____________________________________________

____________________________________________

## IV. Action and Connection System

- ❒ Behavioral: Avoidance, impulsivity, self-harm, or escape behaviors
- ❒ Relational: Mistrust, withdrawal, fawning, conflict, or isolation in relationships

**Description:**

____________________________________________

____________________________________________

____________________________________________

### V. Developmental Integration System

- ❒ Developmental: Early learning that emotions or needs were unimportant or punished, or difficulties with self-care, soothing, or identity

**Description:**

______________________________________________

______________________________________________

______________________________________________

## Step 2: Identify the Triggers

Identify what set off the symptoms and dysregulation. This could be an external event (e.g., tone of voice, location, crowd, smell) or an internal cue (e.g., thought, memory, body sensation, image).

What happened just before the symptoms began?

______________________________________________

______________________________________________

______________________________________________

## Step 3: Skills-Based Response

Choose skills that match your symptoms, domains, and triggers. Check the modules you used and write the specific skills.

**Modules used:**

- ❒ Dialectics
- ❒ Mindfulness
- ❒ Distress tolerance
- ❒ Emotion regulation
- ❒ Interpersonal effectiveness

**Skills used:**

______________________________________________

______________________________________________

______________________________________________

## Step 4: Evaluate and Adapt

After using your skills, reflect mindfully. What happened after skill use?

- ❒ Calmer body
- ❒ Clearer thoughts
- ❒ Softer emotions
- ❒ Reconnection with others
- ❒ Still struggling
- ❒ Other

What skill was most effective?

______________________________________________

______________________________________________

______________________________________________

What could be more effective next time?

______________________________________________

______________________________________________

______________________________________________

**Adaptation plan (choose any):**

- ❒ Use the skill sooner next time.
- ❒ Try a different or additional skill.
- ❒ Ask for support from a therapist, group, or peer.
- ❒ Practice skill during calm periods to build mastery.
- ❒ Other: ____________________

**Description:**

______________________________________________

______________________________________________

______________________________________________

Worksheet

# RISE (Brief Version)

Use this quick version to build skills and respond effectively.

## Step 1: Recognize the Symptoms and Associated Domains of Dysregulation

Which PTSD symptom clusters best fit your experience?

- ❐ Intrusive reexperiencing
- ❐ Avoidance
- ❐ Negative thoughts/mood
- ❐ Arousal/reactivity

### I. Mind and Meaning System

- ❐ Emotional: Overwhelming, blunted, or unpredictable emotions
- ❐ Cognitive: Racing thoughts, self-blame, rigid or catastrophic thinking
- ❐ Meaning and belief: Negative or distorted beliefs about the self, others, or safety

### II. Body-Based System

- ❐ Nervous system: Fight, flight, freeze, or collapse responses
- ❐ Somatic: Muscle tension, pain, nausea, fatigue
- ❐ Interoceptive: Difficulty sensing or trusting body cues (hunger, fatigue, safety signals)

### III. Consciousness and Memory System

- ❐ Dissociative: Zoning out, losing time, feeling detached or unreal
- ❐ Memory: Intrusive images, flashbacks, fragmented recall, gaps in memory

### IV. Action and Connection System

- ❐ Behavioral: Avoidance, impulsivity, self-harm, substance use
- ❐ Relational: Mistrust, isolation, people-pleasing, conflict

 

V. Developmental Integration System

- ❒ Developmental: Early experiences taught that emotions, needs, or boundaries were unsafe or unwanted

## Step 2: Identify the Triggers

______________________________________________

______________________________________________

______________________________________________

## Step 3: Make a Skills-Based Response

**Modules used:**

- ❒ Dialectics
- ❒ Mindfulness
- ❒ Distress tolerance
- ❒ Emotion regulation
- ❒ Interpersonal effectiveness

## Step 4: Evaluate and Adapt

How effective was your response? What worked or didn't work?

______________________________________________

______________________________________________

______________________________________________

What adaptations can you make next time?

- ❒ Use skill sooner
- ❒ Try a different or additional skill
- ❒ Ask for support
- ❒ Practice in calm moments

## RISE Examples

The following four examples show RISE in action. As you review these examples, take note of a number of things. First, all domains (not symptom clusters) have been checked with descriptions of how they could be experienced. *This was done for teaching purposes.* As mentioned earlier, it is much more likely that most people will identify a smaller number of affected domains or focus on what is most dysregulated. In fact, you will see in the examples that not every domain is targeted with skills; instead, the clients tend to focus on the most impactful areas of dysregulation.

Second, the skills identified are a sampling and do not reflect the full scope of skills that could be used in these scenarios. While some skills will be "go-to" ones for many, each client will also have their own custom skills recipe to address their unique profile of symptoms and dysregulation.

Third, when specific skills are mentioned in step 3, those skills are in **bold** type, and the module in which they come from is identified in (parentheses) after the skill. Again, this is for teaching purposes. If the names and definitions of the skills are unfamiliar to you, then read through the examples with the *Master Skills List* handy for reference. You can find that list of skills and their brief definitions in the appendix.

Fourth, you may notice in the examples, and in your own use of RISE, that at times the information that comes up expands beyond a single instance or experience. That's because reflecting on any one experience of trauma symptoms and dysregulation evokes experiences around similar experiences. That's all right, because we know that the aftereffects of trauma are rarely clear-cut; experience is often messy! The good news is that if associated experiences come up, it simply leads to a richer understanding of the many ways people are affected by trauma, and it opens up more doors to skill use.

Finally, each example ends with a brief reflection on the use of the method.

With that in mind, let's review the examples on the pages that follow.

Worksheet

# RISE Example 1: Nightmares About the Trauma

After being sexually assaulted as a teenager, Taylor frequently dreams of being attacked. These nightmares wake her in a panic, leaving her feeling disoriented, sweating, with a racing heart, and afraid to fall back asleep. Although the danger is long past, Taylor's mind and body continue to react as if the trauma is still happening. She believes she will always have nightmares and is on edge rather than relaxed at bedtime, which disturbs her sleep. Because she fears nightmares, there are nights when she avoids falling asleep until she is exhausted.

## Step 1: Recognize the Symptoms and Associated Domains of Dysregulation

Observe what you're experiencing right now, what you've recently noticed, or what you expect to happen again.

**PTSD symptom clusters:** Start by checking the PTSD symptom clusters that best fit your experience and then briefly describe what you noticed.

- ☒ Intrusive reexperiencing (e.g., flashbacks, nightmares, intrusive thoughts)
- ☒ Avoidance (e.g., avoiding reminders, emotions, or situations)
- ☒ Negative changes in thoughts and mood (e.g., guilt, numbness, loss of interest, distorted beliefs)
- ☒ Heightened arousal and reactivity (e.g., anger outbursts, hypervigilance, startle, sleep disturbance)

**Description:**

*I woke up with an awful nightmare that really scared me. It is hard to fall back asleep because my body reacts so much, and most nights I feel keyed up before bed, which makes it difficult to fall asleep in the first place. Sometimes I don't even try to sleep because I hate the nightmares, and I think it's all pointless and I'll always be like this.*

**Systems and domains of dysregulation:** Check the domains within each system that best capture your experience, then briefly describe what you noticed. Focus on the one to three areas you identified on the *Personal Systems Map*.

 

## I. Mind and Meaning System

- ☒ Emotional: Overwhelming, blunted, or unpredictable feelings (fear, shame, grief)
- ☒ Cognitive: Racing thoughts, self-blame, rigid or catastrophic thinking
- ☒ Meaning and belief: Negative or distorted meanings about self, others, or safety ("It's my fault," "The world isn't safe")

**Description:**

*I had intense fear and guilt after waking. My thoughts race around "what if" scenarios related to being hurt, and I always catastrophize. I believe that I'm never safe and that sleep isn't safe.*

## II. Body-Based System

- ☒ Nervous system: Hyperarousal, racing heart, agitation, or feeling frozen or collapsed
- ☒ Somatic: Tension, pain, headaches, nausea, or fatigue
- ☒ Interoceptive: Difficulty sensing or interpreting body cues (hunger, fatigue, safety signals)

**Description:**

*My heart was racing, my muscles were tense, and I was breathing shallowly. I was sweaty and nauseous, and I was kinda confused about whether my body was reacting more to fear or being really tired.*

## III. Consciousness and Memory System

- ☒ Dissociative: Spacing out, feeling detached, losing time, or feeling unreal
- ☒ Memory: Intrusive images, flashbacks, fragmented recall, or gaps in memory

**Description:**

*Sometimes when I wake up, I can't tell what's real for a while. Sometimes the dreams bring back memories, and often I confuse my dreams with things that have actually happened, especially right after I wake up. That happened this time too.*

### IV. Action and Connection System

- [x] Behavioral: Avoidance, impulsivity, self-harm, or escape behaviors
- [x] Relational: Mistrust, withdrawal, fawning, conflict, or isolation in relationships

**Description:**

*I was able to calm down with skills, but instead of going back to sleep, I just loaded up on caffeine and scrolled on social media. The next day I felt so irritable that I couldn't stand people, so I just avoided as many people as possible.*

### V. Developmental Integration System

- [x] Developmental: Early learning that emotions or needs were unimportant or punished, or difficulties with self-care, soothing, or identity

**Description:**

*I've always been alone at night. My parents never came to me when I cried out. I guess I never learned how to deal with bad dreams, and I need to figure that out.*

## Step 2: Identify the Triggers

Identify what set off the symptoms and dysregulation. This could be an external event (e.g., tone of voice, location, crowd, smell) or an internal cue (e.g., thought, memory, body sensation, image).

What happened just before the symptoms began?

*I was watching a true crime show before bed in a dark room. It set off my trauma stuff, I couldn't turn off my brain, and I felt tense in my body. I guess my body can get confused about watching violence on TV and being in danger.*

## Step 3: Skills-Based Response

Choose skills that match your symptoms, domains, and triggers. Check the modules you used and write the specific skills.

**Modules used:**

- ☐ Dialectics
- ☒ Mindfulness
- ☒ Distress tolerance
- ☒ Emotion regulation
- ☐ Interpersonal effectiveness

**Skills used:**

I used **Paced Breathing (TIPP)** and long exhales to slow my heart rate (distress tolerance) and then used **Grounding** techniques (distress tolerance). I was also using **Self-Soothe** with a soft, comforting blanket (distress tolerance). When my body calmed, I did **Check the Facts**: "The trauma is not happening. I'm safe in my room" (emotion regulation).

I'm also practicing **Radical Acceptance**: "It just 'is' that my body learned to fear rest. I'm teaching it that rest is safe" (distress tolerance). That helps me stop spinning my wheels over it. I'm also going to use the **Emotions** part of the **ACCEPTS** skill (distress tolerance) to replace upsetting shows with calm music before bed. That's kinda a **Wise Mind** decision (mindfulness) and an **Opposite Action** (emotion regulation) because I like those crime shows.

## Step 4: Evaluate and Adapt

After using your skills, reflect mindfully. What happened after skill use?

- ☒ Calmer body
- ☒ Clearer thoughts
- ☒ Softer emotions
- ☐ Reconnection with others
- ☐ Still struggling
- ☐ Other________________

What skill was most effective?

**Paced Breathing (TIPP)** and **Self-Soothe** grounded me the fastest. Reminding myself that I'm safe helps a lot too. Trusting myself about that.

What could be more effective next time?

*Avoiding going back to bed, drinking caffeine, and scrolling really didn't help me. I think changing my nighttime routine and doing breathing and* **Self-Soothe** *before bed will help.*

**Adaptation plan (choose any):**

- ☒ Use the skill sooner next time.
- ☒ Try a different or additional skill.
- ☐ Ask for support from a therapist, group, or peer.
- ☒ Practice skill during calm periods to build mastery.
- ☐ Other: ______________________

**Description:**

*I'm going to be more proactive about using calming skills and create a real bedtime routine based on relaxation. I'm also going to avoid just getting up and using caffeine and social media. That really didn't work at all.*

## Teaching Reflection

Taylor's example shows how trauma-related nightmares can expand into several symptom clusters (even though intrusive reexperiencing is the primary one) and dysregulate multiple domains. By following RISE, Taylor learned to recognize where dysregulation happens, identify triggers, apply skills, and evaluate her progress, learning what works and what is not effective.

To make significant progress, notice that she did not have to address everything and instead focused on key areas such as calming her body. In time, rather than falling victim to nightmares, she will be able to use skills to decrease them and their effects. This will make sleep more restful because it feels, and is, less risky.

Worksheet

# RISE Example 2: Substance Use to Cope

Teddy drinks nightly after work, telling himself it helps him "wind down." In truth, he's using alcohol to avoid the intrusive memories and painful emotions that surface when he's alone, especially the sudden images of the roadside explosion that killed two members of his military unit. The fear that rushes through him during those flashes, along with the shame he carries about surviving when his unit members did not, feels overwhelming. What starts as relief quickly turns into a cycle of avoidance, disconnection, and dysregulation across multiple systems.

## Step 1: Recognize the Symptoms and Associated Domains of Dysregulation

Observe what you're experiencing right now, what you've recently noticed, or what you expect to happen again.

**PTSD symptom clusters:** Start by checking the PTSD symptom clusters that best fit your experience and then briefly describe what you noticed.

- ☒ Intrusive reexperiencing (e.g., flashbacks, nightmares, intrusive thoughts)
- ☒ Avoidance (e.g., avoiding reminders, emotions, or situations)
- ☐ Negative changes in thoughts and mood (e.g., guilt, numbness, loss of interest, distorted beliefs)
- ☒ Heightened arousal and reactivity (e.g., anger outbursts, hypervigilance, startle, sleep disturbance)

**Description:**

*I found myself drinking again because it helps me forget. It numbs out my emotions and puts flashbacks on mute.*

**Systems and domains of dysregulation:** Check the domains within each system that best capture your experience, then briefly describe what you noticed. Focus on the one to three areas you identified on the *Personal Systems Map*.

### I. Mind and Meaning System

- ☒ Emotional: Overwhelming, blunted, or unpredictable feelings (fear, shame, grief)
- ☒ Cognitive: Racing thoughts, self-blame, rigid or catastrophic thinking

 

- ☒ Meaning and belief: Negative or distorted meanings about self, others, or safety ("It's my fault," "The world isn't safe")

**Description:**

When I'm sober, the fear and shame can be too much. I guess I'm black and white in thinking that drinking is the only thing that helps. Deep down, I believe that being sober means I'll suffer and be overwhelmed with feelings.

## II. Body-Based System

- ☒ Nervous system: Hyperarousal, racing heart, agitation, or feeling frozen or collapsed
- ☒ Somatic: Tension, pain, headaches, nausea, or fatigue
- ☒ Interoceptive: Difficulty sensing or interpreting body cues (hunger, fatigue, safety signals)

**Description:**

It's subtle, but I feel agitated when I get home, and my body is restless. I ignore that I'm hungry and tired and go drinking. Then I get really disconnected.

## III. Consciousness and Memory System

- ☒ Dissociative: Spacing out, feeling detached, losing time, or feeling unreal
- ☒ Memory: Intrusive images, flashbacks, fragmented recall, or gaps in memory

**Description:**

After drinking, I definitely lose time and feel so detached. I don't remember much, but at least I'm not remembering what happened either.

## IV. Action and Connection System

- ☒ Behavioral: Avoidance, impulsivity, self-harm, or escape behaviors
- ☒ Relational: Mistrust, withdrawal, fawning, conflict, or isolation in relationships

**Description:**

I suppose drinking is my "coping" mechanism. But it makes me feel more alone and disconnected from others.

 

### V. Developmental Integration System

- ☒ Developmental: Early learning that emotions or needs were unimportant or punished, or difficulties with self-care, soothing, or identity

**Description:**

*I was taught that I shouldn't feel anything, except maybe anger. I never learned how to handle emotions.*

## Step 2: Identify the Triggers

Identify what set off the symptoms and dysregulation. This could be an external event (e.g., tone of voice, location, crowd, smell) or an internal cue (e.g., thought, memory, body sensation, image).

What happened just before the symptoms began?

*I came home, was alone, felt restless, and started thinking about the past. The quiet after work can be unbearable.*

## Step 3: Skills-Based Response

Choose skills that match your symptoms, domains, and triggers. Check the modules you used and write the specific skills.

**Modules used:**

- ☒ Dialectics
- ☒ Mindfulness
- ☒ Distress tolerance
- ☒ Emotion regulation
- ☒ Interpersonal effectiveness

**Skills used:**

*I'm going to try to* ***Observe*** *and* ***Describe*** *my feelings, thoughts, and behaviors with* ***Nonjudgmental Stance*** *(mindfulness). Then, I need to use* ***PLEASED*** *(emotion regulation) to eat when I get home, and even though I'm tired, maybe take a little walk to burn off some restlessness and* ***Bridge Burning*** *(distress tolerance) to avoid resorting to drinking. I'll also do* ***Bridge Burning*** *by getting alcohol out of the house.*

*I did **Pros and Cons** (distress tolerance), and I really want to use skills rather than drink, and I'm trying **"Both/And" Thinking** (dialectics) by telling myself that I sometimes get overwhelmed and I can face it with my skills. I'm planning to fill my time with **Build Mastery** and **Build Positive Experiences** (emotion regulation) by playing guitar and getting together with friends to watch TV instead of drink. That means I have to practice **DEAR MAN** (interpersonal effectiveness) to reach out.*

## Step 4: Evaluate and Adapt

After using your skills, reflect mindfully. What happened after skill use?

- ☒ Calmer body
- ☒ Clearer thoughts
- ☒ Softer emotions
- ☒ Reconnection with others
- ❐ Still struggling
- ❐ Other________________

What skill was most effective?

*The best thing is prioritizing self-care and eating and taking a walk. That really lowers urges. Also **Bridge Burning** so that alcohol isn't there and making other plans to occupy my time.*

What could be more effective next time?

*I think I need to practice **Radical Acceptance** around memories and emotions and just learn to balance being with them mindfully, along with getting into healthy distractions when I need to.*

**Adaptation plan (choose any):**

- ☒ Use the skill sooner next time.
- ☒ Try a different or additional skill.
- ☒ Ask for support from a therapist, group, or peer.
- ☒ Practice skill during calm periods to build mastery.
- ❐ Other: ________________

 

**Description:**

I'm going to keep trying new skills as I learn and start practicing calming skills before I leave work and on the ride home. Maybe enter my home in a more relaxed state. Also, I can call my therapist for skills coaching when my urges are high.

## Teaching Reflection

This example shows how trauma-driven avoidance begins as protection but grows into chronic dysregulation and blocks healing. Instead of avoiding his triggers, Teddy uses skills across all five modules to mindfully attend to his emotions and memories, while also engaging in healthy behaviors and distractions that help him feel better. He also finds relief in skills that calm his body and create connection with others.

 

Worksheet

# RISE Example 3: Survivor's Guilt

Leo survived a violent incident that left others severely injured. He often thinks, "Why them and not me?" and "I should have done more." These thoughts keep him trapped between grief and self-punishment, as guilt blurs the line between mourning and self-condemnation. At times, he's overwhelmed with the memories of what happened.

## Step 1: Recognize the Symptoms and Associated Domains of Dysregulation

Observe what you're experiencing right now, what you've recently noticed, or what you expect to happen again.

**PTSD symptom clusters:** Start by checking the PTSD symptom clusters that best fit your experience and then briefly describe what you noticed.

- ☒ Intrusive reexperiencing (e.g., flashbacks, nightmares, intrusive thoughts)
- ☐ Avoidance (e.g., avoiding reminders, emotions, or situations)
- ☒ Negative changes in thoughts and mood (e.g., guilt, numbness, loss of interest, distorted beliefs)
- ☐ Heightened arousal and reactivity (e.g., anger outbursts, hypervigilance, startle, sleep disturbance)

**Description:**

I drown in self-judgment, guilt, and shame that I didn't prevent this. I know it's not rational, but it consumes me. Sometimes the memories don't stop.

**Systems and domains of dysregulation:** Check the domains within each system that best capture your experience, then briefly describe what you noticed. Focus on the one to three areas you identified on the *Personal Systems Map*.

### I. Mind and Meaning System

- ☒ Emotional: Overwhelming, blunted, or unpredictable feelings (fear, shame, grief)
- ☒ Cognitive: Racing thoughts, self-blame, rigid or catastrophic thinking
- ☒ Meaning and belief: Negative or distorted meanings about self, others, or safety ("It's my fault," "The world isn't safe")

 

**Description:**

The guilt and shame overwhelm me, and my thoughts about it are on a near-constant loop. I just believe deeply that it should have been me, and I should have done something to prevent it.

## II. Body-Based System

- ☒ Nervous system: Hyperarousal, racing heart, agitation, or feeling frozen or collapsed
- ☒ Somatic: Tension, pain, headaches, nausea, or fatigue
- ☒ Interoceptive: Difficulty sensing or interpreting body cues (hunger, fatigue, safety signals)

**Description:**

When I think about it, my nervous system ramps up, I feel a great weight in my chest, and I just get out of touch with what my body needs. I go between that ramped-up feeling and then sometimes collapse into grief. It's hard to know what I need.

## III. Consciousness and Memory System

- ☒ Dissociative: Spacing out, feeling detached, losing time, or feeling unreal
- ☒ Memory: Intrusive images, flashbacks, fragmented recall, or gaps in memory

**Description:**

When it's most intense, I feel detached from the moment and "lost in space." At other times, my memories just keep looping and feeding the emotions.

## IV. Action and Connection System

- ☒ Behavioral: Avoidance, impulsivity, self-harm, or escape behaviors
- ☒ Relational: Mistrust, withdrawal, fawning, conflict, or isolation in relationships

**Description:**

I just withdraw from others and have such distance. They don't understand. And I tend to not feel happiness, so I disengage from things that might be fun.

 

### V. Developmental Integration System

- ☒ Developmental: Early learning that emotions or needs were unimportant or punished, or difficulties with self-care, soothing, or identity

**Description:**

*My family was never great at understanding or validating. I didn't get validation and can't seem to provide it to myself. I feel like I don't deserve to be here, and when I laugh or feel joy, it feels like I'm breaking a rule I was taught long ago about not taking up space or having needs.*

## Step 2: Identify the Triggers

Identify what set off the symptoms and dysregulation. This could be an external event (e.g., tone of voice, location, crowd, smell) or an internal cue (e.g., thought, memory, body sensation, image).

What happened just before the symptoms began?

*Most recently, it was seeing the anniversary of the incident approaching. But sometimes it's simply noticing the upset in my body or catching myself having some enjoyment and then feeling guilty for it.*

## Step 3: Skills-Based Response

Choose skills that match your symptoms, domains, and triggers. Check the modules you used and write the specific skills.

**Modules used:**

- ☒ Dialectics
- ☒ Mindfulness
- ☒ Distress tolerance
- ☐ Emotion regulation
- ☒ Interpersonal effectiveness

**Skills used:**

*I'm starting to* ***Observe*** *and* ***Describe*** *(mindfulness) my body and then transitioning to the* ***TIPP*** *skill (distress tolerance) to reset things, using cold water and breathing especially, but sometimes muscle relaxation too.*

 

When things improve physically, I move to **"Both/And" Thinking** (dialectics) and tell myself that I wish I could have done more, and I did everything that was humanely possible. That's starting to help, a little. I'm also using **Radical Acceptance** (distress tolerance) instead of beating myself up, and I'm practicing **FAST** (interpersonal effectiveness) by being fair to myself, not apologizing, and trying to honor the other survivors by living a more meaningful life—one not defined only by what happened.

## Step 4: Evaluate and Adapt

After using your skills, reflect mindfully. What happened after skill use?

- [x] Calmer body
- [x] Clearer thoughts
- [x] Softer emotions
- [ ] Reconnection with others
- [x] Still struggling
- [ ] Other________________

What skill was most effective?

It helps to start with the body, and my work with **Dialectical Thinking**, **Radical Acceptance**, and **FAST** is starting to take hold, though I'm still struggling a lot.

What could be more effective next time?

I think I need to coach myself into **Build Positive Experiences** and use **Radical Acceptance** when I have opportunities to enjoy life. I'm also creating **Encouragement (IMPROVE)** statements such as "It's okay to feel happy." I think I need to be around others more too.

**Adaptation plan (choose any):**

- [x] Use the skill sooner next time.
- [x] Try a different or additional skill.
- [x] Ask for support from a therapist, group, or peer.
- [ ] Practice skill during calm periods to build mastery.
- [x] Other: Volunteer

 

**Description:**

*I'm going to reach out more to others and maybe start volunteering.*

*Definitely try more positive experiences. When I'm in* ***Wise Mind,*** *I know*

*that I deserve good things too.*

## Teaching Reflection

Leo's experience shows how survivor's guilt spans emotional, cognitive, and belief domains while activating the Body-Based System and relational domain too. He's beginning to see the intense guilt as a trauma response and not an indicator of a moral failing. In fact, he's learning that survivor's guilt often disguises love and loyalty, and when survivors hold both loss and life dialectically, they honor others and can transform guilt into gratitude and purpose.

# RISE Example 4: Hypervigilance in Public

After being mugged from behind, Amie avoids sitting with her back exposed in restaurants, constantly scans exits, and feels uneasy even in safe public places. Though she knows she's safe and her assailant is in prison, her body refuses to believe it. Each outing leaves her exhausted, but she feels compelled to stay alert just in case.

## Step 1: Recognize the Symptoms and Associated Domains of Dysregulation

Observe what you're experiencing right now, what you've recently noticed, or what you expect to happen again.

**PTSD symptom clusters:** Start by checking the PTSD symptom clusters that best fit your experience and then briefly describe what you noticed.

- ☐ Intrusive reexperiencing (e.g., flashbacks, nightmares, intrusive thoughts)
- ☒ Avoidance (e.g., avoiding reminders, emotions, or situations)
- ☐ Negative changes in thoughts and mood (e.g., guilt, numbness, loss of interest, distorted beliefs)
- ☒ Heightened arousal and reactivity (e.g., anger outbursts, hypervigilance, startle, sleep disturbance)

**Description:**

*I'm so hyperalert in public and scan constantly for danger. I just cannot relax and settle in at all.*

**Systems and domains of dysregulation:** Check the domains within each system that best capture your experience, then briefly describe what you noticed. Focus on the one to three areas you identified on the *Personal Systems Map*.

### I. Mind and Meaning System

- ☒ Emotional: Overwhelming, blunted, or unpredictable feelings (fear, shame, grief)
- ☒ Cognitive: Racing thoughts, self-blame, rigid or catastrophic thinking
- ☒ Meaning and belief: Negative or distorted meanings about self, others, or safety ("It's my fault," "The world isn't safe")

 

**Description:**

*I'm always anxious and ruminating on "what if" scenarios. I guess I really believe that if I relax, I'll be hurt.*

## II. Body-Based System

- ☒ Nervous system: Hyperarousal, racing heart, agitation, or feeling frozen or collapsed
- ☒ Somatic: Tension, pain, headaches, nausea, or fatigue
- ☒ Interoceptive: Difficulty sensing or interpreting body cues (hunger, fatigue, safety signals)

**Description:**

*My heart is always racing and my body is so tense, though sometimes I just crash, usually when I get home. I have headaches and unexplained aches and pains. Everything in my body I interpret as danger.*

## III. Consciousness and Memory System

- ☒ Dissociative: Spacing out, feeling detached, losing time, or feeling unreal
- ☒ Memory: Intrusive images, flashbacks, fragmented recall, or gaps in memory

**Description:**

*Sometimes I just go into tunnel vision mode and run on autopilot, not really being in the moment. Being in enclosed spaces also brings back bad memories.*

## IV. Action and Connection System

- ☒ Behavioral: Avoidance, impulsivity, self-harm, or escape behaviors
- ☒ Relational: Mistrust, withdrawal, fawning, conflict, or isolation in relationships

**Description:**

*I avoid a lot of places and miss out a lot with relationships. When I do get out, I'm so distracted and disconnected that I'm really not in the moment with people.*

V. Developmental Integration System

- ☒ Developmental: Early learning that emotions or needs were unimportant or punished, or difficulties with self-care, soothing, or identity

**Description:**

I grew up in chaos, where if you weren't watching out, something bad was bound to happen. I don't know what a safety cue is!

## Step 2: Identify the Triggers

Identify what set off the symptoms and dysregulation. This could be an external event (e.g., tone of voice, location, crowd, smell) or an internal cue (e.g., thought, memory, body sensation, image).

What happened just before the symptoms began?

This time it was being in a crowded restaurant. But it can be a lot of things. Any crowd, loud noises, or even just noticing what's in my head or body. It all sets off the alarms.

## Step 3: Skills-Based Response

Choose skills that match your symptoms, domains, and triggers. Check the modules you used and write the specific skills.

**Modules used:**

- ☒ Dialectics
- ☒ Mindfulness
- ☒ Distress tolerance
- ☒ Emotion regulation
- ☒ Interpersonal effectiveness

**Skills used:**

I first tried **Paced Breathing (TIPP)**, placing my hand on my belly, and then **Grounding** techniques (distress tolerance) to slow things down. Then I used **Check the Facts** (emotion regulation) and noticed that people were calm and there was no threat. That led to a **Wise Mind** realization (mindfulness) that my fear can be real and the moment can also be safe. That's **Dialectical Thinking**, too, I think (dialectics).

 

To build on that awareness, I started practicing **Opposite Action** (emotion regulation) by gradually entering avoided places—in short, calm outings first. I tracked my successful outings in a journal to **Build Mastery** (emotion regulation). I also used **One-Mindfully** (mindfulness) and **GIVE** (interpersonal effectiveness) while I was out to focus on others. Finally, I've been practicing **PLEASED** by attending to my eating habits, sleeping, and hydrating regularly to lower baseline arousal levels (emotion regulation).

## Step 4: Evaluate and Adapt

After using your skills, reflect mindfully. What happened after skill use?

- ☒ Calmer body
- ☒ Clearer thoughts
- ☒ Softer emotions
- ☒ Reconnection with others
- ☐ Still struggling
- ☐ Other ____________

What skill was most effective?

Breathing and grounding are super helpful. I'm also liking **Check the Facts** and using **One-Mindfully** to redirect my attention to where I want it to be.

What could be more effective next time?

I think I could use more **Opposite Action** to approach what's scary but safe. I could also be proactive about using distress tolerance skills from **ACCEPTS** and **IMPROVE**. Using skills helps me feel more in control.

**Adaptation plan (choose any):**

- ☒ Use the skill sooner next time.
- ☒ Try a different or additional skill.
- ☐ Ask for support from a therapist, group, or peer.
- ☒ Practice skill during calm periods to build mastery.
- ☐ Other: ____________

**Description:**

*I'm catching the skills bug, and I just want to be proactive in trying as many of the distress tolerance skills as I can. It feels empowering to develop some tools to cope. My goal is to be calm and alert without the fear.*

## Teaching Reflection

Amie is learning that safety isn't the absence of awareness. Rather, it's the ability to stay present without fear. By practicing regulation in real-world settings, she is building confidence to approach rather than avoid, and she is slowly rewiring her systems to have regulation be her new normal, lowering her hypervigilance in time.

CHAPTER 8

# The Phases of Healing in DTRM: Understanding Where You Are in Recovery

Healing from trauma is a process, not an event. DTRM organizes recovery into three flexible phases that move from stability to integration to connection and growth. At each phase, you'll strengthen specific systems of healing, including your mind, body, memory, relationships, and sense of development, by practicing your skills.

However, recovery from trauma is rarely a straight line. You may revisit earlier work when life gets stressful. That's not failure; it is being flexible to be effective. Each return to an earlier phase builds stability, capabilities, and integration that serves your long-term growth.

## Phase 1: Safety, Stabilization, and Regulation: "Extinguishing the Fire"

When trauma symptoms feel overwhelming, the first goal is to find safety inside your body, in your relationships, and in your daily routines. In this phase, you'll learn to calm your body, manage intense emotions, reduce crisis behaviors, and begin to trust that relief is possible. Here's what's happening in your systems in this phase:

I. **Mind and Meaning System:** Your emotions may feel intense or numb, and your mind may feel flooded, racing, or blank. You might be stuck in deeply held negative beliefs about yourself, others, and the world. In this phase, you'll learn to pause, observe, and name what's happening without judgment. This helps you lower the intensity, start to make sense of your experience, and change your perspectives.

II. **Body-Based System:** Your body might feel tense, restless, shutdown, or even in pain. You might have difficulty making sense of what your body is experiencing or what it needs. You'll practice grounding, mindful breathing, and rhythm-based activities to calm your nervous system and rebuild a sense of safety.

III. **Consciousness and Memory System:** You might be checked out or even disconnected from yourself and the present. Flashbacks or intrusive memories can make it feel like the trauma is still happening. The focus here is returning to the present moment and building skills to separate *then* from *now*.

IV. **Action and Connection System:** You might feel unmotivated and unsure how to create stability in your life, and relationships may feel unfamiliar or unsafe. In this phase, you'll begin building safety through structure—by establishing regular routines, attending therapy consistently, and forming small, safe connections that show "I'm not alone." You'll start replacing ineffective coping behaviors with effective ones and learn how to cultivate healthy relationships.

V. **Developmental Integration System:** When you've ignored your body's needs for so long (or never learned how to meet them in the first place), it's hard to know how to nourish yourself now. This phase resets your foundation. You'll work on basic care (sleep, nutrition, movement) and reestablish predictable patterns that make you feel steady. Whatever you missed out on, like learning how to self-soothe, can be addressed now.

### How You'll Practice Skills in This Phase:

- **Dialectics:** Learn to hold two truths at once, such as "I'm hurting *and* I'm trying."
- **Mindfulness:** Focus on one thing at a time to stay in the present moment.
- **Distress tolerance:** Practice crisis tools like STOP, TIPP, and Self-Soothe to stay safe.
- **Emotion regulation:** Identify and name emotions, reduce vulnerability factors, and create more of the emotions you want.
- **Interpersonal effectiveness:** Build self-respect and begin asking for help, expressing your wants and needs, setting boundaries, and learning that relationships can be safe and fulfilling.

### You'll Be Ready for the Next Phase When:

- You can recognize when you're getting dysregulated and use skills to return to calm.
- You feel moments of safety or control, even if brief.
- You've built a basic safety or skills plan and can reach out for support when needed.
- You can stay present long enough to connect with and learn from your experiences.

When you enter phase 2, your systems will shift from survival to curiosity, and you'll begin exploring your experiences, such as your emotions and body sensations, with greater safety and confidence.

## Phase 2: Emotional Integration and Body Awareness: "Rebuilding the Foundation"

Now that you have more stability, the focus shifts increasingly inward. You'll learn to notice emotions, thoughts, and sensations as information and not danger, and you'll use skills to regulate rather than react. This phase guides you to more fully integrate your inner experience across the five systems. Here's what's happening in your systems in this phase:

I. **Mind and Meaning System:** Your emotions have fewer extremes (and you begin to feel more), and your thoughts begin to slow down and organize. You'll start seeing experiences in more balanced ways and recognize that you can feel many things at once without losing control.

II. **Body-Based System:** You'll reconnect with your body as a safe place. Through mindfulness, breathing, and gentle movement, you'll learn to feel sensations without being overwhelmed by them.

III. **Consciousness and Memory System:** You'll be more in the moment, and memories will feel less like flashbacks and more like stories you can reflect on. You may begin understanding how past experiences shape your present experiences without being trapped in them.

IV. **Action and Connection System:** You'll be coping in healthy ways, and you'll start applying skills in relationships by sharing your emotions, setting boundaries, and practicing communication in real time. Connection begins to feel safer and more authentic.

V. **Developmental Integration System:** You'll build life rhythms that support growth and add creativity, mastery, and pleasure into daily living. Stability becomes less about surviving and more about thriving.

### How You'll Practice Skills in This Phase:

- **Dialectics:** Balance thoughts like "I feel scared *and* safe" and "I can hold grief *and* hope."
- **Mindfulness:** Expand awareness by practicing body scans, engaging in movement, and Observing internal states.
- **Distress tolerance:** Use Radical Acceptance and Willingness to face discomfort without avoidance.
- **Emotion regulation:** Effectively use Opposite Action, Build Mastery, and Build Positive Experiences.
- **Interpersonal effectiveness:** Use FAST and GIVE to balance self-respect and connection, and practice DEAR MAN to communicate clearly.

### You'll Be Ready for the Next Phase When:

- You can feel emotions and sensations without being overtaken by them.
- You can use skills proactively, and even automatically, before things escalate into crisis.
- You're comfortable exploring your experiences and talking about them.
- You begin seeing yourself as capable, not just surviving.

When you move into phase 3, your systems will naturally focus on connection and meaning, and you'll be focused on how to live your values, strengthen relationships, and define who you are beyond trauma.

## Phase 3: Relational Healing, Identity Reconstruction, and Meaningful Living: "Rebuilding What Trauma Broke"

Phase 3 is about living fully. You've built safety and integration, and now you'll apply these skills to deepen relationships, live through your values, and build a life that reflects who you truly are.

Note that phase 3 can happen independently of therapy as you continue to live your life and use your skills. Importantly, using skills to regulate and grow doesn't end when you leave therapy; it becomes a healthy lifelong pursuit! Here's what's happening in your systems in this phase:

I. **Mind and Meaning System:** Your emotions are balanced and trustworthy, and your mind feels clearer and more compassionate. You can hold multiple truths and rewrite old stories through the lens of growth and purpose.

II. **Body-Based System:** Your body feels more like home. You can notice tension and release it, experience rest, and enjoy energy and movement without fear.

III. **Consciousness and Memory System:** You feel fully present, and your traumatic memories are part of your story, not fully defining your identity.

IV. **Action and Connection System:** Relationships become more mutual and grounded. You can assert your needs, set limits, and stay connected through conflict. You live more intentionally, acting from your values rather than reactivity.

V. **Developmental Integration System:** This phase supports ongoing growth. You'll focus on long-term goals, creativity, contribution, and the freedom to keep evolving as a whole, resilient person.

### How You'll Practice Skills in This Phase:

- Dialectics: Accept both healing and growth: "I am whole *and* still becoming."
- Mindfulness: Practice relational presence and compassion in daily life by Participating fully and responding Effectively in your interactions.
- Distress tolerance: Use Radical Acceptance to handle life's pain without losing balance.
- Emotion regulation: Continue to engage fully in Build Mastery and Build Positive Experiences to live a satisfying life.
- Interpersonal effectiveness: Integrate all skills fluidly to repair, connect, and communicate with authenticity from a place of self-respect.

### You'll Know You're Living the Work When:

- You can hold both pain and peace within the same moment.
- You view trauma as a chapter in your story and not your identity.
- You navigate relationships with confidence and care.
- You feel guided by your values and a sense of meaning.

Remember that you might revisit earlier phases as new challenges arise. Each return allows you to reregulate and strengthen your systems with more awareness and skill. Healing isn't about erasing the past. It's about integrating it so you can live with freedom, connection, and purpose. With that, let's turn to the skills training curriculum, which contains the five DBT-based modules and their accompanying skills.

# Skills Training Modules

## Introduction to Skills Training

Skills training is where regulation becomes practice. It is the place where insight about trauma turns into action and where surviving begins to transform into living. Within DTRM, skills training gives you a clear, structured pathway to restore balance to the five interdependent systems and eleven domains of dysregulation.

Remember that trauma can interfere with these systems by fragmenting attention, distorting meaning, overwhelming the body, and disrupting your ability to connect. The purpose of skills training is not to suppress these reactions but to approach them with awareness and choice. Skills meet you where dysregulation is occurring and help bring that system or domain back online. As discussed earlier, the skills modules included in this curriculum are:

- Dialectics
- Mindfulness
- Distress tolerance
- Emotion regulation
- Interpersonal effectiveness

Throughout the curriculum, you'll see frequent references to the systems and domains that each skill targets. This mapping helps you understand *where* the skill works and *why* it helps. You'll also use RISE to apply skills in real time, though it is also important to practice skills in unstructured ways too.

Think of skills training as a practice of discovery, not perfection. Skills work best when you use them regularly:

- During calm moments (to strengthen neural pathways)
- During distress (to regulate)
- Afterward (to reflect and integrate what happened)

As you practice, notice which systems and domains get activated most easily and which remain under- or overresponsive, and note the shifts that occur with skills practice. Discuss these observations with your therapist or group, using curiosity rather than judgment to deepen your understanding.

For teaching purposes, I've periodically woven information throughout these modules about how the systems, domains, and neurobiology relate to the skills. It's all right if some of that information—especially related to brain areas—seems too technical or doesn't add to your personal learning experience. *It is not necessary to know or remember the underlying neurobiology to effectively use skills.* Practicing the skills is key, and brain and body changes will happen even if you don't fully understand the underlying mechanisms.[18]

As you work through the modules, notice the overlap between skills and how skills relate to one another. Metaphorically, singular skills are like words, and over time, skills will come together in phrases, sentences, and then paragraphs.

The first module, dialectics, lays the foundation. It helps you build flexibility so you can learn how to hold two seemingly opposing truths at once. This is the heart of both DBT and DTRM: Growth happens not by choosing between acceptance and change but by integrating both. Dialectical skills will prepare you to balance extremes, see complexity, and approach all that follows with an open and adaptive mind.

---

18 For those who are interested, a Trauma Neurobiology Glossary with examples is in the appendix.

CHAPTER 9

# Dialectics Module

## Dialectics: The Art of Holding Two (or More) Truths

Dialectics is at the heart of this treatment. A philosophical concept, dialectics refers to the synthesis or integration of opposing forces to arrive at a more complete truth. This is not just an idea but a practice to be with ourselves, others, and our experiences in a manner that creates flexibility in thought and behavior.

For many trauma survivors, the ability to think and act dialectically has been interrupted by overwhelming experience, as trauma often fractures our inner world, pushing us into polarized, rigid thinking: "I'm either completely safe or in danger" or "I'm either strong or broken." These extremes are protective, efficient, and often necessary survival strategies in the moment. Yet long after the danger has passed, these survival patterns can persist, becoming a default way of understanding the world. Flexibility, which was once a threat to survival, now feels foreign or unsafe.

As a result, survivors of trauma often experience an internal conflict that feels irreconcilable. This breakdown affects every area of functioning. For example, a trauma survivor may:

- Feel emotionally numb or emotionally flooded (emotional dysregulation): "I feel everything all at once, or I feel completely numb."
- View themselves as either all good or all bad (meaning and belief dysregulation): "Maybe I deserved what happened. Maybe it was my fault."
- Live in constant fight, flight, freeze, or collapse (nervous system dysregulation): "My body remembers danger, and I can't ever feel safe."
- Avoid relationships or attach desperately (relational dysregulation): "I trust no one and isolate, or I reach out for others impulsively."
- Inherit developmental beliefs (developmental dysregulation): "My feelings are dangerous" or "I don't matter."

These are not signs of dysfunction; they are natural outcomes of trauma. Trauma teaches the nervous system and the mind to organize experience in stark, binary terms. This is especially true when trauma occurs early in life, repeats over time, or comes from trusted figures. The world becomes divided into opposites, like safe/unsafe, love/harm, and right/wrong, and you become stuck on one side or the other, sometimes flipping between extremes.

Dialectical thinking doesn't ask you to get rid of these parts. It asks you to hold them and find space for complexity. It says, "You can feel betrayed *and* want closeness; you can be angry *and* still care; you can feel overwhelmed *and* still survive this moment." This foundational shift supports you in stepping out of all-or-nothing thinking and behavior and into a more flexible, compassionate understanding of yourself, your relationships, and the world around you. It creates space where all parts of your experience are allowed to coexist. And it is this space—spacious enough for grief and hope, fear and love—that makes healing possible.

When you practice dialectics, your brain begins to integrate again. The parts of your brain that manage survival, called the limbic system, and the parts that make sense of experience, called the prefrontal cortex, start working together. This balance calms the body's alarm system while strengthening insight and choice. Over time, these small shifts in thinking and awareness actually rewire the brain toward flexibility and regulation.

To illustrate this, consider a well-known story that captures how partial truths can obscure the whole. Several blind men encounter an elephant for the first time. One touches its side and says, "It's like a wall." Another, feeling the ear, insists, "It's a fan." A third, holding the trunk, claims, "It's a snake." Each man is convinced his perspective is correct, even as none see the whole animal.

This story mirrors trauma recovery. Each part of our experience, such as fear, anger, longing, or avoidance, might feel like the whole truth. Yet when we step back and listen to every part with respect and curiosity, a fuller picture emerges. Trauma can cause us to cling tightly to one part of the elephant, to one piece of the story. Dialectical thinking allows us to zoom out and integrate other parts into a richer, more complete truth.

## Dialectics Related to the Systems and Domains

Dialectics is an initial step in trauma stabilization. By learning to hold multiple truths, you begin to shift from survival-based reactions to a steadier awareness that makes space for healing. This new balance prepares you for the skills that follow in the mindfulness, distress tolerance, emotion regulation, and interpersonal effectiveness modules, each of which deepens and expands this foundation.

However, restoring dialectical capacity is more than an intellectual task. It is a full-system recalibration in which:

- The Mind and Meaning System regains balance between thoughts, feelings, and beliefs.

- The Body-Based System learns that tension and calm can coexist in one body.
- The Consciousness and Memory System reconnects the past and present without losing stability.
- The Action and Connection System allows both closeness and boundaries.
- The Developmental Integration System grows new ways of self-care and compassion.

The following table illustrates how dialectical awareness supports regulation and integration across the eleven domains in the systems. Notice the "Both/And" Thinking in the statements and examples.

| System | Dysregulation Type | Statements | Example |
|---|---|---|---|
| **I. Mind and Meaning** | Emotional | "I feel like this emotion will destroy me, *and* I can survive it."<br>"I feel out of control, *and* I can influence my emotions." | Ash feels intense sadness after a trigger. He validates his sadness and takes a walk. Over time, he learns that emotions don't have to dictate his behavior, and he can both feel and act with intention. |
| | Cognitive | "My thoughts are racing, *and* I can refocus my attention, over and over."<br>"My thoughts feel overwhelming, *and* I don't have to believe all of them." | Jade is catastrophizing. Her therapist helps her hold the dialectic: "It both feels like everything is coming apart, and it's not a fact." This reduces the intensity of her catastrophic thinking. |
| | Meaning and belief | "I believe I should have done something, *and* I was in an impossible situation."<br>"What happened was terrible, *and* I can create meaning moving forward." | Terrence feels defined by his trauma. In group, he says, "It should never have happened, and I'm using it to fuel my purpose." Meaning doesn't erase pain but reframes it. |
| **II. Body-Based** | Nervous system | "My brain is on high alert, *and* I can calm it with breath and grounding."<br>"My trauma wired me for reactivity, *and* I can rewire through practice." | Chloe freezes during conflict. She learns: "My nervous system is doing its job, and I can train it to feel safer." |
| | Somatic | "My body feels unsafe, *and* I am learning to listen to it with care."<br>"My body feels like a threat, *and* it's also the place where healing happens." | Omar carries tension in his body and sees it as dangerous. Through grounding and breathwork, he balances fear with learning to trust his body. |
| | Interoceptive | "I'm not sure what I need, *and* I can slow down and find out."<br>"I can't always trust what I feel inside, *and* my body gives me useful information." | Aaron mistakes hunger for anxiety. His therapist supports him to say, "These sensations feel confusing, and I can practice noticing what my body needs." Over time, he reengages with his body's cues. |

| System | Dysregulation Type | Statements | Example |
|---|---|---|---|
| **III. Consciousness and Memory** | Dissociative | "Part of me is far away, *and* I can call myself gently back." "I feel disconnected, *and* there is still a part of me that is watching and grounding." | Natalie begins to dissociate in therapy. She says, "A part of me is gone, and a part of me is still here." This allows her to use skills to stay present. |
| | Memory | "I'm remembering what happened, *and* I can stay in the present." "My memories feel unbearable, *and* I can choose how I hold them now." | Eli has intrusive memories of trauma. With grounding, he observes the memory instead of reliving it: "That was then, and this is now." |
| **IV. Action and Connection** | Behavioral | "I want to act on this urge, *and* I can choose something else." "I acted in a way I regret, *and* I can change my behavior now." | Sasha relapses and feels ashamed. Her therapist affirms, "Yes, that happened, and today is a new day." |
| | Relational | "I'm afraid to trust, *and* I want closeness." "I want connection, *and* I'm terrified of being hurt." | James pushes people away while craving connection. He learns: "I can hold both truths and still try." |
| **V. Developmental Integration** | Developmental | "I didn't get what I needed then, *and* I can give it to myself now." "I missed out on a lot, *and* I can still grow." | Keira grieves the parenting she never received. Her therapist helps her hold: "I was not supported, and I can reparent myself now." |

Across all systems and domains, dialectical thinking transforms fragmentation into coherence. It allows you to hold the complexity of trauma and recovery together—to see that distress and healing, fear and strength, grief and growth can coexist.

Integration begins in this "both/and" space, where you recognize that opposing truths can live side by side and that wholeness is not the absence of contradiction but the ability to hold contradiction with compassion. Dialectics is the thread that sews together the torn fabric of trauma. It allows you to say, "This happened, and I'm still here. I was hurt, and I can heal. I feel overwhelmed, and I'm learning to regulate."

Let's turn to more examples of dialectics in action.

## Dialectics in Action

*Understanding* dialectics is the foundation, and *practicing* it brings healing to life. By naming these tensions without flipping between extremes, you learn to observe emotions, thoughts, sensations, and situations without judgment, allowing you to validate your experience without self-blame and make room for both acceptance and change. This practice strengthens the Mind and Meaning System by helping you hold different truths without losing balance or coherence.

To get into the habit of practicing dialectics, the next time a dilemma arises, pause and ask yourself:

- "What are the two (or more) truths I can hold?"
- "Can I validate both?" or "What is the kernel of truth in each side?"
- "What would Wise Mind say?"
- "Can I speak to myself (and others) with 'and' instead of 'but'?"

This might sound like:

- "I want to isolate, and I know I need support."
- "I'm angry, and I don't want to harm this relationship."
- "These sensations in my body are overwhelming, and I know it will pass."

Each time you choose "Both/And" Thinking over "either/or," you strengthen your capacity for flexibility, self-compassion, and regulation. On a neurobiological level, this choice helps calm overactive limbic regions and strengthens prefrontal pathways that allow perspective, balance, and emotion regulation. It also activates the Action and Connection System by aligning your thoughts, emotions, and actions so they move in an integrated fashion.

## Dialectics in Your Body

Notably, you can also practice dialectics in your body. Try noticing two sensations at once, perhaps tension in your chest and calm in your hands. Allow both to be true. By breathing slowly while saying to yourself, "I can feel discomfort and safety," you cue your nervous system to experience integration, not just think about it. This supports the Body-Based System, where your body can learn that opposite sensations can exist safely together.

Here are more examples of bottom-up ways of practicing dialectics:

- **Warmth and coolness:** Notice warmth in one area of your body and coolness in another. Say to yourself, "I can feel warmth and coolness. My body can hold both." This simple awareness helps the brain register contrast without judgment.
- **Tension and softness:** Tighten your shoulders slightly, then release them. Feel the difference and say, "I can experience tension and release; both are part of my body's story."
- **Stillness and movement:** Feel your feet rooted on the ground while gently swaying or rocking: "I can be grounded and in motion." This balance restores safety in movement, often disrupted by trauma.
- **Effort and ease:** Hold a yoga pose or stretch to mild effort, then soften just a little: "I can work and rest at the same time." This teaches the nervous system that effort doesn't always have to mean strain.

- **Alertness and relaxation:** Notice how your eyes can be open and aware while your breath stays slow and calm: "I can be alert and relaxed." Trauma often pairs vigilance with tension; this repairs it with calm.
- **Heaviness and lightness:** Feel the weight of your body supported by a chair or the floor. Then notice the lightness of your breath: "I can feel heavy and light, both anchored and free."
- **Holding and letting go:** Clasp your hands tightly, then slowly open them: "I can hold on and let go." This exercise mirrors the emotional dialectic of protection and release.
- **Pain and comfort:** If you feel physical discomfort, locate one area of the body that feels okay: "I can feel pain here and comfort there." This teaches you that distress can coexist with safety.
- **Heartbeat and breath:** Place one hand on your heart and one on your abdomen. Feel the steady pulse and the rise and fall of breath: "My body can be active and calm; both belong."
- **Energy and fatigue:** On a day you feel drained, notice small pockets of vitality, maybe in your hands or eyes: "I can feel tired and alive." This helps regulate energy perception and counter all-or-nothing fatigue responses.

## Dialectics in Action with Other Skills

Dialectical thinking and action are captured in many of the philosophies and skills you'll learn in the other modules. Here are some examples:

- **Balancing Acceptance with Change:** Accept where you are while simultaneously working toward change.

  *Example:* "It makes perfect sense that I shut down, and I'll find a safe way to stay engaged next time."

- **Wise Mind:** The balanced state where Emotion Mind and Reason Mind meet.

  *Example:* "I feel angry at my friend, and I also value the relationship. Wise Mind says I can express myself calmly."

- **Radical Acceptance:** Fully accept a painful reality while still working toward transformation.

  *Example:* "This happened. I hate it. And I can stop fighting reality and start responding skillfully."

- **Turning the Mind:** Choose acceptance again and again, even when resistance is present.

  *Example:* "I'm still angry this happened, and I'm choosing not to feed the resistance right now."

- **Check the Facts:** Compare your inner emotional experience with external facts.

  *Example:* "I feel rejected, and the facts show she was just distracted and not intentionally ignoring me."

- **Opposite Action:** Balance your internal emotional pull with external behavioral flexibility.

  *Example:* "I feel like avoiding class, and I will go to build mastery and improve my mood."

- **GIVE vs. DEAR MAN:** Attending to others while also getting your wants and needs met.

  *Example:* "I was kind and respectful and was still able to set a boundary."

These examples are just the beginning. As you learn the skills in this manual, actively consider how they might relate to dialectics.

To begin, try practicing the dialectical exercises on the following worksheet.

Worksheet

# Dialectical Exercises

## Balance Acceptance and Change

Balancing acceptance and change is a cornerstone of trauma recovery. Acceptance doesn't mean giving up; it means acknowledging reality as it is, without judgment, and grounding yourself in the present. Change, on the other hand, involves taking steps toward healing and growth. For trauma survivors, this balance might include accepting the limitations of their current circumstances while actively engaging in therapy, self-care, and life-enhancing behaviors.

*Example:* You recognize that while you cannot change the past, you can accept it and choose to work on recovery by participating in treatment and using skills to regulate yourself.

How can you practice both acceptance and change right now?

______________________________________________

______________________________________________

______________________________________________

## What's Going Well?

Trauma often creates a negativity bias, making it hard to notice what's positive. Yet consciously identifying what's going well, even in small ways, can help balance this perspective and support more regulated emotions.

*Example:* Despite the stress of daily life, you might feel grounded by a supportive friendship or comforted by your self-care routine and consistent skill use.

What's going well for you today, even if it's small?

______________________________________________

______________________________________________

______________________________________________

## Compassion for Self and Others

Feelings of shame, guilt, and unworthiness can make self-compassion difficult. Practicing compassion for both yourself and others reduces those painful emotions and helps build a healthier, more balanced view. It reminds you that everyone is doing the best they can with the resources available to them.

*Example:* You may struggle with self-blame for your past actions, yet by practicing self-compassion, you begin to understand those actions in the context of your trauma and see that you were doing your best under very difficult circumstances.

Who can you offer compassion to today, including yourself?

________________________________________

________________________________________

________________________________________

## Work on Incremental Changes

Trauma recovery is a process, not an event. Expecting instant results can lead to discouragement. Focusing on small, consistent changes helps build momentum and confidence, showing that healing is happening, even if slowly.

*Example:* You may not notice immediate results from using a skill, but with repeated practice, you begin to experience positive changes over time.

What is one small step you can take today to support your healing?

________________________________________

________________________________________

________________________________________

## Find a Silver Lining

Finding a silver lining doesn't mean minimizing trauma; it means noticing how growth can arise from difficulty. This practice supports posttraumatic growth by identifying the strengths and insights you've gained through lived experience.

*Example:* Although your trauma was painful, it may have helped you develop resilience, empathy, or a deeper understanding of yourself, which are qualities that now support a more fulfilling life.

What's a silver lining you can find in a recent challenge or problem?

## Perspective Taking

Trauma can narrow your perspective and make it harder to understand others' experiences. Practicing perspective taking can reduce conflict, deepen empathy, and improve relationships.

*Example:* Instead of taking a friend's irritability personally, you consider that they might be struggling with their own stress or trauma. Responding with empathy rather than defensiveness deescalates tension and supports connection.

Is there a recent situation where you can try seeing things from someone else's point of view?

Each of these exercises helps your mind, body, and relationships find balance. The more you practice, the more your nervous system, thoughts, and emotions begin to integrate and regulate together.

## Dialectics and Chronic Invalidation: Healing the "Either/Or" Wound with "Both/And" Thinking

A major barrier to dialectical thinking is chronic invalidation, which reinforces "either/or" beliefs and fractures identity. Invalidation teaches you that you are either too much or not enough, dramatic or detached, to blame or imagining things. This binary worldview fractures your sense of identity, fuels shame, and distorts reality. It sends the message that only one experience is valid, *and it is never yours.*

Dialectical thinking begins to repair this. It engages the Mind and Meaning System, particularly the cognitive and meaning and belief domains, by expanding how the mind interprets experience and finds truth in complexity. It can also regulate the Body-Based System, softening the nervous system responses that accompany rejection, criticism, and shame. Over time, the brain learns that multiple perspectives can exist safely together, calming limbic alarm and strengthening prefrontal integration.

In short, dialectics offers a radical counternarrative to original invalidation: You can be this and that. You can feel what you feel and still be worthy. You can disagree and still be valid.

Dialectics heals the rigid "either/or" thinking at the heart of chronic invalidation, restoring nuance, permission, and the complexity of lived experience. Here's how you can practice this:

- **Validate internal contradictions:** "I can want closeness and be scared of intimacy." Both can be true. Neither cancels the other.
- **Use dialectical self-talk:** "This is really hard, and I'm doing the best I can." Practice this by using No Unnecessary Apologies from FAST (found in the interpersonal effectiveness module).
- **Reject false binaries:** When you notice "either/or" thinking (e.g., "I'm either broken or healed"), pause and reframe: "I'm healing, and it's a process, not a destination."
- **Apply dialectics in relationships:** "I can disagree with you and still care about you" or "I need space, and I want to stay connected."
- **Let dialectics restore trust in your perception:** "I see it differently, and that doesn't make me wrong" or "I feel this deeply, and I can hold space for other perspectives."
- **Move from invalidation to integration:** Reframe an invalidating belief, such as "I'm weak because I still get triggered," to a balanced and validating perspective, like "I have triggers, and I'm strong for surviving and learning to manage them."

Dialectics offers what chronic invalidation denies: truth with flexibility, identity with complexity, and self-trust without conditions. Dialectics teaches you to stop arguing with your experience and start listening to it. In that listening, you begin to reclaim what trauma tried to split apart—namely, your voice, your perception, and your wholeness.

Now let's move to the mindfulness module.

CHAPTER 10

# Mindfulness Module

## Mindfulness: The Universal Skill Set

Mindfulness is a mental state in which you consciously focus your awareness on the present moment by calmly acknowledging and accepting your feelings, thoughts, bodily sensations, and surroundings without judgment. In simple terms:

**Mindfulness is choosing to pay attention to the present moment without judgment.**

For individuals recovering from trauma, mindfulness is a powerful tool for regaining a sense of control over internal experiences. It can allow you to Observe flashbacks, intrusive thoughts, emotions, or bodily sensations without being overtaken by them. Instead of avoiding, suppressing, or reacting automatically, mindfulness gives you space to witness what is happening *so you have the power to choose how to respond.*

Mindfulness does this by directing you to focus your attention with intention. To do this, think of your attention like the lens of a camera: You can zoom in on details or zoom out to take in the full picture. This attentional control keeps you anchored in the now rather than pulled into the past (where trauma lives) or future (where fear tends to grow). Learning to control your attention and mental processes, rather than be controlled by them, is known as "taking hold of your mind."

There is immense healing power in learning how to place your attention where you want it to be. Instead of your mind scattering in response to distress, mindfulness trains you to return to the present moment and to ultimately act from your Wise Mind, which is a space that integrates emotion-based experience with grounded wisdom.

Importantly, mindfulness does not direct you to simply "be present" for the sake of it; sometimes being present can be too painful or overwhelming. Instead, *it teaches you choice about what to be present with and how to be present with it,* which you learn by practicing the core mindfulness skills and Wise Mind.

In DTRM, mindfulness is the foundation of phase 1 (stabilization), and it continues through all other phases of treatment (and life). In fact, mindfulness can be treated as a nearly universally applied set of skills across the systems and domains. Consider that the effectiveness of any of the skills is directly connected to your ability to do them mindfully. In DTRM, we encourage clients to "always bring their mindfulness along."

## Mindfulness Related to the Systems and Domains

With consistent practice, mindfulness reduces suffering across all five systems and eleven domains. That's because cultivating mindfulness is not simply an awareness exercise. It is a full-system practice that restores balance across mind, body, and meaning. Here's how:

- The Mind and Meaning System learns to notice emotions, thoughts, and beliefs without becoming entrenched in them.
- The Body-Based System experiences sensations as information rather than threat.
- The Consciousness and Memory System witnesses experiences with gentle observation, allowing the past and present to coexist without overwhelm.
- The Action and Connection System acts with intention instead of impulse, creating space between stimulus and response.
- The Developmental Integration System learns presence as a new way of caring for the self.

The following table illustrates how mindful awareness supports regulation and integration across the eleven domains in the systems.

| System | Dysregulation Type | Statements | Example |
|---|---|---|---|
| **I. Mind and Meaning** | Emotional | "I feel swept away by this emotion, yet I've found an anchor in Observing my breath." "I feel intense sadness, and I can allow it to move through me like a weather pattern." | Josh feels the weight of sadness in his chest. He names it Nonjudgmentally and focuses on slow, steady breathing. Noticing and naming the emotion calms his body, allowing it to pass instead of taking over. |
| | Cognitive | "My mind is racing, and I simply Observe and Describe my thoughts without a fight." "My thoughts are loud, and I can turn my attention One-Mindfully toward a distraction." | Sam's thoughts spiral into worst-case scenarios. She practices Observe and Describe, noticing, "My mind is planning for danger." The awareness interrupts rumination and allows her to focus elsewhere. |
| | Meaning and belief | "I believe I'm broken, and I can witness that belief without obeying it." "My story feels fixed, and I can watch it change in real time by embracing Effectively." | Terrence notices old narratives surface during meditation. Instead of arguing with them, he Observes their pull, letting them pass like clouds. Over time, mindfulness loosens the hold of trauma-based meaning. |

| System | Dysregulation Type | Statements | Example |
|---|---|---|---|
| II. Body-Based | Nervous system | "My heart races, and it helps to access Wise Mind: It's uncomfortable, and logically I know I'm okay and it will pass." "My body is on alert, and it helps to focus on one thing." | Chloe feels her pulse quicken after a loud noise. She anchors to the present, naming five things she sees, four things she hears, and so on. This mindful grounding steadies her system. |
| | Somatic | "My body feels unsafe, and I can sense my feet on the ground." "My muscles tighten, and it helps to accept and breathe into the tension." | Tyrone scans his body and notices clenching in his jaw. He practices mindful release, exhaling slowly and stretching his mouth into a gentle yawn that he holds briefly. The physical shift signals safety to his nervous system. |
| | Interoceptive | "I don't know what I need, so I pause to listen." "My body's cues confuse me. I stay curious to learn more." | Aaron mistakes anxiety for hunger. He takes a moment to breathe and feel. With the practice of the core mindfulness skills, he learns to discern between emotional and physical signals. |
| III. Consciousness and Memory | Dissociative | "I feel far away, and I notice that I am still here and can return fully with mindful grounding." "Part of me is drifting. I'll take a Nonjudgmental Stance about it, and I can gently return to the moment." | Natalie senses herself fading during session. She feels her feet on the floor and names the colors in the room. These mindful anchors reorient her to the present, and she asks her therapist for some moments of pause. |
| | Memory | "I remember what happened, and I can sort out what happened *then* from *now* with awareness in this moment." "My memories arise, and I can Observe them safely." | Eli has a flashback while driving. He places both hands on the steering wheel, feels its texture, breathes, and pulls over safely. Observing his sensations pulls him back to the present, and he resumes driving when settled in Wise Mind. |
| IV. Action and Connection | Behavioral | "I want to react, and I can choose to pause, work toward Wise Mind, and respond Effectively." "I feel the urge to act, and I am not my urges." | Sasha feels an impulse to text her ex. She engages her Wise Mind and decides it would be an ineffective choice. Over time, the impulse passes. |
| | Relational | "I'm afraid to speak, and I can stay present with that fear without judgment." "I want to withdraw, and I can remain open and Participate." | James feels defensive in a conversation. He notices his body tense, then relaxes his shoulders and listens. Mindfulness keeps connection possible. |
| V. Developmental Integration | Developmental | "I never learned to feel safe, and I can learn now." "I missed out on care with my neglectful family, so I engage in mindful compassion toward myself and my family." | Keira practices a mindful self-hold during moments of sadness. Attending to herself with compassion rewires her capacity for safety and care. |

Across all systems and domains, mindfulness awareness circumvents reaction. It teaches that pain and calm, fear and grounding, and chaos and stillness can coexist (which is also dialectical). Integration begins in this noticing, through the quiet recognition that we are not our thoughts or sensations, as we hold this awareness with compassion.

Beyond moments of being with experience, mindfulness helps you regain flexibility, presence, and balance. It counters the chaos of trauma by helping you take hold of your mind and teaching that emotions, thoughts, sensations, and memories can all show up without taking control of what you do, because *you have the choice of what to focus on*. When you notice without judging, it creates a small, powerful pause between what happens and the choice of how you respond. That pause is where healing begins.

Notably, healing with mindfulness isn't about forcing symptoms to stop; *it's about changing your relationship with them to one that is steady, curious, compassionate, and skillful.* As mindfulness becomes a habit, it strengthens all eleven areas of regulation, and your brain starts reconnecting two key areas: the prefrontal cortex (which helps you make thoughtful choices) and the limbic system (which reacts to threat). This new connection quiets the brain's alarm system and helps you feel safer inside. Over time, your nervous system learns that being present isn't dangerous, and your body begins to relax from the inside out.

Yet even with all these benefits, many trauma survivors believe mindfulness "isn't for them" or worry they're doing it wrong. These misunderstandings can make it hard to even start. The handout that follows looks at these myths so you can find a way to make mindfulness your own.

Handout

# Myths About Mindfulness

There are many common myths about mindfulness that can become barriers to practicing it. As you read through this list, notice which myths resonate with you. For each one, reflect on the fact that follows. Is there a grain of truth in the myth? How does each fact help broaden your understanding of what mindfulness really is?

**Myth:** Mindfulness is only for Buddhists or spiritual people.

**Fact:** Mindfulness is a secular practice that has been used across cultures and belief systems. It's accessible to anyone, regardless of religion, spirituality, or worldview.

**Myth:** Mindfulness is just about relaxation.

**Fact:** While mindfulness can promote relaxation and reduce stress, its primary purpose is to cultivate awareness and presence in the moment. This leads to improved focus, clarity, and self-awareness, all essential in trauma recovery.

**Myth:** Mindfulness is easy.

**Fact:** Mindfulness is simple in concept but not always easy to practice. Like any meaningful skill, it takes time, effort, and patience to develop.

**Myth:** Mindfulness takes too much time.

**Fact:** Mindfulness can be practiced in just a few moments. Even brief exercises like mindful breathing or a body scan can be effective. You can also integrate mindfulness into daily activities like eating, walking, or washing dishes.

**Myth:** Mindfulness is a one-time solution.

**Fact:** Mindfulness is a lifelong practice, not a quick fix. Its benefits grow over time through consistent, intentional practice.

**Myth:** Mindfulness is a cure-all.

**Fact:** Mindfulness is helpful for many mental and physical health concerns, but it's not a substitute for other forms of treatment. It works best as part of a holistic recovery approach.

**Myth:** Mindfulness means clearing your mind of thoughts.

**Fact:** The goal of mindfulness is not to stop thinking but to Observe your thoughts without judgment or attachment. Thoughts will arise, and it's what you do with them that matters.

**Myth:** Mindfulness is only for people with serious mental health issues.

**Fact:** Mindfulness is helpful for those with mental health concerns, but it also benefits anyone who wants to live with more awareness, intention, and balance.

**Myth:** Mindfulness requires a special environment.

**Fact:** Mindfulness can be practiced anywhere, while sitting, walking, commuting, or going about everyday life. You don't need a quiet space, special equipment, or perfect conditions.

**Myth:** Mindfulness is only for people who are already calm and centered.

**Fact:** Mindfulness is especially helpful for people who struggle with anxiety, intense emotions, or difficulty regulating their mood. The goal isn't to suppress your emotions; it's to build awareness and respond skillfully to whatever arises.

**Myth:** Mindfulness is a solitary activity.

**Fact:** Mindfulness connects us to something larger. Many cultures have long understood that healing is both personal and collective, and when you slow down and breathe, you're joining a universal rhythm of awareness that transcends trauma and isolation. Mindfulness reminds us that being present is not only an act of self-care; it is a way of belonging.

In sum, mindfulness is a human endeavor to connect us to the moment so we can live more fully with intention. Beyond understanding these myths and facts, exploring mindfulness practice yourself will clarify what it means for you.

 

## States of Mind

In DBT, mindfulness is taught through the framework of the three states of mind: Emotion Mind, Reason Mind, and Wise Mind. These states are not "good" or "bad." They are simply different ways your mind processes and responds to experiences. Each has strengths and limitations, and the goal is not to avoid any one of them entirely but to increase your time in Wise Mind, where emotion and reason are integrated and balanced. This integration strengthens the Mind and Meaning System, linking your thoughts with your emotions to create coherence. Let's look at each state more closely.

### Emotion Mind

In Emotion Mind, which is largely a bottom-up process, your thoughts, decisions, and actions are driven primarily by feelings. This state reflects the activity of the limbic system and the Body-Based System, where the nervous system and body react first and fast. For trauma survivors, this state can be especially intense when filled with fear, shame, anxiety, rage, or deep sadness. It might feel like you're drowning in overwhelm or acting on impulse to escape distress or pursue relief. Learning to notice Emotion Mind without judgment allows you to reconnect with the prefrontal regions that bring calm and clarity, allowing emotion and reason to begin working together again.

Even though Emotion Mind can lead to ineffective behaviors, especially when emotions are dysregulated, it's important to recognize that emotions aren't the problem. Emotions are essential, as they serve critical functions:

- **Communication:** Emotions communicate our inner experience to others through facial expressions, tone, body language, and words.
- **Information:** Emotions alert us to what matters, like our needs, values, and concerns, and warn us when something feels wrong or dangerous.
- **Safety and survival:** Emotions like fear keep us vigilant and protect us in unsafe situations.
- **Motivation:** Emotions fuel our behavior, from reaching out for connection when we feel lonely to withdrawing for safety when we feel threatened.

The challenge arises when emotions become too intense, rapid, or prolonged, especially in trauma recovery. In this state, actions may become impulsive, based more on survival instincts than long-term goals. The aim is not to avoid or silence Emotion Mind but to balance it with Reason Mind so that emotions can guide rather than control.

## Reason Mind

Reason Mind is your logical, rational state. It is top-down and focused on facts, data, and analysis. In Reason Mind, you make decisions based on logic and observable evidence, which can be particularly helpful when emotions feel overwhelming or unreliable.

For trauma survivors, Reason Mind can be a welcome refuge, as it offers structure, control, and distance from painful emotions. It supports the Mind and Meaning System, particularly the cognitive and meaning and belief domains, helping you organize experiences and restore a sense of order after chaos. It also engages the prefrontal cortex, the part of the brain responsible for planning and reasoning, which helps quiet the limbic alarm system when stress is high.

Reason Mind helps with planning, problem-solving, and managing responsibilities. But living exclusively in Reason Mind can also create problems. It can lead to emotional detachment, numbness, or a sense of disconnection from yourself and others. You might "know" something cognitively but feel completely disengaged from it emotionally.

Healing requires more than logic. To live fully, you must also feel, and that is where Wise Mind comes in.

## Wise Mind

Wise Mind is the state where bottom-up Emotion Mind and top-down Reason Mind come together, integrating your brain and body. It is a place of balance, inner knowing, and integrated awareness. In Wise Mind, you can validate your emotional experience while still considering the facts. You can respond to a situation thoughtfully rather than react impulsively or shut down entirely.

Wise Mind reflects your values and your deeper sense of self. It unites the Mind and Meaning System with the Body-Based System, bringing coherence between thought, feeling, and physiology. On a neurobiological level, Wise Mind represents balanced communication between the prefrontal cortex (your thinking center), limbic system (your emotion center), and insula (your internal awareness center), allowing both awareness and compassion to guide your choices.

It is often intuitive, quiet, and centered, helping you act in alignment with who you really want to be. In trauma recovery, Wise Mind allows you to make choices that honor both your pain and your progress. It offers clarity even in uncertainty and allows you to hold space for contradiction: "This is hard, and I can handle it."

Everyone has a Wise Mind. Even if you don't feel connected to it right now, it's always there and available to be accessed and strengthened through practice. You can begin to access your Wise Mind by asking yourself:

- What state of mind am I in right now? Emotion, Reason, or Wise Mind?

- What would the opposite state of mind say or do?
- What would my Wise Mind say or do in this moment?

Pause, listen to the answers, and choose to respond from Wise Mind. This practice brings you closer to clarity, compassion, and effectiveness, which are cornerstones of healing.

Another thing you can try is finding Wise Mind through your body. To do this, place one hand on your chest and one on your abdomen. Breathe slowly and say to yourself, "Breathing in, I know I am here. Breathing out, I am safe." Feel the steadiness in your breath as a bridge between feeling and thinking. This simple act lets your body participate in the balance your mind is learning.

Worksheet

# States of Mind

Understanding the three states of mind—Emotion Mind, Reason Mind, and Wise Mind—helps you recognize your internal experience and apply skills that lead to more effective choices. Each of these states plays a role in how you react to the world around you. By increasing awareness of these states, especially during moments of stress or trauma activation, you can better regulate your responses and move toward healing.

## Emotion Mind

Emotion Mind occurs when your feelings are in control of your thoughts and actions. In this state, decisions tend to be reactive and impulsive, based on how you feel rather than what's actually happening or what might be most effective. For those recovering from trauma, Emotion Mind is often activated quickly and intensely due to an overactive nervous system or unresolved emotional pain.

*Examples:*

- **Anger and confrontation:** You feel disrespected by a coworker, leading to overwhelming anger and resulting in you yelling or lashing out.
- **Sadness and withdrawal:** After receiving upsetting news from a loved one, you shut down emotionally, avoid others, and neglect responsibilities.
- **Excitement and risky behavior:** After feeling euphoric about a new romantic relationship, you ignore red flags and move too fast, despite concerns.
- **Anxiety and substance use:** Nervous about attending a party, you drink excessively beforehand to avoid feeling anxious.
- **Fear and isolation:** Intense fear of judgment or rejection causes you to cancel plans and avoid even close friends.

Can you identify a time when you were in Emotion Mind?

___________________________________________

___________________________________________

How did it affect your behavior or your relationships?

___________________________________________

___________________________________________

## Reason Mind

Reason Mind is when logic, facts, and evidence guide your decision-making. It allows for clear thinking and planning, especially in situations that require structure or problem-solving. However, leaning too heavily on Reason Mind can lead you to suppress, disconnect from, or overintellectualize feelings that actually need to be acknowledged.

*Examples:*

- **Financial planning:** You create a strict monthly budget based on your income, bills, and savings goals, without letting emotions interfere with spending.
- **Job search:** You prepare for interviews by researching companies, crafting resumes, and practicing responses in a methodical way.
- **Health management:** You track your symptoms, take medications on time, and make logical decisions based on a doctor's advice.
- **Academic goals:** You prioritize schoolwork, manage deadlines, and attend study groups to stay on track with a degree program.
- **Learning a new skill:** You break down a complex task like coding or cooking into steps and consistently practice, regardless of frustration or impatience.

Can you recall a situation where you successfully used Reason Mind?

______________________________________________

______________________________________________

What was the result?

______________________________________________

______________________________________________

## Wise Mind

Wise Mind is the balanced, centered state where both Emotion Mind and Reason Mind come together. It's where your intuition, values, emotions, and logic are all considered in harmony. Wise Mind helps you respond to life thoughtfully rather than react impulsively. For trauma survivors, it is the place of integration where pain can be acknowledged and healing choices can still be made.

 

*Examples:*

- **Managing anger:** You recognize a rising anger response and choose to take deep breaths before calmly expressing your feelings to resolve conflict.
- **Coping with despair:** You feel hopeless but use skills to validate your pain, focus on the present, and reach out for support anyway.
- **Rebuilding relationships:** You balance your hurt and desire for closeness by listening with empathy, sharing honestly, and taking small steps to rebuild trust.
- **Making major decisions:** You weigh the pros and cons of a career move or life change while staying grounded in your emotional truth and practical needs.
- **Navigating complex situations:** When facing a difficult supervisor at work, you choose to regulate your emotions while using assertive communication to advocate for yourself.

Can you think of a time when you acted from Wise Mind?

____________________________________________________________

____________________________________________________________

What helped you access that inner clarity?

____________________________________________________________

____________________________________________________________

With an understanding of the states of mind, you are now ready to begin learning the core mindfulness skills that help you return to Wise Mind more consistently and use it as a foundation for healing.

## The Path to Wise Mind: Core Mindfulness Skills

The journey to Wise Mind, especially for those who have experienced trauma, involves learning and practicing six core mindfulness skills. These skills are divided into two groups: The "What" skills explain *what* you do to reach Wise Mind, and the "How" skills describe *how* you practice mindfulness effectively.

**The What Skills:**

- Observe
- Describe
- Participate

**The How Skills:**

- One-Mindfully
- Nonjudgmentally
- Effectively

These six skills work together like parts of an engine, powering your ability to access Wise Mind. For trauma survivors, these skills make it easier to regulate emotions, reduce reactivity, and think more clearly when navigating difficult moments. And notably, these skills are not just techniques; they are forms of reparenting. Many trauma survivors were never taught how to attend to their inner world without judgment. Practicing Observe, Describe, and Participate with kindness builds that capacity, offering the safety and curiosity that should have been modeled early in life. Let's look at each component skill.

### What Skills

**Observe**

Observation is the first step: You simply notice what's happening, internally and externally, without trying to change anything. This includes noticing your emotions, thoughts, bodily sensations, urges, and environmental cues. It's about turning your attention deliberately to one area of experience without judgment or interpretation. For trauma survivors, this allows you to acknowledge your inner world without becoming overwhelmed by it.

*This is "What" you are doing. Practicing it One-Mindfully is "How."*

**Describe**

Once you've Observed your experience, the next step is to label it in clear, objective terms, staying clear of words that judge or color the experience. Describe what you see, hear, feel, or think, using factual language like "I notice tightness in my chest" or "I'm having the thought that I failed." This creates distance between you and the experience, which is especially helpful when the experience feels intense or consuming.

*This is "What" you are doing. Doing it Nonjudgmentally is "How."*

**Participate**

This skill is about fully engaging in the present moment by immersing yourself in what you're doing without analyzing it or becoming self-conscious. For trauma survivors, Participating fully without judgment restores connection to the present and reduces avoidance. Whether you're talking with someone, doing an activity, or just noticing your breath, Participation helps you live more fully in the moment.

*This is "What" you are doing. Doing it Effectively is "How."*

## How Skills

**One-Mindfully**

This skill helps you focus on one thing at a time. Trauma can fragment your attention, with your mind bouncing between past triggers, present stress, and future worries. One-Mindfully means you choose to focus on what you're doing now, even if your attention drifts. It's the practice of coming back to the moment, again and again. When practicing One-Mindfulness, remember that distractions are natural, and gently treat them as reminders to return to what you choose to focus your attention on.

*This is the "How" of Observing.*

**Nonjudgmentally**

This skill teaches you to notice your experiences without labeling them as "good" or "bad." Trauma often leaves behind layers of self-blame and harsh internal judgments. Practicing Nonjudgmentally, even with judgments, creates space between you and your thoughts or emotions so that you can simply experience them as they are without shame, denial, or overidentification. This is a powerful skill, as attaching judgments to experiences tends to add needless intensification and suffering.

*This is the "How" of Describing.*

**Effectively**

To act Effectively means to do what works, not what you wish would work, what you prefer, or what feels good in the moment. Effectiveness is about being goal focused and values based, especially when emotions or trauma responses are pulling you off course. Doing what works may mean tolerating distress, asking for help, setting a boundary, or trying something new even when it's hard.

*This is the "How" of Participating.*

By combining these core mindfulness skills, you move closer to Wise Mind, a place where emotion and reason come together and where you can make thoughtful, balanced, and values-aligned decisions.

## Let It Slide: Teflon Mind

Teflon Mind is a metaphor for practicing mindful nonattachment. It teaches you to let thoughts, feelings, and sensations move through awareness without clinging to them or pushing them away. Just as food slides effortlessly off a Teflon pan, experiences can arise and pass through consciousness without leaving residue. This practice does not deny or invalidate your experience; it allows you stay present without becoming entangled in intrusive thoughts, overwhelming emotions, or trauma reactivation. Here are some examples of Teflon Mind:

- **Intrusive thought:** "I'm not good enough." Recognize it as a passing thought, not a truth. Let it slide through awareness without engagement.
- **Overwhelming emotion:** A sudden wave of panic arises. Notice the sensation, breathe through it, and let it pass like a tide that naturally recedes.
- **Physical sensation:** A tight chest or nausea emerges. Acknowledge the sensation without resistance, understanding that it will move on when you allow it space to do so.

In early phase 1 stabilization, this skill interrupts reactivity and provides a method for safely observing distressing experiences without escalating. In the integration phase, phase 2, it supports processing by allowing you to notice intrusive or painful material without collapse or avoidance. This practice supports the Mind and Meaning System by creating space between your experiences and your self-understanding. It also activates the Consciousness and Memory System by helping you notice trauma-related experiences while preserving a stable sense of self in the moment.

Teflon Mind helps your brain stay steady and flexible. It strengthens areas like the medial prefrontal cortex and insula, which support awareness and balance by helping you notice and interpret your body's internal signals. These regions also calm the default mode network and limbic system, which are the parts of the brain that can make you get stuck in or overidentify with your thoughts, emotions, or body sensations.

When you practice Teflon Mind consistently, your brain becomes less likely to personalize transient experiences and creates new neural associations between awareness and calm. This reduces emotional spiraling and increases resilience. Mindful labeling functions as a top-down process, while grounding and noticing your breath provide bottom-up support, creating bidirectional regulation. Letting your experiences move through awareness also reestablishes the healthy emotional boundaries that may have been blurred or violated in your early relationships. In this way, the practice offers developmental repair by retraining your mind and body to differentiate between yourself and your experiences, while maintaining connection and safety. Here's how to use this skill:

1. **Notice.** Bring awareness to what is happening. For example, say to yourself, "I'm having a thought about being unsafe." This simple observation allows you to maintain awareness of the thought without overly identifying with it.

2. **Acknowledge.** Validate your experience by recognizing that it makes sense in light of your history. You might say, "This thought is understandable given what I have been through." Validation honors your experience without giving it control.
3. **Let it slide.** Visualize the thought, feeling, or sensation drifting away, perhaps like a leaf floating down a river or a cloud passing through the sky. This imagery reinforces the impermanence of inner experiences and the safety of Observing them without reaction.
4. **Return to the present.** Ground yourself in the here and now. Focus on your breath, the feeling of your feet on the ground, or the sensory details of your surroundings. Returning to the present reorients your nervous system toward safety and restores mindful connection.

Teflon Mind ultimately teaches you that awareness itself is strong enough to hold whatever arises. By allowing your experiences to come and go freely, you reclaim mastery over attention and emotion. Each moment of letting go reinforces regulation, integration, and the deep resilience that comes from living fully in the present.

Handout

# Using Core Mindfulness and Wise Mind to Address Trauma

Core mindfulness is the foundation for accessing Wise Mind to make intentional, healing choices. The examples in this handout show how to use these mindfulness skills to address trauma-related challenges in your daily life. Each of these practices allows different systems and domains of regulation to work together, restoring balance across your body and mind.

When mindfulness becomes a habit, it weaves stability through all eleven domains of dysregulation. You begin to trust your emotions, clarify your thoughts, regulate your body, anchor your memories, act intentionally, relate safely, and nurture your own development.

## Use Deep Breathing

After a flashback or distressing memory, take slow, deep breaths while keeping your eyes open. Focus on something neutral or calming in your environment. This grounds you in the present and soothes your nervous system. Deep, rhythmic breathing supports the Body-Based System by calming sympathetic arousal and strengthening vagal tone,* allowing your body to signal safety to the brain. It also relates to your Consciousness and Memory System by anchoring you in the present moment.

## Scan Your Body

During periods of anxiety or physical tension, bring attention to each part of your body in turn. Breathe into areas of discomfort with curiosity and care. This supports somatic regulation and eases somatic distress. Body scanning activates the somatic and interoceptive domains, reconnecting awareness with bodily experience so your brain can integrate the sensations that trauma once disconnected.

## Try Loving-Kindness Meditation

When anger, guilt, or shame arise, practice saying loving-kindness phrases like "May I feel safe" or "May I treat myself with compassion." This shifts your mindset toward healing rather than self-judgment. Loving-kindness strengthens the Mind and Meaning System, especially the emotional and meaning and belief domains, by cultivating warmth, empathy, and new neural associations of safety and care.

---

* Your vagus nerve is one of the main pathways that connect your brain and body. It helps control your heart rate, breathing, digestion, and the ability to feel calm and connected. After trauma, this system often gets thrown off balance. The body starts to live in survival mode, stuck in fight, flight, freeze, or collapse even when there's no real danger.

Restoring vagal tone requires helping your body's systems relearn how to shift out of survival mode and back into safety. In this context, *tone* refers to your body's ability to flexibly transition from a state of alertness to calm and back again as needed. Healthy vagal tone doesn't mean you never feel stressed; it means your body knows how to come back down when the stress passes.

## Mindful Communication

When discussing trauma, pay attention to your body, emotions, and thoughts. Listen with openness, speak from a centered place, and aim for understanding rather than control. This practice regulates the Action and Connection System, particularly the relational domain, creating pathways for trust and mutual safety in relationships.

## Observe Mindfully

When you're in a chaotic or overstimulating environment, notice any sounds, sights, and sensations without reacting to them. This practice keeps you grounded and less triggered. Observing mindfully reduces hyperarousal by training your brain to notice without immediately becoming defensive or avoidant.

## Mindful Self-Reflection

When intense emotions surface, pause and Observe. Ask yourself what you're feeling and what the emotion is trying to tell you. Reflect with compassion rather than criticism, allowing yourself to find meaning in your inner experience rather than judgment.

## Mindful Movement

Activities like walking, stretching, dancing, or yoga become grounding when done with awareness. Move your body with intention to reconnect and release stored tension. Mindful movement directly regulates the Body-Based System (especially the nervous system and somatic domains), releasing built-up activation while reestablishing safety in motion and embodiment.

## Gratitude Practice

When you're feeling discouraged, identify one thing you're grateful for, even if it's small. Gratitude reorients your mind toward what is supportive, healing, and positive. This practice engages the meaning and belief domain by focusing the brain on sources of safety and hope rather than threat.

## Mindful Listening

When someone is speaking, focus fully on their words and tone. Let go of distractions or inner commentary. Practicing mindful listening makes you feel more connected and less isolated. This strengthens the relational domain of the Action and Connection System, deepening attunement and trust while softening hypervigilance and social withdrawal.

## Mindful Problem-Solving

When faced with a challenge, pause, ground yourself, take stock of facts and emotions, and then brainstorm a Wise Mind approach that honors your needs and boundaries. This process integrates top-down and bottom-up regulation, allowing Reason Mind and Emotion Mind to cooperate. It strengthens connections between the prefrontal cortex (thinking center) and limbic system (emotion center), promoting thoughtful, balanced action.

Handout

# Guided Imagery for Healing from a Painful Event

Guided imagery is a form of mindfulness that uses visualization to activate the body's relaxation response and reshape traumatic associations. Instead of automatically pairing certain sensations or memories with fear, the mind learns to associate them with safety, calm, or support. When you imagine safety, strength, and compassion, your nervous system responds as if those qualities are real in the moment. This practice can reduce stress, support regulation, and promote a sense of peace.

1. **Find a comfortable position:** To begin, sit or lie down somewhere quiet. Take a few deep breaths, and let your body relax.
2. **Ground in the present:** Notice the surface beneath you. Feel the rise and fall of your breath. Gently bring your attention to this moment.
3. **Visualize a safe place:** Picture a location that feels calm, beautiful, and secure. It might be real or imagined. Perhaps it's a beach, forest, cozy room, or place of spiritual meaning.
4. **Engage your senses:** Notice what you see, hear, feel, and even smell in this place. Take your time to bring this place to life. The more sensory details you include, the more your mind anchors to safety.
5. **Invite supportive energy:** Imagine a warm light surrounding you that is protective, soothing, and compassionate. Let it fill this place and your body with calm.
6. **Release the pain:** If distressing thoughts or images arise, imagine placing them on a leaf that floats downstream or releasing them into the light. Allow yourself to let go without judgment.
7. **Affirm healing, then repeat to yourself:**

   "I am safe now."

   "I can let this moment pass."

   "I am learning to trust myself again."
8. **Return slowly:** Bring your awareness back to the room. Notice the present sights, sounds, and sensations around you. Take one more deep breath, feeling grounded and at ease.

You can practice guided imagery daily or anytime you feel triggered. Over time, it helps your body associate mindful presence with safety rather than danger.

## Mindfulness and Chronic Invalidation: Cultivating Internal Validation Through Awareness and Presence

Invalidation is one of the most painful and confusing experiences for trauma survivors. It occurs when your emotions, perceptions, or experiences are dismissed, minimized, or denied by others or even by yourself. Chronic invalidation leads to deep self-doubt, self-criticism, and emotional numbing. It teaches the nervous system that feelings and experiences are dangerous, unreliable, or wrong.

Mindfulness counters invalidation by helping you turn toward your own experience with awareness, curiosity, and compassion. Instead of judging your feelings or seeking external validation, you learn to validate your inner world as it is right now. This shift supports all five systems by restoring trust in your internal signals, thought processes, and embodied wisdom.

Follow these steps to practice validation through mindfulness:

1. **Notice:** Begin by Observing your experiences as they arise, without labeling them as good or bad.

   *Example:* "I feel anxiety, tension in my body, and my heart is racing."

2. **Acknowledge:** Allow the experience to exist without trying to change or fix it.

   *Example:* "It's okay that I feel this way right now."

3. **Name the need:** Ask yourself what this experience might be communicating.

   *Example:* "My body and mind are concerned, and it's showing up in these experiences."

4. **Offer compassion:** Use gentle self-talk or grounding to soothe your distress.

   *Example:* "This is uncomfortable, and I can be with it and kind to myself while I feel it."

5. **Act wisely:** Respond with effectiveness rather than reactivity.

   *Example:* "I can connect with this and use skills to calm my systems."

This practice replaces internal judgment with internal care. Over time, mindfulness teaches you that your experiences make sense, even when they're uncomfortable. You learn to trust your perception, which reestablishes internal safety, a key outcome in trauma recovery. Here are other examples of how mindfulness can counter invalidation:

| Invalidated Emotion | Mindful Response |
|---|---|
| "You shouldn't be so sensitive." | "Sensitivity is part of my experience. It helps me notice things others might miss." |
| "You're overreacting." | "My reaction feels strong because this reminds me of past hurt. That's understandable." |
| "That didn't happen." | "Even if others don't remember it the same way, my body and emotions remember my truth." |
| "You're being dramatic." | "I have needs, and it's okay to express them with clarity and respect." |

Practicing internal validation through mindfulness heals the relational wounds left by chronic invalidation. You become both the witness and the comforter within your own system, grounding in compassion rather than self-doubt. This strengthens the relational domain of your Action and Connection System by rebuilding trust and safety from within that can later extend to others.

Mindfulness teaches that your inner experience always deserves acknowledgment. As you turn toward emotions with curiosity and care, your nervous system learns that being seen is safe. These moments of self-recognition quietly repair disrupted attachment patterns and foster connection where fear once lived.

Through presence and self-validation, you reclaim what trauma took away—namely, the right to trust yourself. This supports the Developmental Integration System by helping the parts of you that felt unseen as a child grow with coherence, confidence, and belonging.

CHAPTER 11

# Distress Tolerance Module

## Distress Tolerance to the Rescue

For individuals who have experienced trauma, distress often leads to ineffective "coping" behaviors that offer short-term relief but ultimately cause long-term harm. These behaviors might include self-injury, substance use, overeating, withdrawal, or aggression. The distress tolerance module offers you skills to survive and manage intense distress without resorting to these ineffective and harmful behaviors. These skills are especially essential during the first phase of treatment, though effective coping behaviors are really necessary for life.

Distress tolerance skills are organized into two main categories:

- **Crisis survival strategies:** These skills provide healthy distractions and make the moment better during overwhelming times. For example, when you're feeling triggered or flooded, you might distract yourself by engaging in a hobby, listening to calming music, or getting some physical activity. You could also choose to Self-Soothe by focusing on pleasant sensory experiences, like smelling a favorite essential oil or using deep breathing to relax your mind and body. Crisis survival skills activate the parasympathetic branch of the autonomic nervous system, countering trauma-related sympathetic overactivation like fight, flight, freeze, or collapse and restoring vagal tone.
- **Reality acceptance skills:** These include skills like Radical Acceptance and Turning the Mind, which involve letting go of the struggle with reality to reduce suffering. For trauma survivors, this can mean accepting the reality of their past trauma and its impact rather than staying stuck in denial or anger. Acceptance does not mean approval; it simply means acknowledging reality so you can heal in the present. It is like recognizing that it is raining: You do not have to like the weather, yet by admitting it is happening, you can reach for an umbrella. Refusing to accept the rain only leaves you standing in it, soaked and suffering. Acceptance prepares you to respond wisely to what is real, rather than fighting a battle you cannot win.

## Guidelines for Using Distress Tolerance Skills

The key to distress tolerance is consistent practice and patience. These skills are not designed to eliminate distress entirely but to get you through the moment without making things worse. Regular use, even during lower-stress times, strengthens these skills so they are more effective during crises. To get the most out of distress tolerance skills, keep the following guidelines in mind:

- **Use for survival, not avoidance.** Distress tolerance skills are designed to survive painful moments, not to avoid or ignore problems that can be solved. When a situation is changeable, and you are in Wise Mind enough to focus on problem-solving, then solve the problem instead of using these skills as an escape.
- **Know when to tolerate and when to act.** Learn to distinguish between situations that require acceptance and those where change is possible. When you are in your window of tolerance, practice mindfully being with lower levels of discomfort, and use distress tolerance skills when the distress is high enough that you need a break or relief to stay within your window of tolerance.
- **Don't confuse tolerance with approval.** Tolerating a situation doesn't mean you approve of it or are giving up. It means you're accepting the reality of the moment so you can cope with it more effectively and without making it worse. Don't equate tolerance with submission and powerlessness; in this context, tolerance is a mindful choice that reflects mastery.
- **Use these skills for short-term survival.** Distress tolerance is about short-term survival, not long-term resolution. These skills help you ride out emotional storms until you're ready to return to problem-solving and healing work. That said, frequent practice of these skills will result in long-term regulation.
- **Build a full tool kit.** Because distress tolerance skills are meant for short-term use, it's important to develop a wide range of strategies. This gives you more flexibility when one skill isn't effective or starts to lose its impact.
- **Practice regularly.** The more you practice these skills, even when you're not in crisis, the more effective they become. The skills work when you work the skills, and practice makes you prepared to handle challenging situations. Also, look for opportunities to practice these skills in session along with your therapist; this is a wonderful opportunity to co-regulate, which creates healing in the relational domain.

## Distress Tolerance Related to the Systems and Domains

Distress tolerance is not simply about surviving crisis. It represents a full-system process that restores steadiness across mind and body. With distress tolerance:

- The Mind and Meaning System learns to hold distress without collapse or avoidance.
- The Body-Based System endures sensations safely, finding strength within discomfort and harnessing the ability to restore balance.
- The Consciousness and Memory System stays present with pain without being consumed by it or checking out.
- The Action and Connection System chooses effective responses over impulsive reactions and enters into relationships with greater regulation.
- The Developmental Integration System develops resilience from which to grow.

The following table illustrates how distress tolerance supports regulation and integration across the eleven domains in the systems.

| System | Dysregulation Type | Statements | Example |
|---|---|---|---|
| **I. Mind and Meaning** | Emotional | "I feel like emotions will drown me, yet I've learned to Ride the Wave (Urge Surfing)."<br>"I feel unbearable pain, yet I can use skills from ACCEPTS and IMPROVE to get through these moments." | Lena feels heartbreak wash over her. Instead of numbing, she focuses on her breath, counting each exhale. The emotion peaks, then softens. She learns that the intensity passes and listens to uplifting music to create different Emotions (ACCEPTS). |
| | Cognitive | "My mind screams that I can't do this, and I can focus on One Thing in the Moment (IMPROVE)."<br>"I think I'll fall apart, and I can use Encouragement (IMPROVE) and distract with Thoughts (ACCEPTS)." | Devon's thoughts spiral during an argument. He takes a break (Vacation from IMPROVE) and uses TIPP by splashing cold water on his face. He then says aloud, "This feeling won't last forever." This breaks the loop of panic. |
| | Meaning and belief | "Sometimes I believe I deserve this pain, and in these moments, I can Radically Accept that change takes time."<br>"When life feels hopeless, I can both use Prayer and practice Meaning (IMPROVE)." | After a setback, Marisol feels worthless. She lights a candle, a small act of care, and whispers, "I'm still here." These small acts represent Self-Soothe and Meaning (IMPROVE) in the midst of despair. |

| System | Dysregulation Type | Statements | Example |
|---|---|---|---|
| II. Body-Based | Nervous system | "My heart is racing, and I can cool it down by meeting it with acceptance and using Imagery (IMPROVE)."<br>"My body floods with adrenaline, and I focus on Sensations (ACCEPTS) to reset." | When panic hits, Mia presses a cold pack to her neck (TIPP). The temperature shift engages her parasympathetic system, signaling safety. She feels her pulse slow. |
| | Somatic | "My body feels like it's breaking, and I can address it with Activities (ACCEPTS) like yoga or stretching."<br>"My stomach knots in fear, and I can ground my feet to the floor and gently sway to comfort myself." | Andre shakes after receiving bad news. He squeezes a stress ball and exhales through pursed lips. The release steadies his hands and slows his breathing. |
| | Interoceptive | "I can't tell whether I'm hungry, scared, or angry. Using Prayer (IMPROVE) in these moments helps, and then I can check back in with my body."<br>"My body screams for escape, and I can Radically Accept the discomfort." | Caleb confuses emotional overwhelm with physical danger. He focuses on noticing his sensations without judgment, repeating, "This is discomfort, not threat." He then turns to tools like Self-Soothe and TIPP to calm his system. |
| III. Consciousness and Memory | Dissociative | "I feel myself disappearing, and I can plant my feet on the floor, feel my body in the chair (grounding), and use Encouragement (IMPROVE) to coach myself."<br>"I'm fading out, and I can bring myself back gently by naming objects in my room (grounding) and distract with Thoughts (ACCEPTS)." | Renee zones out during conflict. She grips a smooth stone from her pocket, feeling its texture and coolness until the room comes into focus again. The sensory anchor reclaims presence. |
| | Memory | "When my mind replays the past, I can use Encouragement (IMPROVE) to remind myself that I'm safe now and choose to engage in Activities (ACCEPTS) I enjoy."<br>"The memory feels intense, and I can use grounding to stay here." | When trauma memories surface, Ian names objects around him—chair, window, light—until the images lose intensity. He reminds himself, "That was then, and this is now." He then uses Comparisons (ACCEPTS) to note that his present life is better than his past. |

| System | Dysregulation Type | Statements | Example |
|---|---|---|---|
| **IV. Action and Connection** | Behavioral | "I want to escape by using drugs, but I have Burned the Bridge to substances and can distract with Thoughts (ACCEPTS) until the urges fall." "I feel the urge to use, and I can use Urge Surfing (Ride the Wave) for an hour and recheck my urge then." | Sophie feels an impulse to self-harm. She uses her skills from her distress tolerance plan. By the time ten minutes pass, the urge has eased. |
| | Relational | "I want to lash out, and I can practice STOP to walk away instead." "I want to withdraw, and instead I practice Contributing (ACCEPTS)." | Marcus feels hurt by a friend's comment. He decides to go for a drive to take a break (Vacation from IMPROVE) and distract. The pause prevents an impulsive text or call and preserves connection. |
| **V. Developmental Integration** | Developmental | "I never learned how to calm myself, and I practice Relaxation (IMPROVE) and other skills now." "No one soothed me then, and I can comfort myself with Self-Soothe today." | Clara wraps herself in a blanket and practices Paced Breathing (TIPP) after a nightmare. The Self-Soothe and TIPP ritual becomes a new kind of caregiving and provides evidence that regulation can be learned. |

Across all systems and domains, distress tolerance transforms crisis into capability. It reminds survivors that pain is not permanent and that the ability to endure creates the conditions for change. Integration begins in the quiet realization that suffering can be met with skill and that survival can evolve into resilience.

Worksheet

# Wise Mind ACCEPTS

Wise Mind ACCEPTS offers seven skills for mindfully distracting from distress in healthy, intentional ways. Rather than suppressing or avoiding emotions, these skills provide safe pauses that engage the mind and body in balanced, constructive activity. Each letter represents a pathway to restore regulation across systems and domains: Activities, Contributing, Comparisons, Emotions, Pushing Away, Thoughts, and Sensations.

## Activities

Engage in activities that provide healthy distraction from distress, such as reading, doing a hobby, creating arts and crafts, or getting physical movement or exercise. Creative and physical engagement redirects attention from the brain's threat response (via the amygdala) back to thinking and problem-solving (via the prefrontal cortex). This can restore a sense of agency and disrupt the cycle of trauma-driven avoidance.

Activity with movement anchors the Body-Based System, replacing immobilization or hyperarousal with rhythmic, regulated action that supports nervous system coherence. Through activity, energy is channeled into present-moment, goal-directed behavior, and the body relearns safety through movement and mastery.

List three new activities you can try this week.

________________________________________

________________________________________

________________________________________

## Contributing

Do something kind or helpful for someone else to shift your focus outward and build meaning, connection, and worth. Acts of contribution like volunteering, helping a friend, or offering kindness regulate the Action and Connection System, especially the relational domain, transforming isolation into connection.

Altruism also helps rebuild healthy attachment patterns that may have been disrupted early in life, speaking to the Developmental Integration System. Through acts of care and reciprocity, you activate the Action and Connection System, integrating empathy with purpose and awakening your capacity for trust and co-regulation.

Describe one way you can contribute today.

## Comparisons

Compare your current situation to others who may be facing greater challenges, or to your own past when life was more difficult, to gain perspective. For example, think about someone with fewer resources or more severe struggles. This skill is meant to expand awareness and not to minimize your pain. You can fully validate your suffering while still finding gratitude or perspective.

Comparisons engage the Mind and Meaning System, broadening your perspective and helping recalibrate your beliefs about suffering, resilience, and worth. Through this process, you deepen compassion for both yourself and others, and you develop new sources of meaning that counter hopelessness and distortion.

Record a couple healthy comparisons that broaden your view without invalidating your feelings.

## Emotions

Generate an emotion opposite to the one you are currently experiencing. If you are anxious, practice calming actions like gentle stretching, deep breathing, or sitting by candlelight. If you are sad or numb, watch a comedy, listen to uplifting music, or reach out to someone supportive.

From a neurobiological perspective, practicing opposite emotions calms the parts of the brain that react automatically to stress and strengthens the pathways that support emotional balance. Acting opposite to your emotion connects mind and body, linking emotional awareness with physical regulation so you can feel your feelings without being ruled by them. Both the Mind and Meaning System and the Body-Based System come into play with this process. Together, these systems build emotional flexibility and teach you that emotions can shift through intentional experience, rather than remaining fixed by trauma conditioning.

List three behaviors that can help create positive emotions today.

______________________________

______________________________

______________________________

## Pushing Away

Create mental distance from distress by temporarily setting it aside. Imagine placing the problem in a box and putting it on a shelf, or remind yourself, "This is a tomorrow problem." This technique builds containment, allowing for respite without avoidance.

This skill relates to the Consciousness and Memory System where temporary, intentional compartmentalization protects against overwhelm in the dissociative domain. Learning to skillfully contain distress teaches flexible control and prevents dissociation.

Describe a time when you practiced pushing away effectively and how it helped.

______________________________

______________________________

______________________________

## Thoughts

Focus your mind on other thoughts to redirect attention from emotional intensity. Work on a puzzle, read something interesting, have a thoughtful conversation, or engage your curiosity about a neutral topic.

This strengthens the Mind and Meaning System, particularly the cognitive domain, by reengaging brain regions that organize perception and restore perspective. The act of thinking intentionally grounds your mind in structure and signals that control and coherence are possible even in distress.

Identify three ways you can redirect your thinking when distressed.

______________________________

______________________________

______________________________

## Sensations

Use strong, healthy physical sensations to ground and reorient yourself when you're feeling overwhelmed in your mind or body. Squeeze a stress ball, take a cold shower, smell something refreshing, or taste something sour. Strong sensory input stimulates the vagus nerve and resets the Body-Based System, bringing you back to a sense of safety. This is a rapid, bottom-up method to regain stabilization when words or logic are inaccessible.

Moreover, safe, predictable sensory experiences such as temperature, pressure, or rhythm can engage the Developmental Integration System by teaching you how to meet your own needs for safety and regulation. These sensations become new anchors for the nervous system, reintroducing the felt sense of being cared for and contained.

Describe how you can engage your senses to create safety and presence.

________________________________________

________________________________________

________________________________________

Worksheet

# IMPROVE the Moment

When distressing emotions or trauma symptoms arise, the IMPROVE skill helps shift your emotional state and reground yourself. The acronym stands for Imagery, Meaning, Prayer, Relaxation, One Thing in the Moment, Vacation, and Encouragement.

## Imagery

Use visualization to create a mental sanctuary. Perhaps it's a safe or peaceful place you can visit in your mind, or you might imagine a calming natural scene, picture yourself thriving in the future, or use guided imagery recordings to promote relaxation. Visualization establishes a sense of internal refuge when external circumstances feel overwhelming.

From a neurobiological perspective, guided imagery engages the prefrontal and sensory networks of the brain to override limbic activation. Visualizing safety helps rewire trauma-related neural networks within the Consciousness and Memory System, creating new associations of calm and control. When combined with breathwork and grounding, imagery strengthens a felt sense of safety in the interoceptive domain, countering body-based fear responses and reinforcing self-regulation.

Search the internet or YouTube for imagery exercises or ask your therapist for resources, and note them here.

________________________________________

________________________________________

________________________________________

## Meaning

Find or create purpose in your experience. Reflect on what you have learned from your challenges, how your pain may connect you to others, or why it is worth using your skills to stay safe and move through this moment. Meaning transforms suffering into growth and reorients you toward hope and purpose.

This skill primarily engages the Mind and Meaning System, particularly the meaning and belief domain. It helps you make sense of your experiences by connecting your thoughts, beliefs, and memories into a clearer story, turning confusing or painful memories into something more understandable and meaningful.

Recall a time you found meaning in a difficult experience.

______________________________________________

______________________________________________

______________________________________________

## Prayer

Connect with a higher power, your spiritual beliefs, or your inner wisdom. This may take the form of traditional prayer, silent reflection, meditation, or compassionate self-talk. The act of prayer can cultivate humility, surrender, and connection to something larger than yourself, promoting perspective and safety.

Prayer also reconnects you to cultural, familial, or collective traditions, restoring belonging and coherence, which are essential components to repair relational and intergenerational trauma. It integrates the meaning and belief domain within the Mind and Meaning System with the relational domain of the Action and Connection System, creating alignment between spiritual meaning and secure attachment.

Describe how prayer or spiritual practice has supported you.

______________________________________________

______________________________________________

______________________________________________

## Relaxation

Calm your body and mind through relaxation practices such as deep breathing, progressive muscle relaxation, meditation, or gentle movement, or simply spend time in activities that soothe you, like baking, gardening, or being with pets. These practices reset the body's physiological balance and open pathways to mindfulness and emotion regulation.

Relaxation decreases sympathetic arousal and activates the parasympathetic nervous system, promoting recovery within the Body-Based System. This shift lowers cortisol (a stress hormone), increases vagal tone, and restores a sense of bodily safety. When paired with mindful awareness of your breath, posture, or temperature, relaxation strengthens interoceptive accuracy, rebuilding trust in your body's signals and fostering calm regulation from within.

Describe different ways you can practice relaxation this week.

______________________________

______________________________

______________________________

## One Thing in the Moment

Stay grounded by focusing on just one thing at a time. You might observe your breath, notice your immediate surroundings, or fully engage in one simple task. The goal is to bring full awareness to the present, countering fragmentation and overwhelm.

This practice synchronizes top-down attentional control from the prefrontal cortex with bottom-up sensory awareness, aligning the Mind and Meaning System and Body-Based System to create full-body mindfulness. Within the Consciousness and Memory System, focusing on present experience stabilizes awareness and reduces dissociative symptoms by keeping you in the moment.

Share one way you can practice doing one thing in the moment.

______________________________

______________________________

______________________________

## Vacation

Take a brief mental break from distress. This could be a literal rest, like a nap, a relaxing bath, or a walk. Or perhaps you try a mental vacation by daydreaming, listening to music, or visualizing a peaceful setting. The goal is to restore balance through a momentary escape that replenishes you.

Taking a brief mental vacation engages both the emotional and cognitive domains of the Mind and Meaning System by creating temporary distance from stress, while also bringing regulation to the Body-Based System. In the first phase of DTRM, this practice offers containment by allowing you to safely disengage from intense emotions, and in later phases it models flexible Self-Soothing and healthy retreat without avoidance.

Brainstorm ways to take a vacation.

___

___

___

## Encouragement

Use positive self-talk and affirmations to replace internal criticism with compassion. Remind yourself of your strength, your capabilities, and the temporary nature of distress. Encouragement cultivates inner nurturing, especially for those who lacked consistent validation or care early in life.

This practice provides repair within the developmental domain by helping you internalize the voice of a compassionate caregiver. It also strengthens the Mind and Meaning System, particularly the meaning and belief domain, by replacing shame-based schemas with supportive narratives. Over time, self-encouragement builds emotional resilience and reinforces a stable sense of self-worth.

Write down three encouraging statements or affirmations.

___

___

___

Worksheet

# Self-Soothe with the Five Senses

Self-Soothing is the ability to calm and comfort yourself during moments of distress, especially in response to trauma-related triggers or intense emotional states. Rather than relying solely on others for support, you develop the internal resources to manage overwhelming emotions and reestablish safety. This skill becomes particularly valuable in everyday life when external support is unavailable or in times of solitude when emotions feel difficult to face.

The sensory practices that follow can help reintroduce safety and comfort in concrete, straightforward ways. These practices are rooted in the Body-Based System, particularly the nervous, somatic, and interoceptive domains. On a neurobiological level, these practices activate the parasympathetic nervous system, triggering the release of oxytocin (the "love hormone") and endorphins ("feel-good" chemicals). This shifts your physiology from threat to safety and strengthens vagal tone.

## Vision

Engage your sense of sight to orient yourself to safety and beauty. Observe the movement of trees, water, or clouds. Create art, sketch, or paint to express yourself. Look at photographs of loved ones or calming landscapes. Practice mindful observation by noticing colors, patterns, and light. Watching a comforting movie can also provide a familiar rhythm that settles you.

Soothing with vision stabilizes the nervous system by orienting you to visual cues of safety in the present.

List several visual experiences that bring you a sense of calm or pleasure.

______________________________________________

______________________________________________

______________________________________________

## Hearing

Use sound to regulate your inner state. Listen to music that soothes or uplifts you, notice natural sounds like birds or wind, play an audiobook, or listen to National Public Radio (NPR), which has become known for hosts with a calm, measured, and "soothing" tone, lovingly referred to as the "NPR voice." You can also sing or hum softly to yourself, paying attention to the vibration in your chest and the rhythm of your breath. Focus on the sound of your exhale to deepen the feeling of calm.

Rhythmic sounds, like humming, chanting, or singing, stimulate the vagus nerve, which shifts your nervous system into a calming, parasympathetic state. Not only does this engage the nervous system domain of your Body-Based System, but these patterns of sound echo early attachment experiences, such as heartbeat, voice tone, and lullabies, providing repair to the Developmental Integration System by reinstating implicit memories of co-regulation and safety.

Identify sounds, songs, or voices that bring comfort and connection.

______________________________________________

______________________________________________

______________________________________________

## Smell

Use scent to evoke calm and familiarity. Light a candle or incense, use essential oils such as lavender or eucalyptus, cook or bake foods that remind you of safety, or spend time outside noticing the natural scent of grass, flowers, or rain.

Olfactory input connects directly to the limbic system, influencing emotion without the need for conscious thought. Soothing smells calm the Body-Based System and can even reencode safety memories by linking pleasant scents to relaxation and presence.

Record a few scents that bring you peace or a sense of calm.

______________________________________________

______________________________________________

______________________________________________

## Taste

Bring awareness to taste as a grounding anchor. Practice mindful eating by slowing down and savoring each bite. Enjoy favorite flavors such as fruit, chocolate, or tea, or notice the texture and temperature of food and drink. Hydrate slowly, paying attention to the sensation of swallowing and warmth or coolness in the body.

Taste anchors your attention in the present moment through sensory pleasure and mindful focus. It enhances your awareness of interoceptive cues and strengthens your connection to your body's signals. Food also carries cultural and communal meaning in many instances, and reclaiming comfort through taste can reconnect you to traditions of nourishment and belonging within a cultural and collective context.*

Name a few foods or drinks that comfort you.

______________________________________________

______________________________________________

______________________________________________

## Touch

Use physical sensation to soothe and reestablish connection with your body. Wrap yourself in a soft blanket, hold a comforting object, or wear clothing that feels good against your skin. Apply gentle pressure by pressing your feet into the floor, squeezing a stress ball, or giving yourself a hug. Experiment with temperature using a warm compress or cool cloth, or try light self-massage to ease tension.

Touch stimulates C-tactile fibers, which are specialized nerve fibers that communicate safety and connection to the brain, releasing oxytocin and calming all domains within the Body-Based System. Safe touch also rebuilds trust in bodily sensations and offers repair to the Developmental Integration System by reintroducing nurturing, nonthreatening contact that strengthens Self-Soothing capacity.

Identify ways you can use touch or texture to comfort yourself.

______________________________________________

______________________________________________

______________________________________________

* Cultural and collective context refers to the shared social, historical, and systemic forces that shape how you experience, express, and recover from trauma. It includes the collective memories, norms, and values of your community or culture. Since many trauma responses are not only personal but also embedded in collective experience, healing can be both individual and communal.

 

# Tackle Your Self-Soothe Barriers

Many trauma survivors encounter real challenges when learning to Self-Soothe. They may judge the practice as childish or indulgent, feel undeserving of comfort due to guilt or shame, believe that soothing is ineffective or pointless, experience numbness that blocks connection with positive sensory experiences, or lack access to safe and quiet environments.

Resistance to Self-Soothing often mirrors early patterns of invalidation or neglect. Choosing to care for yourself despite discomfort provides repair in the Developmental Integration System by providing a new attachment experience within the self that pairs compassion with regulation.

Cultural barriers can come up too. Many people grow up in environments that value endurance, productivity, or self-sacrifice over rest and comfort. Reframing this practice as an act of strength and resilience counters collective messages that equate self-care with weakness. By practicing Self-Soothing, you participate in personal and collective repair, challenging inherited beliefs and building a new foundation of safety.

This worksheet invites you to reflect on those and other barriers so you can develop strategies to overcome them.

**What barriers do you notice when trying to practice Self-Soothing?** Consider whether self-judgment, numbness, lack of privacy, or feelings of unworthiness interfere with your ability to comfort yourself.

______________________________

______________________________

______________________________

**How do these barriers relate to your trauma experiences?** Reflect on early experiences of neglect, punishment, or invalidation that may have taught you to suppress your needs for care.

______________________________

______________________________

______________________________

 

**What thoughts or emotions arise when you consider these barriers?** Notice whether shame, sadness, or resistance comes forward, and allow these reactions to simply be observed.

_______________________________________________

_______________________________________________

_______________________________________________

As you explore your responses, consider which skills can move you through these barriers:

- **Wise Mind** reminds you that self-care is not indulgent but essential to healing. It connects intuitive knowing with reasoned awareness to support balanced choice.
- **Opposite Action** encourages you to engage in soothing behaviors even when guilt or doubt appears. Acting opposite to avoidance rewires associations between care and shame.
- **Radical Acceptance** invites you to acknowledge discomfort or resistance without judgment, choosing compassion instead of criticism. It also allows you to accept sensations and feelings of comfort that are initially experienced as foreign and, paradoxically, uncomfortable.
- **Self-validation** allows you to affirm that your need for comfort is real, human, and deserving of care.

**Which of these skills resonate most strongly with you?** How might you apply them during moments of distress? Identify two or three specific actions you can take to practice Self-Soothing even when resistance arises.

_______________________________________________

_______________________________________________

_______________________________________________

Imagine the benefits of integrating Self-Soothing into your daily life: reduced anxiety and stress, improved regulation, and enhanced self-worth and compassion. Over time, it reconnects you with pleasure, calm, and safety, positively influencing your relationships, work, and overall sense of balance. Every small act of comfort contributes to healing by strengthening the pathways of safety, trust, and self-compassion that form the core of recovery.

 

## SKILL Pros and Cons

Pros and Cons is a powerful decision-making tool that is especially useful when you feel unsure about your next step or tempted to engage in harmful or avoidant behaviors. It helps you anticipate the outcomes of different choices by thoughtfully considering both benefits and drawbacks, guiding you toward informed, values-based decisions that support your healing journey.

Pros and Cons is a dialectical skill that enables you to view decisions from multiple perspectives, and it moves you beyond emotion-driven reactions by engaging your Reason Mind so you can ultimately respond from your Wise Mind.

This skill primarily engages all areas of the Mind and Meaning System to restore capacity for thoughtful reflection, and it also engages the Action and Connection System to translate that insight into adaptive behavior. By activating the brain's prefrontal regions, this skill balances limbic urgency, creating top-down regulation that restores a sense of agency after trauma.

Here's how to use the skill:

1. **Identify the decision.** Start by clearly naming the decision you are facing. For example, you might be deciding whether to attend a therapy session that feels intimidating because you're afraid of experiencing painful emotions. Naming the decision itself brings awareness and creates space between impulse and action.
2. **List the positive consequences (pros).** Identify the potential benefits of making a healthy choice. For instance, the pros of attending the therapy session might include:
    - Making progress in your healing by facing rather than avoiding fears
    - Learning coping tools and insights from your therapist
    - Strengthening the therapeutic relationship
    - Reducing long-term avoidance that increases distress and keeps you stuck
3. **List the negative consequences (cons).** Next, identify the possible drawbacks or challenges of the same choice:
    - Feeling emotionally overwhelmed during or after the session
    - Experiencing increased anxiety or vulnerability
    - Recalling painful memories that may intensify distress in the short-term
4. **Compare short-term vs. long-term consequences.** Weigh how your decision will affect you now compared to later. Avoiding the session might bring immediate relief from fear, but it could also reinforce avoidance patterns and slow your progress. Attending may feel uncomfortable in the moment, but it offers lasting benefits such as reduced symptoms, increased insight, and greater emotional resilience.

5. **Ask: Is it worth it?** Reflect on whether the long-term benefits outweigh the short-term discomfort. Ask yourself, "Is the temporary pain of this choice worth the long-term progress in my healing?" Allow yourself to connect with your Wise Mind as you consider this question.
6. **Decide and take action.** Use your Wise Mind to make a clear decision, then commit to it. Ideally, your action will reflect your long-term goals and deeper values, even when the choice feels difficult in the short term. Following through builds confidence, consistency, and trust in your ability to guide your healing with intention.

Using the Pros and Cons skill in this structured and mindful manner allows you to approach trauma-related decisions with clarity and self-awareness. It encourages regulation, reduces impulsivity, and strengthens your sense of agency.

One last tip: Cognitively weighing the consequences of your decision (a top-down process) becomes even more effective when paired with grounding or breathwork (bottom-up processes), ensuring that you make a decision from a regulated nervous system. When your mind and body work together in this way, choices reflect wisdom, balance, and purpose.

## Trauma-Focused Scenarios for Pros and Cons

Here are some common trauma-related situations where the Pros and Cons skill can support Wise Mind decision-making:

- **Coping with trauma triggers:** Should you face or avoid a trauma trigger? Facing it now may increase distress in the moment but reduce sensitivity and promote growth over time. Avoidance offers short-term relief but reinforces long-term fear.
- **Choosing healthy coping strategies:** Deciding between healthy strategies (like mindfulness or journaling) versus harmful ones (like substance use or self-injury) isn't always easy. While healthy coping builds long-term regulation, it often doesn't offer instant relief. Harmful behaviors provide temporary escape, but at great cost.
- **Setting and maintaining boundaries:** When navigating boundaries with your family, friends, or coworkers, use Pros and Cons to weigh the discomfort of asserting yourself against the long-term benefit of protecting your emotional well-being.
- **Managing trauma-related anxiety:** Evaluate the benefits of grounding, practicing self-care, or reaching out for help versus allowing anxiety to spiral or avoiding situations altogether.
- **Reconnecting with family posttrauma:** Weigh the potential healing benefits of seeking support against the risks of retraumatization or unresolved conflict.
- **Choosing a safe living environment:** Assess living options by comparing the benefits and drawbacks. For example, one apartment may feel emotionally supportive because a trusted friend

lives nearby, yet it might also be close to places that trigger trauma reminders. Another option may offer fewer reminders and a quieter neighborhood but less daily support.

- **Engaging in trauma advocacy or education:** Consider the empowerment and connection that can come from sharing your story against the emotional toll it may take.
- **Managing trauma-impacted relationships:** Evaluate whether to maintain or distance yourself from relationships that may support or harm your recovery.

You can apply this skill to virtually any situation where a decision carries emotional or trauma-related weight. Use it often to slow down, gain clarity, and support your healing with intention.

Worksheet

# Pros and Cons Worksheet 1

Use this worksheet to reflect on a current decision related to your trauma recovery, or any decision. By exploring both the benefits and drawbacks of your choice, you can move toward a Wise Mind decision that supports your long-term well-being.

**Decision to consider.** What choice are you trying to make?

______________________________________________

______________________________________________

**Pros or benefits of taking this action.** List the positive outcomes that could result from making this decision.

______________________________________________

______________________________________________

**Cons or drawbacks of taking this action.** List possible challenges, discomforts, or negative effects.

______________________________________________

______________________________________________

**Short-term vs. long-term consequences.** How might this choice affect you in the short term? How might it support or hinder your healing over time?

______________________________________________

______________________________________________

**Final decision and action plan.** What will you choose, and what is your plan to follow through?

______________________________________________

______________________________________________

By carefully evaluating the outcomes of your choices, you empower yourself to make decisions that support lasting recovery and emotional growth.

# Pros and Cons Worksheet 2

This version of the Pros and Cons worksheet helps you explore a decision by comparing two opposing choices. It gives a more complete picture of the consequences to clarify your path forward. Take time to consider both sides of the decision to respond with clarity, intention, and effectiveness.

| **My Basic Choices Are:**<br>____________________ **versus** ____________________<br>(Example: "Using alcohol to cope" vs. "Using DBT skills instead") | |
|---|---|
| **Short-term pros of:** ____________<br>What are the immediate benefits of this choice? | **Short-term cons of:** ____________<br>What are the immediate drawbacks of this choice? |
| | |
| **Long-term pros of:** ____________<br>What are the long-term benefits of this choice? | **Long-term cons of:** ____________<br>What are the long-term drawbacks of this choice? |
| | |
| **Versus** | |
| **Short-term pros of:** ____________<br>What are the immediate benefits of this alternative? | **Short-term cons of:** ____________<br>What are the immediate drawbacks of this alternative? |
| | |
| **Long-term pros of:** ____________<br>What are the long-term benefits of this alternative? | **Long-term cons of:** ____________<br>What are the long-term drawbacks of this alternative? |
| | |
| **My Decision:** ________________________<br>**Based on your reflection, what choice will you make and why?** | |

## SKILL Bridge Burning and Barrier Building

Bridge Burning refers to the intentional act of cutting off access to behaviors, environments, or relationships that undermine trauma recovery. Examples include ending communication with people who invalidate or obstruct healing, removing objects such as letters or photographs that evoke painful memories, and removing the means of acting on harmful behaviors like self-injury and substance use.

The purpose is not isolation or punishment but protection and foresight—creating firm boundaries that make it more difficult or even impossible to return to harmful patterns, especially during times of vulnerability. Each burned bridge represents an intentional choice to shift from reactivity to self-protection, replacing past helplessness with grounded agency. By eliminating these pathways, you create safer conditions for healing and reduce the likelihood of setbacks. Bridge Burning is especially important in phase 1, when safety must be prioritized by restructuring your environment and limiting behaviors that pose risks.

Bridge Burning operates primarily within the Action and Connection System, engaging both the behavioral and relational domains as you take decisive action to support stability. It also strengthens the Mind and Meaning System, particularly the meaning and belief domain, by reinforcing the belief that you can make self-protective choices. On a neurobiological level, removing access to triggers helps weaken old response patterns that are encoded in the amygdala (the brain's emotional center) and basal ganglia (the brain's habit and reward center), which lowers arousal and relapse risk.

Can you recall a time when you intentionally cut off access to a harmful person or behavior? How did this impact your recovery?

__________________________________________________

__________________________________________________

Bridge Burning carries deep developmental significance. For many survivors, choosing to sever unsafe ties restores the autonomy they lost in childhood and repairs the learned helplessness embedded within the developmental domain, affirming that safety can be created and maintained through deliberate action.

In collectivist or high-loyalty cultures, ending relationships may feel at odds with values of duty and belonging. Framing these choices as acts of self-preservation rather than rejection honors both personal healing and cultural integrity, emphasizing balance and respect rather than abandonment.

While Bridge Burning is often difficult, it represents an act of courage and commitment to self-care. It builds agency and establishes a foundation for long-term regulation and growth.

## Building Barriers When Bridges Can't Be Fully Burned

In some situations, it's not realistic or even possible to completely burn a bridge. That's where Barrier Building comes in. This approach involves putting intentional obstacles in place to reduce risk, manage exposure, and maintain control. Each barrier also serves as an opportunity to practice your skills.

Here are some examples of Barrier Building:

- **Limit interactions:** If you can't avoid someone entirely, set clear boundaries around when you'll communicate, what you'll discuss, and the frequency of these interactions.
- **Change your routine:** Take a different route home from work or school to avoid high-risk locations that might trigger harmful urges (e.g., a liquor store, bar, dealer's home).
- **Set boundaries in triggering environments:** Schedule visits to stressful places only during safe times, bring a support person, or use grounding tools while present.
- **Use mental distancing:** Use mindfulness or grounding exercises to create internal space even when physical distance isn't possible.
- **Reframe conversations:** If you can't avoid triggering discussions, practice redirecting or reframing them to reduce emotional intensity.
- **Secure dangerous items:** If you cannot fully dispose of a self-harm tool (e.g., a razor also used for hygiene), then keep it in an inaccessible place and retrieve it only when urges are low and it's to be used for its intended purpose.
- **Keep a commitment journal:** Regularly write down your reasons for staying committed to change.
- **Make a public commitment:** Let trusted people know about your healing goals to increase motivation and accountability.

Can you think of a time when you successfully built a barrier to prevent harmful behavior? What worked?

____________________________________________________________

____________________________________________________________

Whether you Burn Bridges or Build Barriers, the goal is the same: to support your healing by creating distance from what harms and moving toward what heals.

Worksheet

## Bridge Burning and Barrier Building

Use this worksheet to prevent relapse into harmful behaviors by identifying what triggers can be removed entirely and what needs a boundary.

Describe the harmful behavior you want to address (e.g., self-harm, substance use, toxic relationship).

_______________________________________________

_______________________________________________

What steps can you take to burn the bridge? Be specific about how you will cut off access.

_______________________________________________

_______________________________________________

If full removal isn't possible, how can you build barriers? What boundaries, limits, or supports can you put in place?

_______________________________________________

_______________________________________________

What healthy behaviors or skills will replace the old pattern?

_______________________________________________

_______________________________________________

What benefits will come from these changes for you and others? Think about how this supports your recovery, self-esteem, and relationships.

_______________________________________________

_______________________________________________

Write a personal commitment statement about burning this bridge or building these barriers.

_______________________________________________

_______________________________________________

## SKILL Urge Surfing (Ride the Wave)

Urge Surfing is a mindfulness-based skill to manage impulses and behaviors that arise from trauma responses, dysregulation, or habitual coping patterns. The practice is built on the understanding that urges naturally rise, peak, and fall, like waves. Through mindful awareness, you can learn to Observe these waves rather than act on them, building confidence in your ability to stay present and maintain control even in moments of impulsivity.

Urge Surfing is an important phase 1 skill, though it becomes easier and almost automatic as you work through the phases of recovery. This practice bridges the Body-Based System with the Mind and Meaning System, transforming physiological arousal into conscious observation to Build Mastery across both body and mind.

Neurobiologically, Urge Surfing strengthens the prefrontal cortex's ability to inhibit impulsive neural circuits while increasing interoceptive awareness within the insula. This process teaches the nervous system that it's possible to experience strong urges or sensations without needing to immediately react or escape. Mindful Observation engages top-down cognitive processes, while observing your urges and sensations and allowing them to pass engages bottom-up regulation. The result is an integrated state in which thought, awareness, and physiology work together to restore control and stability.

To practice Urge Surfing, start small and focus on manageable urges to build confidence. That means using this skill when your urges are low. Urges that are too intense require other skills. Even world-class surfers stay out of the ocean when a tsunami is coming in!

Observe the urge as if you were watching a wave in motion, noticing how it rises, peaks, and eventually falls. Stay curious rather than fearful, allowing the experience to unfold without judgment. Resist the impulse to label or criticize yourself for the presence of the urge. Instead, acknowledge it as a natural, temporary expression of activation.

When discomfort arises, let it be part of the experience rather than something to escape. Sitting with discomfort builds emotional tolerance and gradually reduces the power of the urge over time. If the intensity feels overwhelming, pair this practice with additional distress tolerance tools such as grounding, distraction, or Self-Soothing.

Think of an urge you recently experienced. How might you have "surfed" that urge instead of reacting to it? What would it feel like to ride the wave rather than be pulled under it?

________________________________________

________________________________________

From a developmental perspective, Urge Surfing provides a reparative experience that mirrors the early co-regulation ideally provided by caregivers. It teaches you that strong emotions and impulses are survivable and do not require avoidance, collapse, or self-harm. By learning to stay present through activation, you learn to trust yourself and repattern internal safety signals that were disrupted by trauma.

# SKILL The TIPP Skill: Fast-Acting Regulation

The TIPP skill offers a set of rapid, body-based interventions to regulate intense states when distress is overwhelming. It is especially useful during trauma triggers, crises, or moments of acute stress when your nervous system is flooded and higher reasoning feels out of reach.

TIPP is a go-to phase 1 intervention because it rapidly restores safety by "tipping" body chemistry to allow later emotional and cognitive processing. TIPP specifically targets the Body-Based System, engaging the nervous system, somatic, and interoceptive domains to interrupt dysregulation at its physiological root. TIPP also supports the Mind and Meaning System by linking body awareness with mindful intention, strengthening the connection between sensation and conscious regulation.

The TIPP acronym stands for Temperature, Intense Exercise, Paced Breathing, and Progressive Muscle Relaxation. In neurobiological terms, each component of TIPP modulates the autonomic nervous system. Cooling the body's Temperature activates the parasympathetic "dive reflex," which rapidly slows heart rate and reduces arousal. Intense Exercise metabolizes stress hormones such as adrenaline and cortisol, allowing the body to release activation rather than store it. Paced Breathing balances carbon dioxide and oxygen exchange, stimulating the vagus nerve and signaling calm to the brain. Progressive Muscle Relaxation decreases muscle tension while increasing body awareness, helping you restore interoceptive accuracy and comfort in your physical state.

TIPP operates primarily through bottom-up regulation by calming the body first, while mindful awareness adds a top-down layer of coordination. The integration of both systems allows for bidirectional communication between the body and the mind. Additionally, many trauma survivors never learned how to calm themselves through breath, movement, or rhythm in early life. Practicing TIPP helps build this missing foundation in the Developmental Integration System, teaching the body that self-soothing is both safe and achievable.

## Temperature

Cooling your body can immediately shift your physiology from high arousal toward calm. Splash cold water on your face, hold a cold pack to your wrists or neck, or dip your face in a bowl of cold water for a few seconds. These temperature-based techniques stimulate the body's natural dive reflex, lowering heart rate and producing a sense of grounded relief.

## Intense Exercise

Brief, vigorous activity helps discharge excess energy and release stress hormones. Do jumping jacks, push-ups, or run in place for a minute. Take a brisk walk after a trigger, or dance intensely to your favorite song. This rapid activation allows your body to metabolize adrenaline, clearing the system so your nervous system can return to baseline.

## Paced Breathing

Intentional breathing is one of the fastest ways to regulate the nervous system. Try inhaling for four counts, holding for four, and exhaling for six. Use a guided breathing app or pair your breathing with calming imagery such as ocean waves or a safe place. Slowing your breath engages the parasympathetic nervous system, relaxes your body, and restores balance between mind and emotion.

## Progressive Muscle Relaxation

Systematically tensing and releasing muscle groups can release stored stress and bring awareness to how your body holds tension. Start with your feet and move upward, tightening and relaxing each muscle group. You might also squeeze your fists and then release them, noticing the sensation of letting go. Over time, this practice teaches the body that it can shift from tension to ease through conscious awareness and gentle action.

## SKILL The STOP Skill: A Mindful Pause Before Action

The STOP skill means you pause, assess, and respond mindfully to stress or trauma triggers rather than reacting impulsively. It creates a moment of conscious awareness in the space between a trigger and your response to enable you to regain control when emotions or physiological arousal threaten to take over. This skill is particularly valuable for trauma survivors, as it replaces automatic reactions with intentional, values-aligned actions that support stability and healing.

STOP is a useful phase 1 intervention used to interrupt impulsive or trauma-reactive behaviors and establish mindful control before acting. It becomes a bridge to phase 2 by creating the mental and emotional space needed for reflection and intentional choice. STOP engages both the Mind and Meaning System, particularly the emotional and cognitive domains, by recruiting Wise Mind awareness, as well as the Action and Connection System, specifically the behavioral domain, by directing behavior toward goals consistent with your recovery values.

Neurobiologically, the act of stopping activates the prefrontal regions that inhibit amygdala overactivation, reestablishing rational control and reducing your physiological perception of threat. Taking a breath during this pause stimulates the vagus nerve, slowing heart rate and supporting parasympathetic recovery. Through repeated practice, your body learns that pausing does not signal danger but safety, reinforcing self-regulation through both top-down and bottom-up mechanisms.

STOP stands for Stop, Take a Step Back, Observe, and Proceed Mindfully.

### Stop

Immediately pause. Freeze your actions, thoughts, and words, even if only for a brief moment. Stopping halts automatic, trauma-driven reactions that often arise before awareness catches up. This simple act of pausing breaks the link between trigger and response, providing the nervous system a chance to reset.

### Take a Step Back

Create physical, mental, or emotional distance from the situation. This might mean walking away, closing your eyes, or taking a slow, deep breath. Taking a step back interrupts reactivity and restores perspective, creating a sense of internal and external space. This moment of withdrawal allows both body and mind to return to baseline before moving forward.

### Observe

Notice what is happening around you and within you. What are you thinking, feeling, and sensing in your body? What is actually unfolding in this moment? Observation connects the Mind and Meaning System with the Body-Based System, encouraging you to notice emotional, cognitive, and sensory cues without judgment. This process promotes clarity by separating perception from interpretation, allowing for a more accurate understanding of the present moment.

## Proceed Mindfully

Move forward with intention. Consider your goals, values, and recovery path before responding. Proceeding mindfully means aligning your actions with Wise Mind rather than reacting from fear, anger, or avoidance. It transforms the pause into purposeful motion, grounding your next step in awareness and self-compassion.

### Trauma-Focused STOP Skill Scenarios

**An Argument with a Family Member**

S: Pause instead of reacting defensively.
T: Step out of the room or take a deep breath to create space.
O: Notice your emotional state and body cues. Are you responding to the present or a reminder of the past?
P: Respond calmly or choose to disengage to protect yourself and/or the relationship.

**Receiving Difficult News**

S: Do not react immediately with anger or despair.
T: Sit in silence to allow the information to settle.
O: Acknowledge your emotions and physical sensations without trying to suppress them.
P: Choose a healthy response, such as reaching out for support, journaling, or practicing self-care.

**Temptation to Use Unhealthy Coping**

S: Pause before reaching for substances or retreating into isolation.
T: Reflect on how acting on the urge might impact your healing and stability.
O: Notice your body's tension and emotional pain. Offer yourself validation rather than judgment.
P: Use a skill such as distraction, connection, or Self-Soothing instead.

### Helpful Companion Skills

- **Radical Acceptance** helps you acknowledge reality as it is, reducing resistance and grounding you in the present.
- **Mindfulness** sustains focus on the current moment, enhancing your awareness of mind, body, and environment.
- **Self-Soothing** allows sensory comfort to restore regulation after stress.

Remember, STOP integrates both top-down and bottom-up regulation. Cognitively, it allows you to take perspective and stay mindful, while physiologically it calms arousal through breathing, posture, and controlled movement. Developmentally, it also repairs early deficits in impulse control and emotion regulation by teaching you to create a safe pause that caregivers may not have modeled.

Through consistent practice, STOP becomes a reliable internal signal for safety and choice. It restores agency to moments once ruled by fear or habit, creating a foundation for stability, reflection, and integration across all systems of recovery.

# SKILL Grounding Techniques: Cultivating Presence and Calm

Trauma can disrupt your sense of being safely rooted in the present, leading to dissociation, numbness, or feelings of unreality. Grounding techniques are essential for restoring safety, stability, and embodied awareness in the here and now.[19] These practices bring the mind back into contact with your body and environment, reorienting your awareness toward the present moment and reestablishing a felt sense of reality.

Grounding is fundamental to phase 1 (stabilization), when you must learn to reduce dissociation and hyperarousal before the deeper work of integration can occur in the second phase. Grounding activates the Body-Based System while supporting the Consciousness and Memory System, especially the dissociative domain, by strengthening the link between body awareness and conscious experience.

On a neurobiological level, grounding redirects focus away from limbic circuits (which trigger fear and stress) and toward the sensory cortex and insula (which support movement and awareness). This shift interrupts dissociation and strengthens the connection between the body and conscious awareness. Grounding combines top-down and bottom-up regulation: Mindful awareness and labeling cognitively guide the experience of grounding, while sensory input and movement calm your nervous system. Over time, this teaches your brain and body that you can find safety within the present moment, even when distress arises.

Here are some ways to practice this skill.

## Sensory Engagement

Grounding through the senses draws awareness back into the body. Notice what you see, hear, smell, touch, and taste. Observe your surroundings in vivid detail, noting colors, shapes, patterns, and textures. Focus on movement, such as the sway of trees or shifting light. Listen for layered sounds, breathe in nearby scents, feel textures or fabrics beneath your hands, and slowly savor a sip of water or food. Choose one object and Describe it fully to yourself, or do a "color and shape inventory" of the space around you. Each sense offers an entry point to presence, allowing experience to unfold through perception rather than thought.

## Sensations (from ACCEPTS)

Use deliberate sensory *intensity* to reconnect with your body. Listen to emotionally evocative music, brush your hair with full attention, or taste something sharp like mint or citrus. Alternate between warm and cool sensations, such as holding a cold pack and then touching a warm mug. Knead clay or squeeze a

19 Although grounding is listed in this module, these techniques represent core mindfulness skills in action.

stress ball, noticing the tactile feedback. These practices activate the somatic and interoceptive domains of the Body-Based System, replacing emotional numbness with embodied awareness.

## Bodily Awareness

Shift your focus to how your body feels in space. Notice the weight of your body in the chair, your feet pressed into the floor, or your hands resting in your lap. Press your palms together or shift your weight mindfully. Conduct a slow body scan, breathing into areas of tension and inviting relaxation. These exercises rebuild the dialogue between the body and mind that trauma often severs, reminding you that you can inhabit your body safely.

## Mindful Breathing

Regulate through the breath. Try practices such as 4-7-8 or box breathing to balance your nervous system. Imagine inhaling calm and exhaling tension. Place a hand on your belly to feel your breath move, using it as a physical anchor. Breath-centered grounding engages the vagus nerve, which restores regulation across the nervous system domain.

## Movement-Based Grounding

Use intentional movement to reestablish connection with your body. Stretch, walk slowly, practice yoga poses, or dance while paying attention to each motion. Sway gently or practice balancing exercises. Standing tall and aligning your posture can shift your mood and mindset. Movement activates your motor and sensory systems, supporting your body and emotions in working together.

## Mantras and Affirmations

Use words to anchor your awareness. Repeat grounding statements such as "I am safe," "This is now, not then," or "I am here." Combine affirmations with breathing or gentle movement. Writing affirmations and keeping them visible can reinforce safety cues and self-compassion throughout the day.

## Nature Connection

Grounding in nature reconnects your body and mind by immersing you in a variety of sensory experiences. Step outside and notice your surroundings. Feel your feet on the earth, touch the texture of a leaf or rock, and listen to natural sounds like wind or birds. Nature-based grounding soothes you in the moment and fosters a sense of belonging within the environment.

## Hand-Based Techniques

Hands are powerful grounding tools due to their rich sensory input. Rub your palms together to generate warmth and awareness, tap your fingers rhythmically, or hold a comforting object and focus on its texture and temperature. Placing your hand over your heart and feeling your heartbeat, as well as the heat exchange between your hand and body, can restore calm and reconnect you to your body's steady rhythm.

Across cultures, grounding echoes long-standing practices that use rhythm, touch, and breath to restore equilibrium. Drumming, chanting, tactile prayer beads, and meditative rituals are collective expressions of embodiment that have historically promoted resilience. Integrating these traditional forms of grounding honors ancestral pathways of regulation and cultural wisdom.

Ultimately, grounding is both a skill and a philosophy of presence. Each practice invites your mind and body to return home to the moment, restoring the bridge between safety, awareness, and connection. Through consistent use, grounding becomes a reliable anchor across all systems of recovery, supporting regulation, integration, and the calm confidence of being fully present in the here and now.

## SKILL Radical Acceptance: Embracing Reality in Trauma Recovery

Radical Acceptance is one of the most challenging yet transformative skills in trauma recovery. It invites you to fully acknowledge reality, even when it is painful or unjust, without resistance. Importantly, this skill does not mean approving of the pain or condoning harm; rather, it asks you to stop waging an internal war against what has already happened. Acceptance allows the energy you once spent on resistance to be redirected toward healing, growth, and presence. In this way, Radical Acceptance becomes a gateway to peace and empowerment, even amid loss or injustice.

While pain is an inevitable part of the human experience, suffering arises when people refuse to accept painful truths. These formulas capture its essence clearly:

**Pain + Resistance = Suffering**

**Pain + Acceptance = Manageable**

Radical Acceptance begins with facing what is true. When you're confronted with a painful or unfair situation, you have four choices: (1) You can change what you can by setting boundaries, ending harmful relationships, or developing new coping skills; (2) you can change your perspective by reframing your experience to identify growth or strength; (3) you can accept what cannot be changed and let go of the fight against reality; or (4) you can continue to suffer by refusing to acknowledge what is. Acceptance, then, is not surrender but empowerment. It's a clear-eyed recognition that energy spent fighting reality cannot also be used for healing. When you accept what exists, you can respond wisely instead of reactively.

### Reframes of Common Misconceptions

Radical Acceptance is often misunderstood:

- Acceptance is acknowledgment; *it is not approval.*
- Acceptance means choosing to stop the struggle against what is; *it is not giving up.*
- Acceptance makes meaningful change possible; *it does not preclude change.*

Within DTRM, Radical Acceptance spans all phases. Early in treatment, it helps you notice difficult internal experiences without struggling against them, which lessens distress and fosters a sense of safety. In phases 2 and 3, it supports you in making sense of your experiences so you can find coherence, compassion, and strength within your stories.

This skill primarily engages the Mind and Meaning System, activating the cognitive, emotional, and meaning and belief domains to transform painful experiences into understanding and meaning. It also strengthens the Consciousness and Memory System, especially the memory domain, by integrating intrusive or fragmented memories into coherent awareness.

From a neurobiological perspective, Radical Acceptance may engage the medial prefrontal and anterior cingulate cortices, which are the brain regions associated with regulation and flexibility, while reducing activation in the amygdala. When you consciously choose acceptance from the top-down, you also calm your body's physiology from the bottom-up, bringing together insight and safety into a single act of integration.

## Turning the Mind

Radical Acceptance is not a single act but a practice of intentionally turning and returning to reality every time resistance arises. Recognizing when you are saying, "This shouldn't be happening" becomes the cue to pause and shift your stance.

You must choose acceptance consciously, even when it feels unnatural. This is called Turning the Mind. You repeat the shift as often as needed, just as a driver continually adjusts the steering wheel to stay on course when the suspension is out of alignment. Each act of turning toward acceptance cultivates emotional flexibility, compassion, and peace.

Here's how to Turn the Mind:

- Recognize resistance when it appears.
- Choose acceptance intentionally.
- Repeat as needed whenever resistance returns.
- Use mindfulness to Observe without judgment.
- Validate your pain while remaining grounded in action.
- Move forward with clarity and self-compassion.

When you're faced with a difficult truth, such as a relationship that will not change, a loss that cannot be reversed, or an event that can never be undone, Turning the Mind is the moment you choose to shift your perspective. It becomes the turning point between being ruled by the trauma and living freely alongside it. A survivor who once replayed, "Why did this happen?" might begin to say, "This did happen, and I can still create a meaningful life." Another may stop resisting reminders of their trauma, allowing distress to pass through without defining their identity.

Turning the Mind toward Radical Acceptance restores a sense of mastery that trauma often erodes. It teaches you that you can face painful truths without falling apart, which supports developmental needs for coherence and agency within the Developmental Integration System. In broader contexts, Radical Acceptance extends beyond you as an individual. It becomes a collective stance that acknowledges the realities of historical and systemic trauma while affirming the possibility of healing and reclamation.

Ultimately, Radical Acceptance does not erase pain or injustice, but it transforms your relationship to them. By continually reorienting your mind toward reality and accepting it as it is, you reclaim your energy, dignity, and choice. It frees your mind from the bondage of resistance. In this state of alignment, you can integrate pain into wisdom, suffering into strength, and survival into wholeness.

## SKILL Willingness vs. Willfulness

Willingness and willfulness represent distinct ways of meeting the world: One opens the door to healing, while the other keeps it closed. Willingness is the capacity to remain open, flexible, and responsive to what is needed in the moment, even when it is difficult. It is about doing what works in a given situation instead of struggling against it. When you are willing, you face experiences as they are rather than as you wish they would be.

Willfulness, in contrast, is resistance marked by a refusal to cooperate with reality. It may take the form of defiance, rigidity, avoidance, or shutdown in the face of discomfort or perceived loss of control. Willfulness often emerges when you fixate on how things "should" be instead of accepting what *is*.

Here are some examples of Willingness versus willfulness:

| Scenario | Willfulness | Willingness |
|---|---|---|
| A friend cancels plans at the last minute. | "I knew this would happen. Forget it! I'm done with people." | "I feel disappointed, and I'm willing to communicate or reschedule instead of withdrawing." |
| A trauma reminder pops up unexpectedly. | "I shouldn't have to feel this. I'm fighting these feelings and trying to push them away." | "This is a memory surfacing. I don't like it, and I'm willing to use grounding and let it move through." |
| You receive feedback from your therapist or partner. | "That's not true. I'm not listening to you. You're wrong." | "I don't agree with everything, and I'm willing to consider what you're saying to see whether any part is useful." |
| You feel overwhelmed and want to avoid all responsibilities. | "I refuse. I'm checking out and ignoring everything." | "I'm overwhelmed, and I'm willing to take one small step to move forward." |

Willingness engages the Mind and Meaning System, particularly the cognitive and meaning and belief domains, by reshaping how you perceive and respond to experiences. It also activates the Action and Connection System, specifically the behavioral and relational domains, by guiding your behavior toward values and connection rather than avoidance.

On a neurobiological level, the shift from willfulness to Willingness reduces defensive arousal and enhances prefrontal flexibility, making it easier to respond adaptively. Cognitively, choosing Willingness is a top-down decision that becomes more sustainable when paired with bottom-up practices, such as mindful breathing and maintaining an open, relaxed posture that aligns intention with physiological calm. Skills like Half-Smile (which involves softening the facial muscles into a gentle, accepting expression) and Willing Hands (which means resting your hands open on your lap or at your sides rather than holding them clenched or tense) directly signal safety to the nervous system. These subtle posture shifts activate the social engagement system, reduce limbic reactivity, and make it easier for Willingness to take hold in both your mind and body.

Developmentally, many trauma survivors learned willfulness as a way to protect themselves against coercion, betrayal, or helplessness. By practicing Willingness, they can restore trust in their own choices and act with intention. It teaches them that choosing to cooperate or engage with others doesn't require giving up power through fawning or submission; it can be an act of empowerment that reflects autonomy.

Worksheet

## Willingness vs. Willfulness

Reflect on the examples in the following table and identify how choosing Willingness over willfulness can support your trauma recovery.

| Example | Willfulness | Willingness | Your Thoughts |
|---|---|---|---|
| Following routines | Rejecting structure and routine, resulting in conflict or instability | Cooperating with structure and routine to create predictability and safety | |
| Participation in therapy or treatment programs | Avoiding help, rejecting support, or sabotaging recovery | Engaging in therapy or skill-building opportunities | |
| Interactions with therapists and peers | Reacting with anger, withdrawing, or becoming defensive | Cooperating, listening, and showing respect | |
| Conflict resolution | Escalating arguments or avoiding accountability | Choosing calm communication and problem-solving | |
| Personal hygiene and self-care | Neglecting basic needs through hopelessness or avoidance | Maintaining care routines and honoring your body | |
| Exercise and physical health | Resisting physical activity despite knowing its benefits | Engaging in movement to release stress and strengthen the body | |
| Learning and skill development | Avoiding challenges through distraction or resignation | Investing in growth and mastery | |
| Substance use recovery | Continuing harmful habits and resisting change | Asking for help and attending treatment | |
| Planning for the future | Giving up or refusing to imagine possibilities | Setting goals and cultivating hope | |

Each moment of Willingness represents a turning toward life, even when it feels uncertain or uncomfortable. Choosing Willingness means embracing collaboration with yourself, others, and the process of recovery. It is not compliance born of fear but participation grounded in purpose.

## Distress Tolerance and Chronic Invalidation: Surviving What Was Never Acknowledged

Chronic invalidation, whether from families, relationships, or larger systems, teaches you not to trust your own experience. When your emotions and experiences are dismissed, mocked, or punished, you learn to hide your pain, question your instincts, and seek permission to feel. Over time, you may begin to equate distress with danger because no one ever showed you how to stay present with pain safely. The body remembers this lesson, tightening in anticipation of rejection or shame, while the mind turns against itself, doubting what it knows to be true.

Distress tolerance restores what chronic invalidation eroded. It brings calm to the body, clarity to thought, coherence to memory, stability to relationships, and confidence to development. Each moment that is met with acceptance and skill builds internal validation in the belief that your pain is real *and* that you have the capacity to meet it.

Distress tolerance becomes an act of dignity. It allows you to hold pain and strength together and to remain steady without abandoning yourself. This inner steadiness restores the relational domain, teaching your system that connection begins within. It also nurtures the Developmental Integration System, helping the parts of you that learned to suppress or mask grow into authenticity and self-trust.

Through repetition, these practices transform what once felt unbearable into something you can navigate with compassion, courage, and choice, with the message that your distress is real, that you can care for it, and that you can survive and thrive with dignity.

Each time you practice, you rewrite the nervous system's memory of isolation into one of connection, within yourself and with the world. In doing so, you reclaim the most essential freedom: to meet suffering with presence and to choose life, even when it hurts.

CHAPTER 12

# Emotion Regulation Module

## Whole-System Regulation and Recovery

Emotions are part of what makes us human. They tell us what we need, warn us of danger, connect us to other people, and bring understanding to ourselves. But when you have experienced trauma, emotions can feel overwhelming, unpredictable, or even unsafe. You might feel too much, too little, or both at once. Over time, this can lead to emotional confusion and patterns of shutting down, overreacting, or feeling out of control.

Emotional dysregulation is not a sign of weakness. It is a natural response to trauma that affects your whole system: your thoughts, your body, your behaviors, your relationships, and how you make meaning of your experiences. That's why emotion regulation is about much more than "managing feelings." It's about restoring emotional balance from the inside out, bringing regulation to all systems and domains.

In this module, you will learn how to understand emotions and respond to them skillfully. The goal is not to get rid of emotions but to feel them safely, recognize their purpose, and use them as guides for healing and growth. To do this you will learn how to:

- **Identify emotions:** Learn a Cycle of Emotions Model and how to recognize and influence emotions.
- **Reduce emotional vulnerability:** Create daily self-care habits that support stability and lower the likelihood of intense emotions.
- **Build a sense of mastery:** Practice behaviors that lead you to feel capable, confident, and in control.
- **Create positive experiences:** Engage in activities and relationships that build positive emotions, helping counteract trauma's pull toward negativity or emotional numbing.
- **Break mood-driven behavior cycles:** Notice when emotions start to lead you toward choices that make things worse, and choose actions that lead to relief, balance, and connection instead.

Emotion regulation skills help you stay present, steady, and in control, even when feelings are intense. They also remind you that emotions are not the enemy and that they can be useful messengers that guide you toward healing once you know how to listen.

Beyond this, you will find that emotion regulation skills work far beyond the emotional realm, touching all other systems and domains too.

## Emotion Regulation Related to the Systems and Domains

Emotion regulation goes beyond simply understanding and influencing your emotional life. Because emotions touch all aspects of experience, the effects of emotion regulation reverberate through each system. With these skills:

- The Mind and Meaning System learns to identify, name, and balance emotions with clarity and compassion, as well as change perceptions of emotions and what they mean.
- The Body-Based System learns to recognize and listen to bodily signals as messages of emotion and to soothe them with care rather than react to them with fear.
- The Consciousness and Memory System learns to be present with feelings and acknowledge feelings connected to the past while remaining grounded in the present.
- The Action and Connection System learns to transform emotion into purposeful, values-based action that strengthens confidence, connection, and the capacity for joy.
- The Developmental Integration System learns that emotional wisdom grows through practice, patience, and consistent self-care, which is the foundation for lifelong balance and resilience.

Let's look at how emotion regulation supports recovery and integration across the eleven domains.

| System | Dysregulation Type | Statements | Example |
|---|---|---|---|
| I. Mind and Meaning | Emotional | "My feelings sometimes feel too big, and I can use Mindfulness of Current Emotion to name and allow them." "I'm afraid of my anger, and I can use Opposite Action to avoid acting unskillfully on it." | Ava feels frustration rising after receiving criticism. Using Check the Facts, she recognizes the criticism was meant to be constructive rather than harmful, lowering her intensity. She practices Opposite Action by expressing herself calmly, transforming reactivity into assertiveness. |
| | Cognitive | "My thoughts race with emotion, and I can use Check the Facts to evaluate them." "My mind assumes danger, and I can use the Cycle of Emotions Model to see what event prompted it and what my interpretations are to guide choices." | Noah feels anxious when a friend doesn't reply to a message. He traces the steps in the Cycle of Emotions Model and realizes his interpretation ("They must be upset") lacks evidence. This quiets his worry, and his emotion naturally decreases. |
| | Meaning and belief | "I believed emotions were uncontrollable, but emotion regulation skills give me power to influence them for the better." "I came to believe emotions were unsafe. I now see that they can show me what I value." | Selene grew up hearing "Don't cry." In therapy, validation affirms that sadness makes sense in response to loss, changing her interpretations. Over time, she sees emotions as meaningful signals rather than threats, integrating feeling with belief. |
| II. Body-Based | Nervous system | "My adrenaline spikes, and I can use Opposite Action and PLEASED to go for a run." "My body feels keyed up, and I can Build Mastery by doing a yoga routine I found on YouTube." | Kayla feels nervous before presenting. She uses Opposite Action and gives the talk anyway. Each success builds mastery, teaching her nervous system she can tolerate and manage activation. |
| | Somatic | "My body feels tense, yet I can use self-care skills (PLEASED) to improve how it feels." "My body feels heavy with fatigue. I use Opposite Action to get out of my home and go for a walk." | Sawyer feels agitated before a meeting. He engages PLEASED by eating, hydrating, resting, and exercising. Meeting his physical needs helps stabilize his emotions. |
| | Interoceptive | "When I can't tell what I'm feeling, I can Observe sensations to name the emotion." "My cues feel mixed, and I can practice Mindfulness of Current Emotion to interpret them." | Luis feels heavy and restless but unsure why. Using the Cycle of Emotions Model, he identifies sadness underlying his fatigue and validates it as a normal response. Accurately labeling his feelings restores clarity and calm. |

| System | Dysregulation Type | Statements | Example |
|---|---|---|---|
| **III. Consciousness and Memory** | Dissociative | "When I feel disconnected, I use Opposite Action to turn toward the present to counter avoiding it." "When I start to go numb and check out, I find that naming the emotion slows the drift and brings me back." | Renee detaches from others during conflict. She names the fear that arises in intense conversations, Observes its qualities, and stays with it instead of pushing it away, rebuilding emotional continuity and presence. |
| | Memory | "Memories bring up old feelings, and I follow my skills plan to be prepared." "When my past pain resurfaces, I Check the Facts to see how it relates to now." | Tariq hears a song linked to grief. He visualizes soothing himself and uses slow breathing and self-validation. He then practices Opposite Action to reach out for support rather than shut down. |
| **IV. Action and Connection** | Behavioral | "I want to act on my emotion, and I can use Opposite Action to respond wisely." "I feel discouraged, and I can Build Positive Experiences to counteract those feelings." | Marina feels angry after a difficult conversation. She pauses, Checks the Facts, practices Opposite Action by staying at work, and uses Build Positive Experiences by connecting with a coworker and accomplishing a goal. |
| | Relational | "I feel rejected, and I can Check the Facts before reacting." "I want to withdraw, yet I practice Opposite Action by reaching out." | Evan's partner forgets their anniversary. He names his hurt, Checks the Facts, and shares his feelings openly instead of withdrawing, softening defensiveness and fostering reconnection. |
| **V. Developmental Integration** | Developmental | "My home lacked care growing up, and I find that practicing self-care (PLEASED) is a form of parenting myself." "Childhood was chaos. Having a therapist who is calm and regulated when I'm in distress helps a lot." | Keira strengthens her foundation for stability with PLEASED by maintaining consistent sleep, meals, and movement. She adds Build Mastery by completing tasks like cooking and budgeting. Over time, structured care replaces early life instability. |

Across systems and domains, emotion regulation transforms emotional chaos into understanding, agency, and coherence. Each skill in this module speaks to restoring integration across systems, and through repetition, you internalize the truth that emotions are not enemies to conquer but teachers that lead the way toward balance, wisdom, and healing.

## Cycle of Emotions Model

Understanding how emotions develop allows you to influence them more skillfully. Especially in the aftermath of trauma, becoming aware of each part of the emotional process can interrupt unhelpful patterns and create more effective responses.

The Cycle of Emotions Model includes six key components, as shown and described below.

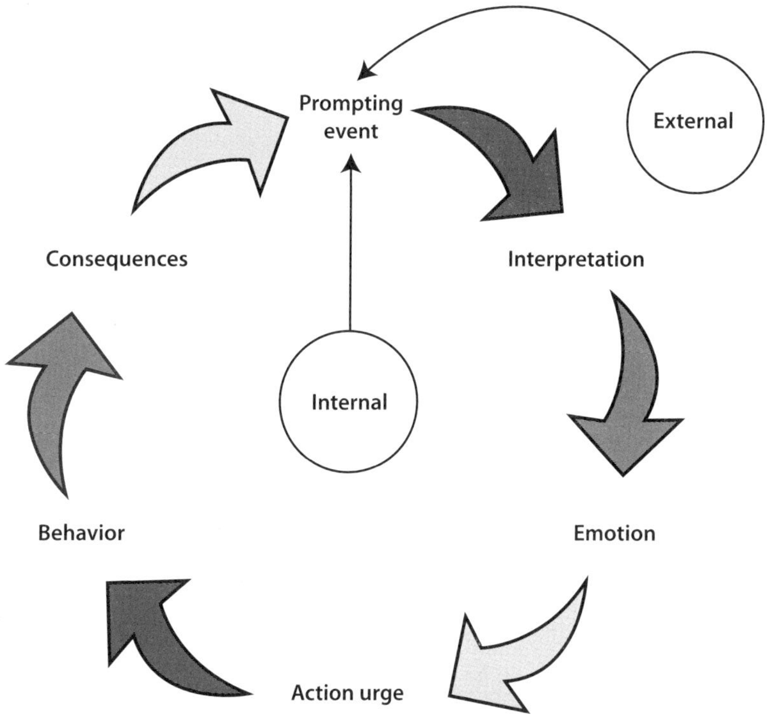


1. **The prompting event:** This is the situation or experience that initiates the emotional cycle. It might be an external event (e.g., seeing a trauma reminder) or an internal one (e.g., experiencing an intrusive memory or thought). The Body-Based System detects potential threat through the nervous system and interoceptive domains, activating protective signals before you're even aware of them.
2. **Your interpretation:** How you interpret the event strongly shapes your emotional response. For example, if you interpret a loud sound as threatening (based on past trauma), it will likely generate intense anxiety or fear. This step involves the Mind and Meaning System, especially the cognitive and meaning and belief domains, where perception and meaning are formed. Learning to slow down and notice your interpretations helps bring the prefrontal cortex online, balancing the brain's emotional and thinking centers.
3. **The resulting emotion:** The interpretation, body's threat response, or both can lead to an emotional reaction. Common trauma-related emotions include fear, shame, anger, and sadness.

These emotions can be understood as primary emotions, meaning they are immediate, natural responses to perceived threat or loss (such as fear when sensing danger or sadness in response to loss). Trauma often adds a layer of secondary emotions, like shame or anger at yourself for having the primary emotion. For example, someone might first feel fear during a flashback (primary emotion) and then feel ashamed for reacting so intensely (secondary emotion). These reactions involve the Mind and Meaning System's emotional domain while often interacting with body-based activation and memory cues. Through mindful awareness, you can notice and name your emotions without being overwhelmed by them, giving you space to differentiate between your initial feelings and the emotions that follow.

4. **The action urge:** Every emotion creates an action urge, which is an internal push to behave in a particular way. Fear may prompt escape, while anger may prompt confrontation. This urge reflects communication between the Body-Based System (bodily arousal) and the Action and Connection System (readiness to act). Recognizing the urge provides space to choose rather than react automatically.
5. **Your behavior:** This is the action you take (or don't take) in response to the action urge. For instance, after a sudden firework display triggers past memories of trauma, you might avoid leaving your house for the rest of the evening. Your actions are shaped by the behavioral domain in the Action and Connection System, but it's also influenced by relational safety and developmental learning within the relational and developmental domains. Practicing new responses allows the brain to form new pathways for regulation and trust.
6. **The consequences:** Your behavior produces consequences, positive, negative, or mixed, which then feed into the next emotional cycle. For example, if you avoid your trauma triggers, it may bring short-term relief but long-term anxiety and missed growth opportunities. This is where the Mind and Meaning System consolidates learning and the brain encodes new experiences in the memory domain. Over time, consistent skillful choices strengthen neural connections that support stability and emotional balance.

The cycle is continuous: How one emotional experience ends shapes how the next begins. By becoming aware of each step in the cycle, you can make skillful choices that promote emotional balance and healing.

In the next section, we'll explore specific ways to influence this cycle and begin transforming your emotional experience.

## Ways to Influence Your Emotions

Understanding the cycle of emotions helps you identify key opportunities to influence your emotional experiences. Each component of the cycle offers a chance to make more skillful choices that support emotion regulation and trauma recovery.

Let's examine each of the six components and how you can respond more effectively:

1. **The prompting event:** While you can't control all events, you often *can* choose which ones you engage with. You can increase your exposure to events that support healing, such as connecting with supportive people or doing meaningful activities, and limit those that increase distress. Prioritize experiences that build positive emotions and mastery and develop skills to better manage challenging events.
2. **Your interpretation:** Your thoughts and beliefs shape how you respond emotionally. Trauma can distort interpretation, often making safe situations feel threatening. Skills like Check the Facts, Nonjudgmental Stance, and dialectical thinking challenge and change unhelpful interpretations, reducing emotional intensity.
3. **The resulting emotion:** Emotions result from a combination of events, interpretations, and behaviors. While you can't choose your emotions directly, becoming more aware of them gives you greater influence over how you respond. Use mindfulness and other skills to acknowledge emotions without being overwhelmed by them or ignoring them.
4. **The action urges:** Emotions naturally create urges to act, but not all action urges are helpful. Increase your awareness of urges and ask yourself, "Is acting on this urge effective?" If not, use Urge Surfing or Opposite Action to shift your response.
5. **Your behaviors:** Your behavior powerfully influences how emotions unfold. Choosing skillful, values-based behaviors leads to better emotional outcomes. Acting on ineffective urges, on the other hand, often worsens emotional suffering.
6. **The consequences:** The outcomes of your behaviors feed into the next emotional cycle. Skillful choices often lead to positive consequences that support regulation and healing. Unskillful behaviors can result in increased dysregulation. If you make an unhelpful choice, practice self-compassion and course correct.

By intentionally working with each step in the cycle, you can gain greater control over your emotional experiences. In the next example, we'll look at how this model plays out in a trauma-related situation.

Worksheet

# Applying the Cycle of Emotions Model

This example shows how a trauma survivor may move through the emotional cycle and what opportunities exist to change the outcome through skillful choices.

1. **Prompting Event**

   This is the internal or external situation that starts the emotional cycle.

   *Example:* Taylor is walking in a park and sees someone who resembles a person from their past trauma. This visual reminder triggers an intense emotional reaction. The Body-Based System, especially the nervous system domain, immediately detects potential danger through the body's sensory networks. The amygdala signals "threat," activating the fight, flight, freeze, or collapse response before conscious thought occurs.

   What cues or sensations first signaled that something felt unsafe? How might noticing these early help create space for Taylor to respond differently?

   ______________________________________________

   ______________________________________________

   ______________________________________________

2. **Interpretation of the Event**

   This is how the person makes sense of what just happened. Interpretations may be automatic and shaped by trauma-related beliefs.

   *Example:* Taylor thinks, "That person could hurt me just like before." This interpretation reflects a trauma-driven belief that people who resemble past perpetrators are dangerous, even if that's not true in the present moment. This happens because the Mind and Meaning System, especially the cognitive and meaning and belief domains, interprets incoming sensory information based on past experiences. Mindfulness and grounding exercises can help bring the prefrontal cortex back online to help reappraise this interpretation.

   What other, more balanced interpretations could Taylor explore? How might mindfulness or Checking the Facts shift their perspective?

   ______________________________________________

   ______________________________________________

   ______________________________________________

3. **Emotion**

   The interpretation generates an emotional response. Recognizing and naming the emotion(s) helps manage this response.

   *Example:* Taylor experiences intense fear and panic. Their heart races, muscles tense, and breathing becomes shallow, even though they are in a safe environment. This response arises in the emotional and interoceptive domains, where the body and brain communicate sensations of fear. The goal here is to label emotions and locate them in the present rather than the past.

   What skills could help manage Taylor's emotional reaction in the moment?

   ______________________________________________

   ______________________________________________

   ______________________________________________

4. **Action Urge**

   Every emotion creates an urge to act. Some urges prompt effective actions, and some do not.

   *Example:* Taylor feels an overwhelming urge to leave the park immediately and find a place they perceive as safe. This urge reflects activation across the Body-Based System (bodily arousal) and Action and Connection System (movement and behavioral readiness). Recognizing the urge is the first step to evaluate whether the action supports safety or reinforces avoidance.

   Is this urge helpful or unhelpful? How might you assess its effectiveness in the short and long term?

   ______________________________________________

   ______________________________________________

   ______________________________________________

5. **Behavior**

   This is the response chosen, whether acting on the urge or choosing an alternative behavior.

   *Example:* Taylor quickly leaves the park and avoids returning, even though being in the park was previously a positive part of their routine. This avoidance behavior, which reinforces anxiety, reflects patterns in the behavioral and relational domains, where learned safety habits guide actions. Practicing alternative, approach-oriented behaviors strengthens new neural pathways in the prefrontal cortex (which supports thoughtful decision-making) and motor-action systems (such as the premotor cortex, supplementary motor area, and basal ganglia, which organize and initiate purposeful behavior), supporting more adaptive responses over time.

What other behavioral options could Taylor consider instead of avoidance? What skills might support these choices?

________________________________________

________________________________________

________________________________________

6. **Consequences**

   Behaviors produce outcomes, both immediate and long term, that affect future emotional cycles.

   *Example:* Leaving the park provides temporary relief, but Taylor later feels frustrated and disappointed. The avoidance reinforces fear and makes it harder to enjoy public places or positive routines, limiting their recovery. This step involves the Mind and Meaning System, as well as the memory domain, where experiences are encoded and patterns are reinforced, for better or worse. Each time Taylor practices a skillful action, the brain experiences new learning, gradually reducing the power of trauma triggers.

   What skillful steps could Taylor take to move forward from this moment? How might they reengage with the park in a gradual and supported way?

   ________________________________________

   ________________________________________

   ________________________________________

By learning to recognize and intervene at each step in the emotional cycle, you can seize opportunities to increase regulation. Each new skillful choice supports the rewiring of neural pathways across the five systems and eleven domains, promoting posttraumatic growth and greater emotional freedom.

Worksheet

# Trauma-Focused Scenarios with the Cycle of Emotions Model

Applying the Cycle of Emotions Model brings theory to life. By walking through real-world examples, you can see how emotions unfold moment by moment and how trauma can shape each stage of that process. The good news is every point in the cycle offers an opportunity to notice what is happening, to understand why it's happening, and to choose a more skillful response.

For each trauma-focused scenario here, describe at what points in the cycle a different choice could have been made, what felt effective or ineffective, and what skills would have allowed the person to respond more effectively.

## Scenario 1: Flashback Trigger

1. **Prompting event:** A child screams in a mall, creating a loud, startling noise that triggers a flashback for an adult nearby.
2. **Interpretation:** "It's happening again. I'm not safe."
3. **Emotion:** Intense fear.
4. **Action urge:** Hide or flee to safety.
5. **Behavior:** Escapes to a secluded place.
6. **Consequences:** Disconnection and anxiety about public spaces.

Looking back at the entire cycle, where did you notice opportunities to pause and make different choices? What was effective, or ineffective, in this example? What skills were used or could have made a positive difference?

____________________________________________________________

____________________________________________________________

## Scenario 2: Criticism and Shame

1. **Prompting event:** A supervisor gives corrective feedback, echoing the harsh tone and criticism the client frequently received from an abusive parent who shamed them growing up.
2. **Interpretation:** "I'm incompetent; I'm failing."
3. **Emotion:** Shame, guilt, worthlessness.

 

4. **Action urge:** Withdraw and avoid all interactions with the supervisor and coworkers.
5. **Behavior:** Isolates and disengages from work.
6. **Consequences:** Increased depression and avoidance of growth opportunities.

Looking back at the entire cycle, where did you notice opportunities to pause and make different choices? What was effective, or ineffective, in this example? What skills were used or could have made a positive difference?

_______________________________________________

_______________________________________________

## Scenario 3: Memory Trigger

1. **Prompting event:** A college student smells a particular cologne at a party, the same scent that was present during a sexual assault in high school.
2. **Interpretation:** "Something bad is about to happen again. I'm not safe."
3. **Emotion:** Anxiety, fear, nausea, tension, and dread.
4. **Action urge:** Leave immediately.
5. **Behavior:** Exits the party and isolates in their dorm room.
6. **Consequences:** Increased hypervigilance and avoidance of social spaces.

Looking back at the entire cycle, where did you notice opportunities to pause and make different choices? What was effective, or ineffective, in this example? What skills were used or could have made a positive difference?

_______________________________________________

_______________________________________________

## Scenario 4: Trust Betrayal

1. **Prompting event:** A friend shares a private story without consent, mirroring past experiences where the client's boundaries were violated and confidences were used against them.
2. **Interpretation:** "No one is trustworthy; betrayal is inevitable."
3. **Emotion:** Anger, sadness, betrayal.
4. **Action urge:** Harshly confront and cut off the friend.

5. **Behavior:** Aggressively confronts the friend, which is followed by a rupture.
6. **Consequences:** Relationship loss and deeper isolation.

Looking back at the entire cycle, where did you notice opportunities to pause and make different choices? What was effective, or ineffective, in this example? What skills were used or could have made a positive difference?

_______________________________________________

_______________________________________________

## Scenario 5: Social Anxiety

1. **Prompting event:** Someone receives an invitation to a social event, which brings up memories of past experiences where they were mocked, excluded, and humiliated in group settings.
2. **Interpretation:** "I'll be judged or rejected."
3. **Emotion:** Anxiety, fear of exclusion.
4. **Action urge:** Decline the invitation.
5. **Behavior:** Avoids the event.
6. **Consequences:** Missed opportunity and reinforced isolation.

Looking back at the entire cycle, where did you notice opportunities to pause and make different choices? What was effective, or ineffective, in this example? What skills were used or could have made a positive difference?

_______________________________________________

_______________________________________________

## Scenario 6: Feeling of Helplessness

1. **Prompting Event:** A client receives news that a loved one is seriously ill, echoing earlier life experiences where they felt powerless during family crises or were unable to protect someone they cared about.
2. **Interpretation:** "There's nothing I can do. I'm powerless."
3. **Emotion:** Sadness, helplessness, despair.
4. **Action Urge:** Avoid and numb out.

5. **Behavior:** Isolates and engages in overeating and excessive sleep.
6. **Consequences:** Increased disconnection and helplessness.

Looking back at the entire cycle, where did you notice opportunities to pause and make different choices? What was effective, or ineffective, in this example? What skills were used or could have made a positive difference?

___

___

## Scenario 7: Self-Blame

1. **Prompting event:** A client recalls being sexually abused by an older cousin during childhood, a memory that reliably triggers thoughts that they "should have stopped it."
2. **Interpretation:** "It was my fault; I should've stopped it."
3. **Emotion:** Guilt, shame, self-hatred.
4. **Action urge:** Engage in self-punishment.
5. **Behavior:** Withdraws from loved ones and engages in self-injury.
6. **Consequences:** Reinforced shame and emotional isolation.

Looking back at the entire cycle, where did you notice opportunities to pause and make different choices? What was effective, or ineffective, in this example? What skills were used or could have made a positive difference?

___

___

## Scenario 8: Rejection Sensitivity

1. **Prompting event:** A friend cancels plans unexpectedly, echoing earlier experiences where important people were inconsistent, unavailable, or withdrew affection without warning.
2. **Interpretation:** "They don't care. They're pulling away."
3. **Emotion:** Hurt, anger, insecurity.
4. **Action urge:** Retaliate by ignoring the friend.

 

5. **Behavior:** Gives friend the silent treatment.
6. **Consequences:** Increased loneliness and interpersonal distance.

Looking back at the entire cycle, where did you notice opportunities to pause and make different choices? What was effective, or ineffective, in this example? What skills were used or could have made a positive difference?

______________________________________________________________________

______________________________________________________________________

## Scenario 9: Hypervigilance

1. **Prompting event:** A stranger walks behind a client at night, triggering memories of earlier situations in which they were followed, threatened, and harmed and had little ability to protect themselves.
2. **Interpretation:** "They're going to harm me."
3. **Emotion:** Fear and anxiety spike.
4. **Action urge:** Escape quickly.
5. **Behavior:** Crosses street or alters route.
6. **Consequences:** Increased sense of safety and distance from a potential threat.

Looking back at the entire cycle, where did you notice opportunities to pause and make different choices? What was effective, or ineffective, in this example? What skills were used or could have made a positive difference?

______________________________________________________________________

______________________________________________________________________

## Scenario 10: Avoidance of Intimacy

1. **Prompting event:** A client receives a date invitation from someone they genuinely like, which stirs memories of past relationships where vulnerability led to betrayal, coercion, and emotional harm.
2. **Interpretation:** "If I get close, I'll get hurt."
3. **Emotion:** Anxiety, sadness, dread.

 

4. **Action urge:** Avoid the risk.
5. **Behavior:** Declines or cancels the date.
6. **Consequences:** Missed opportunity for connection and reinforced fear of intimacy.

Looking back at the entire cycle, where did you notice opportunities to pause and make different choices? What was effective, or ineffective, in this example? What skills were used or could have made a positive difference?

______________________________________________________________________

______________________________________________________________________

The goal of applying this model is not to control emotions but to understand and collaborate with them. Each repetition of mindful awareness and skillful response restores connection across systems and domains. Over time, what once felt like threat becomes information, what once felt like chaos becomes coherence, and what once led to reactivity gives way to stability and choice. This is how you learn safety and how healing becomes a lived experience.

Worksheet

# Cycle of Emotions Model

Use this worksheet to explore how emotions and emotional patterns arise through the Cycle of Emotions Model. It can help you reflect on a recent emotional experience or one you are currently experiencing.

1. **The Prompting Event**
   What happened? Be specific. Who was involved? What occurred? Where and when did it take place?

   ______________________________

   ______________________________

2. **Your Interpretation**

   What thoughts, judgments, self-talk, or beliefs were triggered by the event? Were these interpretations influenced by past experiences, especially trauma-related beliefs or assumptions?

   ______________________________

   ______________________________

3. **The Resulting Emotion**

   What emotions did you feel? How did these emotions show up in your body? What physical sensations did you notice (e.g., heart rate, breathing, muscle tension)? Did your facial expressions or body language change? Were there any underlying or secondary emotions?

   ______________________________

   ______________________________

4. **The Action Urge**

   What impulse or urge did your emotion create (e.g., to leave, lash out, shut down, seek reassurance)? Would acting on this urge align with Wise Mind?

   ______________________________

   ______________________________

 

5. **Your Behavior**

   What did you actually do or not do? Was your response effective or ineffective in the moment? Did your behavior align with your values and long-term goals?

   ______________________________________________

   ______________________________________________

6. **The Consequences**

   What happened as a result of your behavior? How did your response affect your emotions, thoughts, and relationships afterward? Did this situation reinforce a familiar pattern or begin to shift it?

   ______________________________________________

   ______________________________________________

Worksheet

# Mindfulness of Current Emotion: Understanding Common Emotions and How They Are Experienced

Mindfulness of Current Emotion means noticing what you feel, right now, without judgment, resistance, or avoidance. By observing emotions as they arise in the mind and body, you build awareness of how they express themselves cognitively, physically, and behaviorally. This awareness is the foundation for regulation and choice.

The following is a guide to common emotions, including how they vary in intensity, physically appear in the body, are expressed in communication, and can be engaged with in effective ways. As you read through the list, pause and bring mindful awareness to your own experiences. Notice which emotions feel most familiar or uncomfortable. Gently Observe where each emotion might show up in your body—for example, in your breath, posture, or facial expression.

Allow yourself to name what you're feeling without trying to change it. Practicing Mindfulness of Current Emotion in this way strengthens the connection between the Body-Based System (where emotions are sensed and expressed) and the Mind and Meaning System (where they are understood and contextualized), teaching both your brain and body that emotions can be safely noticed, felt, and released.

## Happiness

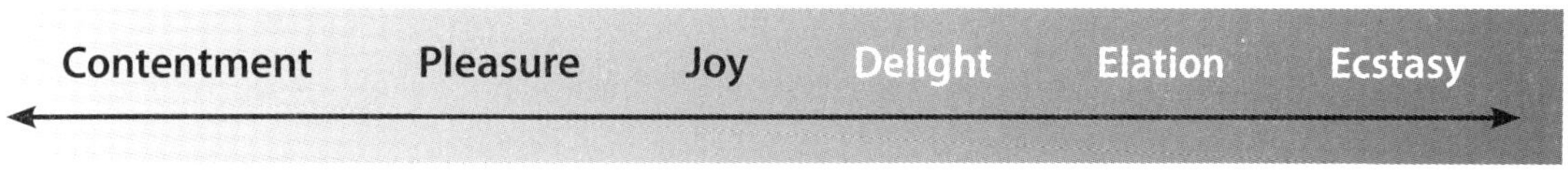


- **Physical experiences:** Feeling energized yet calm, relaxed muscles, a sense of lightness or warmth in the chest.
- **Communication:** Smiling at others, sharing joyful stories, warm tone of voice, open body posture, affectionate gestures (e.g., hugs).
- **Effective engagement:** Practice gratitude, engage in joyful or meaningful activities, and share happiness with others to build connection and safety.

Which areas of dysregulation make it difficult to experience or trust happiness?

______________________________________________________________________

______________________________________________________________________

 

## Sadness

Disappointment — Sorrow — Grief — Anguish — Despair — Heartbreak

- **Physical experiences:** Crying, fatigue, appetite changes, heavy limbs, insomnia or oversleeping.
- **Communication:** Quiet or low speech, social withdrawal, tearfulness, reduced eye contact, slower movements.
- **Effective engagement:** Talk to someone you trust, allow space for grief, engage in mild physical activity, and write in a journal.

How does trauma deepen or prolong sadness in your body and mind? What domains are impacted?

______________________________________________

______________________________________________

## Anger

Annoyance — Irritation — Frustration — Rage — Fury — Wrath

- **Physical experiences:** Clenched jaw, increased heart rate, tight muscles, flushed skin, restlessness.
- **Communication:** Raised voice, abrupt movements, glaring, sarcasm, or confrontational language.
- **Effective engagement:** Use deep breathing or grounding techniques, take a break, engage in physical movement, and reflect on whether anger relates to past trauma.

What systems are activated by anger? Does your nervous system escalate quickly or shut down?

______________________________________________

______________________________________________

## Anxiety and Fear

Apprehension — Nervousness — Panic — Dread — Terror — Horror

- **Physical experiences:** Rapid heartbeat, shallow breathing, tension, sweating, feeling frozen or nauseous.
- **Communication:** Verbal exclamations of fear or concern, lack of eye contact, avoidance of places or people, nervous jokes or hesitant speech.
- **Effective engagement:** Use grounding skills, practice positive self-talk, slowly expose yourself to feared situations, and distinguish past trauma from current safety.

Which domains are overwhelmed during fear responses—interoceptive, cognitive, nervous system?

______________________________________________

______________________________________________

## Surprise

Startle — Amazement — Astonishment — Bewilderment — Shock — Stupefaction

- **Physical experiences:** Widened eyes, raised eyebrows, open mouth, sharp inhale, temporary stillness.
- **Communication:** Verbal exclamations, animated storytelling, laughter, facial expressions of shock or joy.
- **Effective engagement:** Take time to process the surprise, talk it through, and use grounding if the surprise feels unsafe.

Does surprise activate trauma-based alarm? What dysregulation systems flare up or help you adapt?

______________________________________________

______________________________________________

## Disgust

Dislike | Distaste | Revulsion | Repugnance | Abhorrence | Loathing

- **Physical experiences:** Wrinkled nose, gag reflex, nausea, recoiling, frowning, narrowing the eyes.
- **Communication:** "Yuck" or "ew" sounds, rejecting something explicitly, body withdrawal, grimacing.
- **Effective engagement:** Validate the disgust and choose what is effective: move away from genuine threat, or stay present with curiosity when safe.

Is this response rooted in trauma? How do your somatic or memory domains contribute to it?

______________________________________________

______________________________________________

## Curiosity

Interest | Inquisitiveness | Eagerness | Fascination | Intrigue | Obsession

- **Physical experiences:** Leaning forward, wide eyes, alert posture, fidgeting or tapping.
- **Communication:** Asking questions, enthusiastic engagement, listening actively, sharing ideas.
- **Effective engagement:** Pursue interests, share discoveries, and stay present without obsession. Use curiosity to explore healing.

Do fear or anxiety suppress your curiosity? Which domains limit or activate exploration?

______________________________________________

______________________________________________

## Embarrassment

Sheepishness  Awkwardness  Discomfort  Self-Consciousness  Humiliation  Mortification

- **Physical experiences:** Blushing, lowered gaze, slouching, shrinking.
- **Communication:** Apologizing, nervous laughter, self-deprecating humor, low voice, avoidance, changing subjects quickly.
- **Effective engagement:** Practice self-compassion, normalize the feeling, and talk with someone supportive.

How does trauma intensify shame or embarrassment? What domains are activated—relational, meaning, developmental?

______________________________________________

______________________________________________

## Jealousy

Desire  Covetousness  Resentment  Possessiveness  Envy  Greed

- **Physical experiences:** Tight chest, clenched jaw, restlessness, stomach tension, furrowed brow.
- **Communication:** Comparisons, suspicion, passive-aggressiveness, withdrawal, probing questions.
- **Effective engagement:** Identify insecurities, build self-worth, and communicate your needs clearly and kindly.

Does this emotion stem from past betrayal or abandonment? What dysregulation domains maintain it?

______________________________________________

______________________________________________

Worksheet

# Trauma, Emotions, and Skills

Trauma profoundly affects how we experience and express emotions, often amplifying them or leading to avoidance, shame, or reactivity. These shifts and the resulting dysregulation occur across the five systems and eleven domains.

Skills restore balance across these systems by teaching you that emotions represent information, not threats, and that every feeling, no matter how painful, can become a pathway to healing.

Here is a summary of how trauma impacts each emotion and how skills support recovery. *Note that the skills listed just scratch the surface, so explore the breadth of options across all modules.*

## Happiness

After trauma, happiness can feel unsafe, undeserved, or fragile. The emotional domain may associate joy with coming vulnerability, while the meaning and belief domain may link happiness with guilt, fear, or anticipated loss. You may also suppress or mute joy to avoid disappointment or to prevent feeling conspicuous. Helpful skills include:

- **Mindfulness:** Notice moments of happiness as they arise, however small, and anchor your awareness in the Body-Based System by connecting with sensations of warmth, ease, or lightness. Let yourself register the experience without rushing past it.
- **Opposite Action:** Invite small experiences of pleasure or joy at the very moments when your instinct is to pull away, shut down, or dismiss positive emotion. This helps your nervous system learn that it is safe to stay present with happiness and that joy can coexist with protection and grounding.

What helps you feel safe allowing yourself to experience happiness fully?

_______________________________________________

_______________________________________________

## Sadness

In the wake of trauma, sadness is often prolonged or heavy. The emotional domain carries waves of loss, while the memory domain may replay painful events that sustain grief, and the meaning and belief domain may interpret sadness as weakness or punishment. Helpful skills include:

- **Radical Acceptance:** Acknowledge sadness without judgment, activating the Mind and Meaning System to transform pain into acceptance.

 

- **Build Positive Experiences:** Intentionally create small moments of connection or pleasure that counter despair and engage the behavioral domain.

How can you allow sadness to move through you without becoming lost in it?

______________________________________________________________________

______________________________________________________________________

## Anger

Anger may feel explosive, suppressed, or chronic as a result of trauma, often rooted in betrayal or injustice. The Body-Based System remains activated while dysregulation in the relational domain may cause harm in relationships. Helpful skills include:

- **Check the Facts:** Determine whether anger fits the facts or stems from past experiences to regulate the Mind and Meaning System.
- **Opposite Action:** Use Relaxation from IMPROVE and Self-Soothing to settle the nervous system or channel energy into assertive, values-based action.

How do you express anger in ways that protect rather than harm your peace or relationships?

______________________________________________________________________

______________________________________________________________________

## Anxiety and Fear

The nervous system domain becomes hypersensitive after trauma, signaling danger when none exists, and the interoceptive domain confuses internal sensations, like a racing heart, with threat. Further, when memory fragments in the Consciousness and Memory System, fear can make it feel as if the past is happening now. Helpful skills include:

- **Grounding:** Use your senses to orient to the present (rewiring the Consciousness and Memory System) and calm the body (strengthening the Body-Based System).
- **Opposite Action:** Gradually approach avoided situations to retrain the behavioral domain and desensitize the nervous system.

What helps you remind your body and mind that you are safe in this moment?

______________________________________________________________________

______________________________________________________________________

## Surprise

After trauma, surprise may activate startle or panic responses instead of curiosity or delight. The nervous system and interoceptive domains register surprise as potential danger. Helpful skills include:

- **STOP Skill:** Pause, breathe, and observe before reacting, allowing the Mind and Meaning System to come online with higher reasoning.
- **Mindfulness:** Notice sensations of surprise and label them neutrally, teaching the Body-Based System that uncertainty can be tolerated.

How do you stay grounded when something unexpected happens?

______________________________________________________________

______________________________________________________________

## Disgust

Following trauma, disgust can arise as a protective response to violation or contamination, often encoded in the somatic domain as nausea, tension, or withdrawal, while the cognitive domain may link disgust to shame or self-loathing. Helpful skills include:

- **Mindfulness of Current Emotion:** Gently name and Observe disgust as it appears in your body without judging or resisting it. This engages the Mind and Meaning System to separate the physical sensations of disgust from the stories of shame attached to them. Naming the emotion brings clarity to sensations that once triggered avoidance.
- **Opposite Action:** If the source of disgust feels safe and tolerable from Wise Mind, remain present and soften avoidance by taking a small, deliberate step toward what feels repellent or contaminated. This retrains the Body-Based System to tolerate activation without collapse, transforming disgust from a threat signal into a cue for mindful care.

What helps you distinguish between disgust rooted in trauma and what is appropriate to the present moment?

______________________________________________________________

______________________________________________________________

## Curiosity

Trauma can cause the meaning and belief domain to equate curiosity with danger, while the developmental domain may associate exploration with punishment or loss of control. This restricts openness to new experiences. Helpful skills include:

- **Build Mastery:** Choose small, safe opportunities to explore, like a new walking route, a different recipe, or a new song or podcast. Let yourself stay with the feeling of mild interest for just a moment longer than usual. This strengthens the Action and Connection System by pairing exploration with safety and competence.
- **Mindfulness of Current Emotion:** When curiosity arises, pause and notice it. Observe the shift in your body, such as a slight leaning in, a softening, or a moment of focus. Name it as curiosity to help the Consciousness and Memory System link this emotion with the present moment rather than past danger.

How might curiosity become a source of empowerment in your healing process?

______________________________________________

______________________________________________

## Embarrassment

After trauma, embarrassment can feel sharper and more exposing than it would for others. The relational domain may interpret even small missteps as threats to belonging, while the meaning and belief domain may connect embarrassment with old messages of not being good enough or of being judged harshly. This can lead to withdrawal, self-criticism, or replaying the moment long after it has passed. Helpful skills include:

- **Radical Acceptance:** Acknowledge that mistakes, awkward moments, and misunderstandings are part of being human. Allowing this reality to be true reduces emotional intensity and helps the emotional domain settle. Acceptance doesn't mean you approve of what happened; it simply means you stop fighting what is already real.
- **Nonjudgmental Stance:** Notice the stories your mind tells about the embarrassing moment, especially those shaped by past shame. Practice describing what happened without labels like "stupid," "ridiculous," or "I should've known better." This engages the meaning and belief domain in a new way, loosening old shame narratives and strengthening self-trust.

 

How do you support yourself when embarrassment triggers old feelings of inadequacy?

______________________________________________

______________________________________________

## Jealousy

Jealousy often reflects a fear of loss, exclusion, or being replaced. After trauma, especially relational trauma, the relational and developmental domains may replay early attachment wounds, making jealousy feel more urgent or threatening than the current situation warrants. You may imagine worst-case scenarios, monitor for signs of rejection, or struggle to trust reassurance. Helpful skills include:

- **Check the Facts:** Pause to ask whether your fears fit what is actually happening now or whether they echo past experiences of betrayal, abandonment, or inconsistency. Noticing the difference calms emotional intensity and allows the relational domain to respond to the present rather than old patterns.
- **Interpersonal Effectiveness:** Use skills such as DEAR MAN and GIVE to express your needs in a clear, respectful way. Naming your feelings without blame and asking directly for reassurance, boundaries, or clarity supports regulation in the Action and Connection System. These skills turn jealousy from silent worry or reactive behavior into honest communication that strengthens connection.

How can you use DBT skills to transform jealousy into honest communication and deeper connection?

______________________________________________

______________________________________________

## Integration Across Systems

Each emotion involves a unique interplay of the five systems. The Body-Based System carries the sensations of emotion; the Mind and Meaning System interprets them; the Consciousness and Memory System connects them to time and awareness; the Action and Connection System guides behavior and relationship; and the Developmental Integration System determines how you mature through them. Skills work because they reestablish communication among these systems, so emotions move fluidly through the mind and body rather than getting trapped in survival patterns.

## SKILL Check the Facts

Check the Facts is a skill that directs you to pause, question your interpretations, and ground yourself in the reality of the present moment. For trauma survivors, it can be a powerful way to recognize when emotions are being shaped or intensified by past experiences.

In this approach, you'll still use the traditional DBT steps of Checking the Facts, but you'll also learn to notice *where* dysregulation is happening within you to inform your response. That's because trauma doesn't only influence your emotions; it reshapes how you think, sense, remember, relate, and behave. By noticing which systems are activated, you can choose skills that match your unique experience in the moment. This awareness transforms emotional reactivity into an opportunity for greater understanding and regulation.

Here are the steps to Check the Facts with dysregulation awareness:

1. **Name the emotion and rate the intensity**
    - Identify the emotion you're feeling and rate its intensity on a 0–10 scale.
    - Notice whether this emotion feels familiar or linked to past trauma. To do so, ask yourself, "Does this reaction belong to now, or does it feel like then?"
2. **Describe the trigger**
    - What happened that led to this emotion?
    - What were your immediate thoughts, beliefs, or assumptions?
    - Consider whether your interpretation might be influenced by earlier experiences of threat, shame, or loss.
3. **Check the Facts from Wise Mind**
    - What are the objective, observable facts of the situation?
    - What evidence supports or contradicts your interpretation?
    - Ask yourself, "Am I assuming, overgeneralizing, or catastrophizing?"
    - Can you use dialectical thinking to hold both realities (e.g., "This reminds me of the past, *and* it might be different now")?
4. **Decide whether the emotion and intensity fit the facts**
    - Does this emotion match what's happening in the present?
    - Is the intensity appropriate to the current situation?
    - If not, what other interpretations or responses might fit better?

5. **Identify areas of dysregulation**

   For each of the eleven domains, notice what might be activated and how it appears in your experience.

| System | Domain |
|---|---|
| **Mind and Meaning** | Emotional: Was your emotion extreme, blunted, or difficult to regulate?<br>Cognitive: Were your thoughts racing, rigid, or shutdown?<br>Meaning and belief: Were old trauma beliefs triggered ("I'm not safe," "It's my fault")? |
| **Body-Based** | Nervous system: Did your body shift into fight, flight, freeze, or collapse?<br>Somatic: Did you feel pain, tightness, fatigue, or trembling?<br>Interoceptive: Did you misread internal signals like heart rate, breath, or hunger as danger? |
| **Consciousness and Memory** | Dissociative: Did you feel foggy, detached, or outside your body?<br>Memory: Were flashbacks, intrusive images, or trauma-linked associations triggered? |
| **Action and Connection** | Behavioral: Did you react impulsively, avoid, or shut down?<br>Relational: Did you withdraw, assume rejection, or misread others' intentions? |
| **Developmental Integration** | Developmental: Did this situation activate younger parts of you, or a sense of being "small," unworthy, or powerless? |

6. **Act skillfully**

   If your emotion and the intensity fit the facts and your action is effective, proceed with Wise Mind. If not, choose targeted skills to restore regulation before responding from Wise Mind.

Worksheet

# Checking the Facts with Trauma-Linked Dysregulation

This worksheet includes examples showing how emotional interpretations can differ from present reality, as well as how dysregulation may appear across systems and domains. Note that these examples show ways in which each system can be activated for teaching purposes. In practice, not all of them will necessarily be affected.

When you use Check the Facts, focus on your most dysregulated systems and domains, and remember that it is usually most useful to begin with bottom-up skills.

## Scenario 1: A flashback is triggered by loud noise

A door slams and panic surges through your body. It feels like danger is happening again.

**Activated Systems:**

- **Mind and Meaning:** Emotional flooding; "I'm not safe."
- **Body-Based:** Startle reflex, racing heart, tense muscles.
- **Consciousness and Memory:** Flashback or sensory replay.
- **Action and Connection:** Escape or freeze response.
- **Developmental Integration:** Feeling small or helpless.

Check the Facts: Is the sound truly threatening, or does it resemble something from the past?

List skills to try within each system:

- **Mind and Meaning:** How can you counter the thoughts or beliefs that are making you feel unsafe?

  ______________________________

- **Body-Based:** What can you do to calm your body?

  ______________________________

- **Consciousness and Memory:** What grounding techniques can you use to stay in the present moment?

  ______________________________

 

- **Action and Connection:** What actions can you take to reestablish control?

  ______________________________________________

- **Developmental Integration:** How can you reassure yourself in the face of fear?

  ______________________________________________

## Scenario 2: A missed phone call means you've been rejected

A friend doesn't answer your call, and you immediately feel forgotten and rejected.

**Activated Systems:**

- **Mind and Meaning:** Emotional hurt; "I'm unlovable."
- **Body-Based**: Stomachache, restlessness.
- **Consciousness and Memory:** Activation of past abandonment memories.
- **Action and Connection:** Withdrawal, avoidance.
- **Developmental Integration:** Old attachment fear of being left.

Check the Facts: Could they be busy, driving, or out of battery?

List skills to try within each domain:

- **Mind and Meaning:** How can you counter the thoughts or beliefs that are making you feel rejected?

  ______________________________________________

- **Body-Based:** What can you do to soothe physical tension or discomfort?

  ______________________________________________

- **Consciousness and Memory:** What grounding techniques can you use to stay in the present instead of ruminating on past abandonment?

  ______________________________________________

- **Action and Connection:** What actions can you take to reestablish healthy connection without avoiding or withdrawing?

  ______________________________________________

- **Developmental Integration:** How can you reassure yourself that you are not unworthy of love?

  ______________________________________________

## Scenario 3: Feedback from a friend feels like an attack

A friend offers constructive feedback, but it feels like harsh criticism.

**Activated Systems:**

- **Mind and Meaning:** Shame; "I'm failing."
- **Body-Based:** Tension, heat, urge to flee.
- **Consciousness and Memory:** Checking out or remembering past criticism.
- **Action and Connection:** Defensive withdrawal or argument.
- **Developmental Integration:** Feeling like a scolded child.

Check the Facts: Was their tone kind? Were they addressing your behavior, not your character?

List skills to try within each system:

- **Mind and Meaning:** How can you counter the thoughts or beliefs that are making you feel ashamed or criticized?

  ______________________________

- **Body-Based:** What can you do to reduce reactivity?

  ______________________________

- **Consciousness and Memory:** What grounding techniques can you use to avoid getting lost in past critical experiences?

  ______________________________

- **Action and Connection:** What actions can you take to respond thoughtfully rather than defensively?

  ______________________________

- **Developmental Integration:** How can you validate your current competence?

  ______________________________

## Scenario 4: Eye contact avoidance means you're being judged

Someone at a gathering avoids eye contact, and you assume they dislike you.

**Activated Systems:**

- **Mind and Meaning:** Sad and angry; "They think I'm weird."

 

- **Body-Based:** Tight chest, shallow breathing.
- **Consciousness and Memory:** Echo of social rejection.
- **Action and Connection:** Self-conscious, withdrawal.
- **Developmental Integration:** Sense of exclusion or "not fitting in."

Check the Facts: Could they be shy, distracted, or anxious themselves?

List skills to try within each system:

- **Mind and Meaning:** How can you counter the thoughts or beliefs that are making you feel rejected or judged?

  ______________________________

- **Body-Based:** What can you do to ease bodily tension?

  ______________________________

- **Consciousness and Memory:** What grounding techniques can you use to stay in the present rather than reliving prior rejection?

  ______________________________

- **Action and Connection:** What actions can you take to remain engaged?

  ______________________________

- **Developmental Integration:** How can you comfort the part of you that feels left out or unimportant?

  ______________________________

## Scenario 5: Group cancelation feels like a personal rejection

Your therapy group is suddenly canceled, and you feel excluded or unwanted.

**Activated Systems:**

- **Mind and Meaning:** Sadness; "I don't belong."
- **Body-Based:** Fatigue, heaviness.
- **Consciousness and Memory:** Reminder of past invalidation.
- **Action and Connection:** Pulling away and skipping future sessions.
- **Developmental Integration:** Feelings of abandonment or invisibility.

Check the Facts: Could it be a scheduling or logistical issue?

List skills to try within each system:

- **Mind and Meaning:** How can you counter the thoughts or beliefs that are making you feel excluded or unwanted?

  ______________________________

- **Body-Based:** What can you do to counter feelings of fatigue and heaviness?

  ______________________________

- **Consciousness and Memory:** What grounding techniques can help you avoid replaying past feelings of abandonment?

  ______________________________

- **Action and Connection:** What actions can you take to maintain connection and not pull away from future sessions?

  ______________________________

- **Developmental Integration:** How can you attend to these early abandonment fears while staying connected to what is real now?

  ______________________________

Checking the Facts through the lens of the five systems helps you understand *why* your body and mind respond as they do. Each system communicates valuable information, including signals about safety, belonging, and meaning.

By identifying which systems are activated, you can apply skills with precision, meeting yourself where regulation has been lost. Over time, this builds trust between your brain, body, and Wise Mind, allowing reactions once rooted in survival to become opportunities for awareness, healing, and choice.

# SKILL PLEASED for Self-Care

Self-care is essential for those recovering from trauma, as it often disrupts the connections between mind and body, leaving you feeling exhausted, tense, and emotionally fragile. Consistent self-care repairs those connections by supporting regulation across your systems and domains. When used proactively and consistently, PLEASED will positively impact every facet of your being.

The PLEASED acronym stands for Physical Health, List Resources and Barriers, Eat Balanced Meals, Avoid Drugs and Alcohol, Sleep Enough (But Not Too Much), Exercise Regularly, and Daily Habits. By practicing PLEASED, you teach every part of yourself that you are worthy of tending to and capable of recovery.

## Physical Health

Trauma often manifests through body symptoms such as chronic pain, fatigue, digestive issues, or tension. Attending to your physical health is about receiving regular medical checkups, managing any health conditions, and taking medications as prescribed. This provides a foundation of safety and stability for recovery. When you attend to your body's well-being, it communicates to your nervous system that it is safe to rest, recover, and function in balance. Maintaining physical health directly supports regulation within the Body-Based System, especially the nervous system and somatic domains.

*Examples:*

- **Schedule routine medical checkups** (primary care, dental, vision) to monitor ongoing health needs and reduce uncertainty that fuels anxiety.
- **Take medications consistently as prescribed**, using a pillbox or reminders to support follow-through and stabilize physical functioning.
- **Address chronic symptoms** such as headaches, muscle tension, stomach pain, or sleep disturbances with a provider instead of pushing through or ignoring them.
- **Notice body signals early**, such as fatigue or pain, and respond with rest, hydration, or movement rather than forcing yourself past your limits.
- **Create a simple daily health routine**, like taking a morning walk, stretching, or drinking water regularly, to give your nervous system predictable cues of safety and regulation.

## List Resources and Barriers (for Each Area of This Acronym)

Identify both the resources and challenges you have when it comes to engaging in effective self-care. This allows you to problem-solve from a place of Wise Mind rather than overwhelm. Resources may include therapy, supportive people, or access to healthy food and exercise equipment. Barriers might involve time, finances, or access to care. Engage your resources and problem-solve your barriers.

*Examples:*

- **Identify supportive people** who can help you stay accountable, such as a therapist, friend, or family member, and note whether lack of support is a barrier.
- **Recognize your available tools,** like insurance coverage, access to transportation, or nearby clinics, and clarify when limited access is a barrier that needs planning.
- **Take stock of practical resources,** such as having healthy food at home, a quiet space to practice skills, or access to a gym, while acknowledging barriers like cost or limited time.
- **Notice emotional resources and barriers,** including motivation, confidence, or burnout, and use DBT skills to work through emotional blocks to self-care.
- **Plan around predictable obstacles,** such as a busy schedule, childcare needs, or chronic pain, by identifying small, realistic adjustments that keep you engaged in self-care consistently.

## Eat Balanced Meals

Trauma can disrupt your appetite or create cycles of emotional eating and deprivation. Instead, it is important to eat balanced meals consisting of lean proteins, whole grains, fruits, and vegetables, as well as to stay hydrated, in order to regulate your blood sugar and support the neurotransmitters tied to mood and focus. Nutrition fuels the brain and stabilizes the emotional, somatic, and interoceptive domains. Regular nourishment signals that safety and care are present, calming survival responses and supporting sustained energy.

*Examples:*

- **Aim for three steady meals a day,** even if they're simple, such as eggs and fruit for breakfast, a sandwich and veggies for lunch, and a protein with rice and greens for dinner, to keep blood sugar stable.
- **Build a balanced plate** by including a lean protein (chicken, beans, tofu), a whole grain (brown rice, quinoa), and at least one fruit or vegetable at each meal.
- **Stock easy grab-and-go foods** (yogurt cups, cut fruit, nuts, whole-grain wraps) so you can nourish yourself even on stressful days.
- **Use hydration cues,** such as carrying a water bottle or setting reminders, to ensure you're drinking regularly throughout the day.
- **Notice trauma-related eating patterns,** such as skipping meals when stressed or eating past fullness to numb emotions, and gently redirect toward regular, balanced nourishment.

Note: Seek the support of a dietitian, nutritionist, and/or therapist if your eating patterns are significantly disordered.

## Avoid Drugs and Alcohol

Substance use may temporarily numb pain, but it disrupts all five systems over time. It dysregulates the nervous system, clouds the cognitive domain, fragments memory, and strains relationships. Choosing sobriety (or at least moderation) restores clarity, stability, and trust in your ability to cope. This act of care reengages the Developmental Integration System by allowing continued emotional growth and self-leadership.

*Examples:*

- **Replace end-of-day drinking or substance use with a grounding routine,** such as a warm shower, a short walk, or stretching, to give your nervous system a healthier way to decompress.
- **Identify the emotions or trauma reminders that prompt urges to use,** and practice skills like Mindfulness of Current Emotion or Self-Soothe instead of reaching for substances.
- **Ask a trusted person for support,** such as checking in when cravings arise or making shared plans that reduce isolation during high-risk times.
- **Create substance-free zones,** like keeping alcohol out of the house or avoiding certain environments until regulation skills feel stronger.
- **Use urges as information,** noticing what your body or mind is trying to escape, and choose a skillful response such as Paced Breathing (TIPP), Opposite Action, or calling a support person.

Note: Consider a substance use evaluation and/or treatment if you are not able to successfully reduce or eliminate substances on your own.

## Sleep Enough (But Not Too Much)

Sleep directly impacts the Consciousness and Memory System and the nervous system domain. Too little rest heightens reactivity, while too much can reinforce avoidance behaviors. As a general rule, aim to get between seven and ten hours of sleep per night. Simple habits like having a consistent bedtime, limiting screens, and creating a calming wind down routine signal to your body and mind that it is safe to rest. Rested brains integrate memories more effectively and sustain balanced moods. See the *Trauma-Informed Sleep Hygiene Plan* later in this module for more specific information.

*Examples:*

- **Set a consistent sleep schedule,** going to bed and waking up at roughly the same time each day to steady your circadian rhythm.

- **Create a calming presleep routine,** such as dimming lights, drinking herbal tea, engaging in light stretching, or reading something soothing.
- **Limit screens thirty to sixty minutes before bed** since blue light and stimulating content can increase arousal and delay sleep.
- **Use grounding skills at night,** like Paced Breathing (TIPP) or placing a hand on your chest, to help settle your nervous system when trauma-related thoughts or sensations arise.
- **Avoid oversleeping by scheduling a morning anchor,** such as a walk, a call with a friend, or a planned breakfast, to reduce trauma-driven withdrawal or shutdown.

## Exercise Regularly

Movement discharges stored stress energy and strengthens regulation within the Body-Based System. Aim to engage in twenty to sixty minutes of physical activity a few days per week. This can include walking, dancing, yoga, swimming, or stretching, all of which stimulate endorphins, stabilize mood, and rebuild your body's capacity for safety and vitality. Exercise also engages the Body-Based System, reminding you that your body can be a source of strength, agency, and grounding.

*Examples:*

- **Start with short, low-pressure movement,** such as a ten-minute walk around the block, to gently activate your nervous system without triggering overwhelm.
- **Use mindful movement,** like yoga or tai chi, to pair physical activity with breath awareness and grounding.
- **Incorporate enjoyable activities,** such as dancing to a favorite song or swimming, so movement feels like a source of pleasure rather than a chore.
- **Reduce shutdown states by using brief movement bursts,** such as marching in place, stretching your arms overhead, or shaking out tension, to counter freeze or collapse reactions.
- **Build consistency with small routines,** like a morning stretch sequence or an evening bike ride, reinforcing that your body can move, regulate, and come back into balance.

## Daily Habits

Consistency is what transforms effort into healing. Make these PLEASED skills a daily habit to support integration across all five systems. Engaging in regular, small actions cues your memory and behavioral domains to consolidate new, healthy patterns. Over time, these habits rebuild the developmental domain, nurturing the adult capacities that trauma may have interrupted.

## Trauma-Informed Sleep Hygiene Plan

Sleep is a powerful way to support recovery from trauma. Healthy sleep restores the Body-Based System by calming the nervous system, strengthens memory integration in the Consciousness and Memory System, and improves emotional balance within the Mind and Meaning System. Conversely, when sleep is disrupted, trauma symptoms such as hyperarousal, irritability, and dissociation can intensify.

The following strategies are designed to help you create predictable, soothing rhythms that promote safety, rest, and regulation for the benefit of all systems:

- **Keep a consistent sleep schedule.** Go to bed and wake up at the same time each day, even on weekends. Regularity strengthens your body's circadian rhythm to establish a reliable pattern of activation and rest for the nervous system domain. Predictability teaches your body and mind that it's safe to let go and recharge.
- **Create a safe and calming sleep environment.** Your sleep space should cue safety and relaxation. Keep the room cool, dark, and uncluttered (or in a manner that feels safe and calm to you, such as using calming sounds or soft lighting if needed). A peaceful environment communicates safety to the Body-Based System, allowing your body to exit fight, flight, freeze, or collapse mode before rest.
- **Prioritize comfort.** Choose pillows, blankets, and bedding that feel soothing to the touch. The somatic domain responds strongly to tactile comfort, like soft textures and warmth, that signal the body to settle. Over time, your bed becomes associated with safety and rest rather than tension or alertness.
- **Build a presleep ritual.** Create a calming routine that prepares both the Consciousness and Memory System and the nervous system for rest. Reading, journaling, stretching, or breathing practices can help slow thought loops and release daily tension. Doing the same steps each night builds a predictable rhythm that communicates safety and stability. A calming sleep routine can also decrease the frequency and intensity of nightmares.
- **Limit naps.** Short naps can be restorative, but too much daytime sleep confuses the nervous system's sleep-wake cycle. If you nap, keep it under thirty minutes and avoid late-day rest to preserve nighttime depth and continuity of sleep.
- **Avoid stimulants.** Reduce caffeine, nicotine, and energy drinks, especially in the afternoon or evening. These activate the Body-Based System, making it difficult to transition into rest. Replace stimulating habits with calming ones like herbal tea, stretching, or mindful breathing.
- **Be mindful with food and drink.** The interoceptive domain, which drives your awareness of internal sensations, affects sleep more than many people realize. Heavy or spicy foods can disrupt digestion, while hunger can trigger alertness. Choose light, balanced snacks before bed

and avoid alcohol, which fragments sleep and interferes with emotional processing during REM (dream) cycles.

- **Avoid stressful activities before bed.** Conflict, intense work, or stimulating media before sleep can activate you and leave the body on high alert. Protect this time as a transition from effort to rest. Choose gentle, grounding activities that bring calm before rest.
- **Get daytime physical activity.** Movement during the day helps regulate the somatic domain, releasing stored stress energy and improving sleep quality. Exercise promotes the release of endorphins, balances mood, and supports natural fatigue by evening. Even a short walk or stretch helps the body prepare for deeper rest.
- **Stay mentally engaged during the day.** Mental stimulation through learning, problem-solving, or creativity engages the cognitive domain and can prevent nighttime restlessness. When your mind feels productive and purposeful during the day, it's less likely to spin with intrusive thoughts at night.
- **Manage stress daily.** Integrating calming activities throughout the day, such as deep breathing, grounding, yoga, or meditation, keeps the nervous system regulated and the emotional domain balanced. Regular stress relief ensures that by evening, your body is not carrying an overload of activation into bedtime.
- **Use light intentionally.** Light exposure supports the Body-Based System, especially the interoceptive and nervous system domains, by reinforcing the body's natural circadian rhythms. Morning sunlight helps awaken your internal clock and increase alertness. As evening approaches, dimming lights and reducing screen brightness signals to your body that it is time to rest. These cues regulate energy, mood, and sleep-wake cycles, strengthening the body's ability to stay balanced.
- **Limit screen time before bed.** Blue light from screens interferes with melatonin production and delays sleep onset. Turn off devices thirty to sixty minutes before bed or use night mode if necessary. Giving your Consciousness and Memory System time to unwind allows you to integrate the day's experiences and prepares you for restorative sleep.
- **Medication and medical support.** If sleep remains disrupted, consult your medical provider. Some medications and trauma-related conditions affect the nervous system and memory domains, leading to nightmares or insomnia. A medication review may be needed to restore sleep patterns.

Consider how you will improve your sleep hygiene and track how your sleep habits affect your well-being. Remember that improving sleep supports regulation, restores balance, and rebuilds resilience, strengthening your capacity for healing.

## Build Mastery: Reclaiming Control Through Action

Trauma often leaves people feeling powerless, defeated, or disconnected from who they were or could be. Over time, these experiences can create patterns of avoidance, self-doubt, and shame. The Mind and Meaning System loses confidence and clarity, the Body-Based System stays tense or shutdown, and the Action and Connection System struggles to begin or sustain activity.

Mastery restores balance by gently reactivating these systems through intentional, achievable steps. Where:

- Trauma teaches helplessness, mastery teaches effectiveness.
- Trauma erodes confidence, mastery rebuilds it one success at a time.
- Trauma fragments purpose, mastery reconnects effort with accomplishment.

Each time you do something difficult and succeed—even something as simple as getting out of bed, completing a task, or making a meal—your body, brain, and mind receive an important message: "I can do this. I am capable. I am healing."

These actions do not need to be dramatic. Small, consistent wins are often the most effective, especially when trauma has disrupted motivation, focus, or daily functioning. In addition, what feels small to you may feel monumental to another. Choose activities that stretch you gently yet remain achievable. Here are examples of Build Mastery:

- **Maintain a daily routine.** Get out of bed, shower, make your bed, or cook a meal. Trauma often interrupts the behavioral domain, leading to disorganization or avoidance. Pair with Opposite Action to initiate routines.
- **Participate in therapy.** Attend therapy sessions, complete a skills worksheet, or talk about something hard. Engaging in therapy rebuilds trust and strengthens the relational domain, creating new corrective experiences of safety and support.
- **Learn something new.** Try a new hobby, craft, or skill such as painting, playing an instrument, or gardening. Learning activates the Mind and Meaning System and reinforces the Developmental Integration System so you can reclaim curiosity and confidence in your capacity to grow.
- **Join a group or volunteer.** Connect with others through a group, club, or act of service. This reengages the Action and Connection System, counteracting isolation and restoring belonging in the relational domain.
- **Exercise or move your body.** Engage in movement that feels right for your energy and ability. Physical movement regulates the Body-Based System by releasing stored tension in the somatic domain, and it allows you to reclaim your body as a source of strength rather than threat.

- **Set and complete a goal.** Choose a SMART goal that is specific, measurable, attainable, relevant, and time-based—then follow through. Setting and achieving goals strengthens and rebuilds motivation pathways in the Action and Connection System.
- **Practice mindfulness.** Spend even two to five minutes Observing your breath sensations or your surroundings. Mindfulness strengthens the Consciousness and Memory System by keeping you anchored in the present and less vulnerable to intrusions.
- **Seek feedback.** Ask for supportive feedback from someone you trust and use it to grow. This challenges avoidance in the relational domain and builds tolerance for vulnerability, expanding your ability to connect safely with others.

Worksheet

# Build Mastery

Each time you do something that feels meaningful, challenging, or skillful, you strengthen your confidence and capabilities. Small wins matter, as each one rewires your brain for safety and self-trust. Track your Build Mastery with the following steps.

1. What is your mastery goal for today (or this week)?

   ______________________________

   ______________________________

2. Why did you choose this activity (how does it connect to your healing, values, or goals)?

   ______________________________

   ______________________________

3. Before starting the activity . . .

   How do you feel?

   - ❐ Calm
   - ❐ Anxious
   - ❐ Sad
   - ❐ Tired
   - ❐ Numb
   - ❐ Hopeful
   - ❐ Other: ______________

   Emotion intensity (0–10): ________

   What's happening in your body (e.g., tightness, energy, numbness, warmth)?

   ______________________________

   ______________________________

4. After completing the activity . . .

   How do you feel?

   - ❐ Proud
   - ❐ Relieved
   - ❐ Grounded
   - ❐ Encouraged
   - ❐ Still struggling
   - ❐ Other: ______________

   Emotion intensity (0–10): ________

What do you notice in your body (e.g., steadier breathing, relaxed shoulders, warmth in your chest, loosened jaw, less tension in your stomach)?

______________________________________________

______________________________________________

5. What did this activity teach you about what you can do?

______________________________________________

______________________________________________

Which parts of you felt stronger or more regulated?

- ❒ Your emotions or thoughts (Mind and Meaning)
- ❒ Your body (Body-Based)
- ❒ Your awareness and presence (Consciousness and Memory)
- ❒ Your behaviors or relationships (Action and Connection)
- ❒ Your confidence in yourself (Developmental Integration)

Remember, Building Mastery isn't about doing everything perfectly; it's about proving to yourself, one small step at a time, that healing and confidence can grow through action.

## Build Positive Experiences: Reclaiming Joy, Connection, and Hope After Trauma

Trauma robs people of joy, safety, and connection, often replacing them with fear, vigilance, and isolation. Over time, these patterns condition the mind and body to expect pain instead of pleasure. The skill Build Positive Experiences retrains your mind and body by creating intentional moments of happiness and connection that are truly profound, especially in the Body-Based System. These profound effects include:

- **Activation of calm and connection:** Joyful moments awaken the parasympathetic nervous system, especially the ventral vagal pathways that steady the heartbeat, deepen the breath, and relax tension. Your body begins to remember what calm connection feels like: open, grounded, and at ease.
- **Expanded window of tolerance:** Enjoyable experiences stretch your capacity to feel a wider range of sensations and emotions without becoming overwhelmed. They strengthen your nervous system's ability to move fluidly between energy and rest to adapt to life rather than react to it.
- **Creation of new body memories:** When trauma teaches your body to expect danger, happiness teaches it to expect possibility. Pleasant moments leave behind sensory "footprints" of ease that include muscles softening, warmth spreading, and laughter rising, all of which slowly replace old patterns of tension and threat.
- **Improved awareness of internal cues:** Positive emotions invite gentle curiosity toward sensations like warmth, lightness, or expansion. By noticing and naming these experiences, you improve interoceptive awareness so that excitement and safety no longer feel confusing or alarming.
- **Integrated mind and body:** When the body feels good, the mind can think clearly. Positive experiences create synchrony between the brain regions that regulate emotion, attention, and body awareness, restoring the inner communication that trauma disrupts.
- **Release of chemistry of connection:** Joy, affection, and shared laughter boost oxytocin and endorphins, the body's natural bonding and pleasure chemicals. These moments remind your system that connection and vitality are not threats: They are signs of health, resilience, and life returning to balance.

In short, Build Positive Experiences has incredible benefits that span all the systems and domains.

## Types of Positive Experiences

There are several different types of positive experiences, including those you can have now or in the immediate future, those you can plan for in the short term, and those you can plan for in the long term.

**Immediate positive experiences:** These are small, in-the-moment choices that bring enjoyment. They anchor you in the present, which can reduce flashbacks, anxiety, and dissociation.

*Examples:*

- **Pleasant sensations:** Mindfully savor a snack, notice and feel the sunlight, or enjoy your pet's warmth, love, and companionship.
- **Spontaneous connection:** Smile or share a kind word with someone nearby.
- **Nature:** Watch clouds move, listen to birds, or feel the ground beneath your feet.

**Short-term positive experiences:** These are activities you intentionally schedule for the near future. The act of planning creates structure in the Action and Connection System and activates motivation, specifically within the behavioral domain, countering hopelessness and avoidance. To create these experiences, think of interests, hobbies, and activities you enjoy or used to enjoy. Then plan them into your schedule and follow through with them.

*Examples:*

- **Scheduled support:** Plan a visit or call with someone you trust.
- **Creative projects:** Paint, cook, garden, or write for enjoyment and expression.
- **Movement and exercise:** Engage in gentle or energizing activity that allows your body to release stress.

**Long-term positive experiences:** These are meaningful activities that connect to your values and long-term goals. They engage the Developmental Integration System by building purpose, identity, and direction that go beyond symptom relief by creating a life you can truly enjoy. To create these experiences, make a list of your long-term goals and break them down into manageable steps. Make a plan to do the first step and then keep moving forward, one step at a time.

*Examples:*

- **Educational pursuits:** Take a class, read about a passion, or explore a new field.
- **Skill building:** Learn an instrument, trade, or language.
- **Spiritual or reflective exploration:** Reconnect with beliefs, rituals, or practices that foster meaning and peace.

Worksheet

## Overcoming Barriers to Build Positive Experiences

Trauma often distorts how we interpret positive experiences, creating beliefs like:

- "I don't deserve this."
- "It won't last."
- "It's not safe to feel good."

These are trauma-conditioned responses, not facts. They reflect dysregulation in the meaning and belief domain, where your past experiences shape how you interpret what is happening now. These distorted beliefs are reinforced by the emotional and nervous system domains, which make positive experiences feel unreliable, unearned, or even threatening, even though that doesn't reflect your current reality.

To challenge these barriers:

- **Use Opposite Action:** Engage in something pleasant even when joy feels undeserved. This helps retrain the behavioral domain toward reward.
- **Practice Mindfulness:** Stay present with positive sensations without clinging to them or fearing loss, strengthening the Consciousness and Memory System.
- **Remind Yourself:** You do not need to earn joy; you only need to allow it. Every moment of genuine pleasure is an act of repair and reclamation.

What small, positive experiences help you feel safe, connected, or alive?

______________________________________________

______________________________________________

Which systems or domains do you notice are most affected by positive experiences?

______________________________________________

______________________________________________

How can you intentionally include one positive experience each day this week?

______________________________________________

______________________________________________

Worksheet

## Build Positive Experiences

Positive experiences balance the effects of trauma by introducing moments of safety, pleasure, and connection. Even small enjoyable moments teach your brain and body that it's possible to feel good again. Over time, these experiences strengthen the systems that support hope, motivation, and regulation.

1. What is one activity you can plan or schedule this week that might bring joy, comfort, or peace?

   ______________________________________________

   ______________________________________________

   When will you do it?

   ______________________________________________

   ______________________________________________

   Who might you include (if anyone)?

   ______________________________________________

   ______________________________________________

2. Why did you choose this experience (how does it connect to what matters to you or what you want more of in life)?

   ______________________________________________

   ______________________________________________

3. Before starting the experience . . .

   How do you feel?

   - ❒ Calm
   - ❒ Anxious
   - ❒ Sad
   - ❒ Tired
   - ❒ Numb
   - ❒ Hopeful
   - ❒ Other: ____________________

   Emotion intensity (0–10): _________

   What's happening in your body (e.g., tension, energy, numbness, warmth)?

   ______________________________________________

   ______________________________________________

4. After the experience . . .

   How do you feel?

   - ❐ Peaceful
   - ❐ Energized
   - ❐ Connected
   - ❐ Grateful
   - ❐ Neutral
   - ❐ Other: ____________________

   Emotion intensity (0–10): ________

   What do you notice in your body (e.g., lighter breathing, a sense of warmth in your chest, loosened muscles, soft eyes, a calm or steady heartbeat)?

   ______________________________________________

   ______________________________________________

5. What did this positive experience teach you or remind you of?

   ______________________________________________

   ______________________________________________

   Which parts of you felt engaged or supported?

   - ❐ Your emotions or thoughts (Mind and Meaning)
   - ❐ Your body (Body-Based)
   - ❐ Your awareness and presence (Consciousness and Memory)
   - ❐ Your behaviors or relationships (Action and Connection)
   - ❐ Your confidence in yourself (Developmental Integration)

Positive experiences don't erase pain, yet they create new patterns of safety and connection that make happiness possible. Every enjoyable moment, no matter how small, rewires your systems in profound ways.

 

# Build Positive Experiences: Attend to Relationships

Trauma often damages trust, safety, and connection, leaving people feeling guarded, alone, or afraid to depend on others. Yet rebuilding safe, reliable connections is one of the most powerful ways to heal across systems. For example, the Action and Connection System learns new ways to approach, communicate, and maintain closeness; the Mind and Meaning System redefines what trust and safety mean; and the Body-Based System experiences co-regulation through shared calm and compassion.

This worksheet will help you strengthen your relationships with intention, safety, and skill.

## Current Positive People

Who in your life right now brings a sense of comfort, care, encouragement, and enjoyment? These might be friends, family, peers, or others who are emotionally safe. Recognizing these supports activates the relational domain, reminding you that connection already exists.

These people currently support me in my life:

______________________________________________

______________________________________________

## Past Positive People

Are there people from your past who once offered safety, support, and enjoyment and whom you might want to reconnect with? Focus only on relationships that were healthy, nurturing, or hopeful. Reconnection reawakens the developmental domain by reintroducing safe attachment experiences into the present.

These are people from my past I may want to reconnect with:

______________________________________________

______________________________________________

 

## Nurturing and Repairing Relationships

For each person you listed, consider what you can do to care for the relationship, including gently repairing it if needed. Healing in relationships often restores balance within the Action and Connection System by turning intention into action. You might:

- Reach out with a message or call
- Plan regular check-ins
- Express appreciation or gratitude
- Offer an apology or make amends
- Set new, healthier boundaries

My steps to nurture or repair important relationships:

______________________________________________

______________________________________________

## Reconnect with One Person from Your Past

Choose one person you'd like to reconnect with. Consider what you could say and what steps you could take to rebuild trust if needed. Practicing relational courage in this way strengthens the behavioral domain and reconditions the nervous system to tolerate closeness safely.

Name of person: ______________________________________________

My plan to reach out and reconnect:

______________________________________________

______________________________________________

How I'll maintain and nurture this relationship:

______________________________________________

______________________________________________

 

## Building New Relationships

If your current circle is small, that's okay. Trauma often narrows the relational domain by teaching you to withdraw from or mistrust others. Gradually expanding your network builds new patterns of safety and belonging across the Action and Connection System and the Developmental Integration System.

Here are some places or programs where I will look for new relationships:

- ❒ Therapy or support groups (e.g., local recovery meeting, skills group)
- ❒ Faith or spiritual communities (e.g., church, meditation groups)
- ❒ Classes or educational spaces (e.g., art workshops, fitness classes)
- ❒ Community centers or local events (e.g., recreational clubs, street festivals)
- ❒ Online spaces for recovery or shared interests (e.g., mental health forums)
- ❒ My neighborhood or workplace (e.g., neighborhood meetups, social committees)
- ❒ Other: ______________________________

## Skills for Building Relationships

Building relationships requires awareness (of your own feelings, needs, and reactions, as well as those of others), setting healthy boundaries, and communicating skillfully. Consider practicing these skills:

- **Interpersonal effectiveness skills** (DEAR MAN, GIVE, FAST) to express your wants and needs clearly, care for the relationship, and maintain self-respect.
- **Mindfulness skills** to stay present, notice cues of safety, and listen with full attention.
- **Emotion regulation and distress tolerance skills** to manage fear, shame, or anger, or other intense experiences that can surface during connection.

The skills I'll use and how I'll apply them:

______________________________________________________________________________

______________________________________________________________________________

Remember that you don't need to be fully healed to connect because healing *happens* in connection. Every effort to attend to relationships, no matter how small, supports regulation across systems and domains and moves you closer to trust, belonging, and recovery.

## SKILL Opposite Action: Action That Restores Safety and Control

When intense emotions such as fear, sadness, anger, guilt, or shame arise, a traumatized nervous system often reacts as if danger is still present. You may respond by freezing, hiding, fighting, or shutting down, which are reactions that may once have been lifesaving but now keep trauma-related suffering alive long after the threat has ended.

Opposite Action[20] guides you to interrupt these instinctive patterns by choosing behaviors that are *opposite* to what trauma's survival rules tell you to do. For example, instead of isolating and numbing with alcohol when sadness arises, you might journal or reach out to a loved one. Rather than allowing your emotions to dictate your behavior, you act with awareness and intention to restore safety, regulation, and choice. Through this practice, Opposite Action gently retrains your nervous system to act from safety and intention instead of threat. Where:

- Trauma wires the body for defense, Opposite Action teaches regulation.
- Trauma limits meaning and hope, Opposite Action restores purpose and choice.
- Trauma isolates, Opposite Action rebuilds trust, connection, and belonging.

Opposite Action is not about denying or pretending away emotion. It is about using action to reshape what trauma once controlled. Each time you take a healing step such as approaching instead of avoiding, softening instead of attacking, or reaching out instead of withdrawing, you reclaim power from fear and shame.

Over time, the body learns what the mind begins to understand: Safety is possible, change is possible, and you are capable of choosing differently. You do not need to wait to feel ready before you act; acting differently is what begins to create readiness. Healing starts in the moment you move toward what trauma once taught you to fear.

---

20 Opposite Action was originally and is perhaps more commonly referred to as Opposite-to-Emotion Action. While these names refer to the same skill, Opposite Action more accurately describes the mechanism of this skill—namely, that one is acting opposite to certain behaviors connected to emotions rather than to emotions themselves.

# Using Opposite Action by Emotion

| Emotion/ State | Typical Pattern | Opposite Action | Examples | Outcome |
|---|---|---|---|---|
| **Anxiety or fear** | Avoidance of feared people, places, or sensations. | Approach gradually and safely to teach the body that fear can subside without danger. | • Visit a low-stress environment before tackling larger fears.<br>• Talk about the fear in therapy rather than avoiding the topic.<br>• Return to a once-feared space for short, planned intervals. | These Opposite Actions eventually calm the nervous system domain, integrate safety learning in the memory domain, and strengthen confidence in the behavioral domain. |
| **Sadness or depression** | Isolation, inactivity, loss of interest. | Move toward gentle activity and social contact even when motivation is low. | • Get dressed, open curtains, or prepare a meal.<br>• Reach out to a supportive person.<br>• Reconnect with a hobby for ten minutes. | These Opposite Actions activate the Body-Based and Mind and Meaning Systems, translating energy into forward movement and reengaging pleasure pathways. |
| **Anger** | Aggression, argument, or self-directed hostility. | Pause, ground, and respond thoughtfully. | • Take slow breaths before speaking.<br>• Journal or engage in physical movement to discharge energy.<br>• Choose assertive but calm communication. | These Opposite Actions regulate arousal in the nervous system, clarify thought in the cognitive and meaning and belief domains, and model effective behavior in the Action and Connection System. |
| **Guilt** | Withdrawal, overapologizing, or self-punishment. | Repair when guilt is justified; stay engaged and practice self-care when it's not. | • Make amends when appropriate.<br>• Continue self-care even when guilt says you don't deserve it.<br>• Set boundaries without apology. | These Opposite Actions build integrity and balanced accountability within the meaning and belief domain, while also fostering self-respect and repair in the relational domain. |
| **Shame** | Hiding, secrecy, silence, or self-hate. | Move toward safe connection and visibility. | • Share your experience with a therapist or trusted person.<br>• Name shame out loud to reduce its power.<br>• Practice self-compassion through affirming language. | These Opposite Actions restore belonging within the relational domain and repair distorted beliefs about the self within the Mind and Meaning System. |
| **Low motivation or apathy** | Hopelessness, procrastination, or giving up. | Take any small, manageable step toward engagement. | • Walk for five minutes.<br>• Clean one small area.<br>• Begin, rather than finish, a task. | These Opposite Actions stimulate both the Action and Connection and the Developmental Integration Systems, rebuilding your ability to take initiative, follow through, and feel hope. |

Opposite Action works because emotion and behavior continuously influence each other. After trauma, this loop often gets stuck in survival mode: Fear leads to avoidance, and avoidance reinforces fear. Choosing an action that is opposite to your emotion interrupts that cycle and activates new neural pathways. As intentional behavior replaces automatic reactions, the prefrontal cortex strengthens its role in calming the limbic system, helping the brain's emotion regulation networks come back into balance. With repetition, these small, deliberate choices expand your capacity to experience positive emotion, connection, and calm.

## Bottom-Up Opposite Action: Using the Body to Shift Emotion and Restore Safety

Trauma does not live only in thoughts or interpretations. It also lives in the body. Long after danger has passed, your nervous system may brace, collapse, flinch, tighten, or shut down in ways that feel automatic and out of your control. These responses once protected you, yet now they can keep you stuck in survival mode even when you are safe.

Traditional Opposite Action works through the mind: You identify the emotion, check whether the behavior it's pulling you into is effective, and then choose a behavior opposite to the emotion's action urge if a more effective action is needed. By contrast, bottom-up Opposite Action starts in the body through the Body-Based System. In both approaches, the healing happens through behavior. However, one begins with the mind guiding the body, and the other begins with the body guiding the mind.

Bottom-up Opposite Action teaches you to interrupt bodily survival patterns by changing your posture, breath, movement, and facial expression in ways that signal safety to the nervous system, making it possible to then choose an intentional action. Instead of collapsing when shame arises, you might lift your posture and soften your expression. Instead of bracing or tensing when fear shows up, you might slow your breathing and open your hands. Instead of withdrawing into numbness, you might stretch, walk, or gently reengage with your environment. Even small physiological shifts can interrupt threat responses and restore your ability to think clearly, stay present, and choose your next step. In short, where:

- Trauma tightens and protects; bottom-up Opposite Action opens and releases.
- Trauma shuts down or collapses; bottom-up Opposite Action reintroduces movement and vitality.
- Trauma disconnects you from your body; bottom-up Opposite Action rebuilds grounding and internal safety.

The chart that follows shows bottom-up Opposite Actions categorized by emotion. Some examples appear more than once; that's because many body-based practices regulate multiple emotions through overlapping pathways in the nervous system. Definitions of the practices can be found in the appendix.

And remember, this approach is not about forcing yourself to feel differently. It is about helping your body send new signals that support calm rather than fear, openness rather than collapse, and engagement rather than withdrawal. These body-first shifts gently retrain your nervous system, making regulation more possible even before your mind has caught up. One last tip: Practice each of these interventions when you are regulated to get a "feel" for them, which will greatly increase their effectiveness.

| Emotion/ State | Typical Pattern | Bottom-Up Opposite Action | Examples/Practices | Outcome |
|---|---|---|---|---|
| **Anxiety or fear** | Bracing, shrinking, scanning for threat, or preparing to flee. | Use posture and breath to cue safety and interrupt threat responses. | • Safe Posture Practice<br>• Slow, deep exhale breathing<br>• Grounded stance<br>• Gentle orienting<br>• Relaxed jaw and tongue release<br>• Eye gaze softening or widening<br>• Grounding touch<br>• Steady, balanced walking<br>• Cooling-based reset<br>• Power-down movement | These shifts calm the nervous system domain, settle hyperarousal, and let the body relearn that it is safe enough to remain present. |
| **Sadness or depression** | Stillness, withdrawal, curling inward, loss of energy. | Bring gentle activation and openness into the body. | • Full-body stretch<br>• Safe Posture Practice<br>• Rhythmic walking or movement<br>• Warmth-based soothing<br>• Gentle movement<br>• Grounding touch<br>• Eye gaze softening<br>• Half-Smile<br>• Expansion instead of contraction<br>• Stepping outdoors | These actions reintroduce energy and allow the body to shift from shutdown to engagement. |
| **Anger** | Clenching, tightening, glaring, pacing, or preparing to fight. | Release tension and slow the body's activation. | • Willing Hands<br>• Relaxed jaw and tongue release<br>• Half-Smile<br>• Gentle movement (or stillness)<br>• Cooling-based reset<br>• Gentle orienting<br>• Eye gaze softening<br>• Voice modulation<br>• Nervous system reset<br>• Power-down movement | These practices coax the body into exiting fight mode so communication and clarity become possible. |
| **Guilt** | Shrinking inward, collapsing posture, tension, heaviness. | Use grounding and openness to counter self-punishment and withdrawal. | • Safe Posture Practice<br>• Warmth-based soothing<br>• Grounding touch (heart or stomach)<br>• Slow, deep exhale breathing<br>• Eye gaze softening<br>• Gentle orienting<br>• Rhythmic walking<br>• Half-Smile<br>• Willing Hands<br>• Full-body stretch | These shifts support access to self-compassion and balanced accountability rather than self-punishment. |

| Emotion/ State | Typical Pattern | Bottom-Up Opposite Action | Examples/Practices | Outcome |
|---|---|---|---|---|
| **Shame** | Hiding, secrecy, collapsing inward, making the body small. | Expand, open, and lift the body to counter collapse. | • Safe Posture Practice<br>• Half-Smile<br>• Willing Hands<br>• Full-body stretch<br>• Expansion instead of contraction<br>• Eye gaze softening<br>• Warmth-based soothing<br>• Gentle orienting<br>• Slow, deep exhale breathing (expanding chest)<br>• Steady, balanced walking (out of hiding) | These practices restore a sense of belonging and counter shame-driven body patterns. |
| **Low motivation or apathy** | Hopelessness, slowed movement, immobility, giving up. | Introduce small movements and sensory engagement to activate the system. | • Steady, balanced walking (for 3–5 minutes)<br>• Full-body stretch<br>• Gentle bilateral movement<br>• Rhythmic rocking or swaying<br>• Stepping outdoors<br>• Temperature shift<br>• Grounded stance<br>• Power-down movement (if agitation appears)<br>• Safe Posture Practice<br>• Sensory grounding | These practices encourage forward motion and rebuild the capacity to initiate action. |
| **Helplessness or collapse** | Immobility, shutting down, losing energy, dissociating. | Reintroduce small, safe movements and orienting cues. | • Grounded stance<br>• Nervous system reset<br>• Rhythmic rocking or movement<br>• Slow, deep exhale breathing<br>• Stepping outdoors<br>• Full-body stretch<br>• Gentle bilateral movement<br>• Slow, deliberate walking<br>• Warmth-based soothing | These practices gently reverse shutdown states and rebuild access to presence and agency. |
| **Numbness or dissociation** | Disconnection from the body, fogginess, spacing out, feeling unreal. | Activate sensory and motor systems to return to the moment. | • Sensory grounding<br>• Temperature shift<br>• Steady, balanced walking<br>• Gentle movement<br>• Bilateral tapping<br>• Rhythmic rocking or swaying<br>• Gentle orienting<br>• Safe Posture Practice<br>• Power-down movement (if agitation breaks through numbness) | These actions reconnect awareness to the body and stabilize attention in the present moment. |

With practice, bottom-up Opposite Action allows you to reclaim regulation at the level where trauma took hold. When survival responses flood the body faster than the mind can respond, bottom-up practices give you a direct way to influence your emotional state by shifting your physiology first. These skills reconnect you with your body as a source of information, stability, and agency. With repetition, your nervous system begins to expect safety rather than danger, presence rather than collapse, and choice rather than automatic survival responses. Each small shift in posture, breath, or movement is a signal to the brain that life is different now, which creates healing from the inside out.

Worksheet

# Opposite Action

Emotions are powerful forces that sometimes lead us to take actions that keep trauma responses going, like avoiding, isolating, or shutting down. With Opposite Action, you can notice what your trauma urges you to do and choose a different response instead. Each time you practice this skill, you show your brain and body that you can act from safety, not fear.

## 1. Identify the emotion and urge

**Emotion you're noticing:**

- ❒ Anxiety/fear
- ❒ Sadness/depression
- ❒ Anger
- ❒ Guilt
- ❒ Shame
- ❒ Low motivation/apathy
- ❒ Other: ______________________

**What this emotion urges you to do:**

- ❒ Avoid people, places, or feelings (fear/anxiety)
- ❒ Withdraw, stay in bed, or isolate (sadness/depression)
- ❒ Lash out, argue, or turn pain inward (anger)
- ❒ Apologize excessively, hide, self-punish, or give up a behavior it's okay to do (guilt)
- ❒ Hide, stay silent, or disconnect (shame)
- ❒ Do nothing or give up (low motivation/apathy)
- ❒ Other: ______________________

## 2. Choose an Opposite Action

What could you do that's opposite to your emotion-driven urge and that moves you toward safety, connection, or growth? For example:

- Fear ⇨ Approach gradually instead of avoiding.
- Sadness ⇨ Get active or reach out for support.
- Anger ⇨ Breathe, step back, or respond calmly.
- Guilt ⇨ If the guilt is justified, take constructive action to make repairs. If the guilt is unjustified, continue doing the action (until it no longer elicits guilt) while coaching yourself that it's okay.

- Shame ⇨ Share with a trusted person or practice self-compassion.
- Low motivation ⇨ Do one small action, even if you don't feel like it.

______________________________________________

______________________________________________

## 3. Take the step

When and how will you practice this Opposite Action?

______________________________________________

______________________________________________

What might make it hard, and how can you prepare or get support?

______________________________________________

______________________________________________

## 4. Reflect after acting

How do you feel now?

- ❒ Calmer
- ❒ Proud
- ❒ Hopeful
- ❒ Connected
- ❒ Still uneasy
- ❒ Other: ____________________

What did you notice in your body or thoughts after taking the action?

______________________________________________

______________________________________________

What did you learn from doing this?

______________________________________________

______________________________________________

What's one small Opposite Action you could try tomorrow?

____________________________________________________________

____________________________________________________________

Remember, you don't need to wait until you feel ready, as acting differently *creates* the readiness. Each small opposite step tells your systems, "I am safe enough to try," which brings you closer to recovery.

 

## Emotion Regulation and Chronic Invalidation: Reclaiming the Right to Feel

For many trauma survivors, emotional invalidation is not just an echo of the past; it is part of the trauma itself. When your feelings were dismissed, punished, or ignored, your systems learned that emotion was unsafe. Over time, you may have learned to suppress, disconnect from, or overcontrol your emotions in order to feel acceptable, all while losing trust in your own emotional truth.

Whereas invalidation disrupts the natural flow of emotion across the systems and domains of regulation, emotion regulation skills begin the process of repair. They offer ways to notice, name, and work with emotions instead of fighting or fearing them. Through practice, these skills rebuild the belief that emotions are not the enemy: They are sources of information that guide you toward balance, connection, and healing.

Emotion regulation restores what invalidation fractured. It invites calm where there was tension, clarity where there was distortion, and wisdom where there was fear. Each moment of mindful awareness strengthens your capacity to experience emotions fully without being overwhelmed. You learn that emotions rise, peak, and pass and that you can meet each one with understanding and choice.

Emotion regulation becomes an act of truth telling. It honors your body's signals and reawakens the meaning that trauma once silenced. The Mind and Meaning System learns that feelings carry wisdom; the Body-Based System remembers that sensation is safe; the Consciousness and Memory System learns to stay present and integrate the past rather than being ruled by it; the Action and Connection System rediscovers that expression builds closeness, not rejection; and the Developmental Integration System grows toward maturity, self-compassion, and inner leadership.

Each time you allow emotions to move through your awareness rather than control you, you are teaching your system new patterns. Over time, you reclaim the essential freedom to feel what is true and to respond with balance, compassion, and integrity.

CHAPTER 13

# Interpersonal Effectiveness Module

## Relating Effectively to Yourself and Others

Interpersonal relationships can be one of the most sensitive and painful areas of life when you're recovering from trauma. While connection is essential for healing, trauma often disrupts how we relate to others and how we relate to ourselves in the context of others.

People with trauma histories may struggle with:

- Mistrust, hypervigilance, or shutting down around others
- People-pleasing (fawning) or submission to avoid conflict
- Emotional outbursts or withdrawal during interpersonal stress
- Difficulty asserting needs, setting boundaries, or tolerating rejection
- Feeling unsafe, unseen, or unworthy in relationships

These patterns are not flaws; they are adaptations to past harm. But over time, they can lead to loneliness, instability, and disconnection from your values.

The interpersonal effectiveness module allows you to begin the process of reclaiming your voice, agency, and authenticity in relationships. It teaches you communication strategies, yet it also reaches deeper into the parts of your systems affected by trauma that shape how you see others, protect yourself, and decide who you are in relationships. This module helps you rebuild emotion regulation skills, shift unhelpful behavioral patterns, clarify how you make meaning in relationships, and strengthen your sense of safety with others. It can even support repair of early attachment injuries. It is not just about "getting along" with others; it's about restoring dignity, connection, and confidence.

## Interpersonal Effectiveness Related to the Systems and Domains

Interpersonal effectiveness is not simply about getting your needs met. It is a process that has these effects across the five systems:

- The Mind and Meaning System learns to balance self-respect with compassion for others.
- The Body-Based System experiences safety in presence, allowing you to express your needs without shutting down or lashing out.
- The Consciousness and Memory System stays grounded in the present moment and learns to differentiate past relational trauma from present interaction.
- The Action and Connection System uses skills to set boundaries, negotiate needs, and maintain respect.
- The Developmental Integration System relearns trust, interdependence, and belonging.

The following examples illustrate how interpersonal effectiveness supports regulation and integration across the eleven domains.

| System | Dysregulation Type | Statements | Example |
|---|---|---|---|
| **I. Mind and Meaning** | Emotional | "I feel afraid to speak up, and I can express myself with calm."<br>"I feel angry in conflict, and I can use an Easy Manner (GIVE) when communicating." | Tanya feels hurt when her coworker dismisses her idea. She takes a breath, uses GIVE, and responds with respect and clarity. Emotion informs communication rather than hijacking it. |
| | Cognitive | "My thoughts are spinning, but using a DEAR MAN script clarifies what I want."<br>"I assume I'll be misunderstood, and I can clarify what I mean if needed." | Leo thinks his friend will ignore his request for help. He practices DEAR MAN, focusing on the facts and his needs to think and communicate clearly. |
| | Meaning and belief | "I believe I have to please others to be safe, yet I will prioritize and honor my own needs."<br>"I was taught to stay quiet, and now I find meaning in speaking up for myself and others." | Aria hesitates to set boundaries with her sister. She reminds herself that saying no can coexist with love. Each boundary reinforces new meaning around safety and self-worth. |

| System | Dysregulation Type | Statements | Example |
|---|---|---|---|
| II. Body-Based | Nervous system | "My pulse races when I feel criticized, so I use mindfulness to accept rather than fight it." "My body prepares for danger, and knowing this means I need to work bottom-up skills to feel comfortable in social situations." | Zoe feels her heart pounding when feedback comes. She pauses, touches her wrist, and silently says, "I'm safe now." The physical reassurance allows her to listen fully. |
| | Somatic | "My body tenses when I assert myself, so I soothe myself before a difficult discussion." "My chest tightens in conflict, and I can ground my feet and breathe deeply." | Omar feels a surge of adrenaline during a disagreement. He unclenches his fists and takes slow breaths. His calm body steadies the tone of the conversation. |
| | Interoceptive | "I can't tell whether I'm angry or anxious, and I can pause to figure it out before responding." "My body's cues are mixed. When I feel irritable, I make sure I'm not just 'hangry.'" | Julian senses agitation rising but isn't sure why. He takes a break, checks in with his body, and realizes he's hungry. A snack and a moment of reflection prevent escalation. |
| III. Consciousness and Memory | Dissociative | "I feel like I'm not here when my friend gets intense. I use DEAR MAN to set boundaries about this when I need to." "I start to drift away in conversations, so sometimes I take a break to reground in the present." | Nina feels spacey during a tense discussion with her partner. She looks around, names the colors she sees, and then refocuses on the here and now. Presence restores connection. |
| | Memory | "I remember past rejection, and I can recognize this is different." "My history of hurt with people arises, and I find the courage to engage despite those memories." | When a colleague raises their voice, Aiden flashes to childhood criticism. He breathes, names the memory silently, and reminds himself, "This is not then." He then uses FAST to be Fair to himself and make No Unnecessary Apologies for being triggered. |
| IV. Action and Connection | Behavioral | "I want to yell or shut down. Instead, I listen and Validate (GIVE) the other person. It's like magic!" "I feel the urge to withdraw, and I can stay engaged respectfully." | Sasha feels dismissed in group. She uses DEAR MAN to state her perspective calmly. The skillful assertiveness transforms conflict into collaboration. |
| | Relational | "I fear being abandoned, and I can build trust slowly." "I crave closeness and can still Validate (GIVE) others' boundaries." | Noah constantly wants reassurance from his partner. Using FAST, he Sticks to his Value of independence and chooses to tolerate uncertainty. |

| System | Dysregulation Type | Statements | Example |
|---|---|---|---|
| **V. Developmental Integration** | Developmental | "I grew up in chaos, so I practice interpersonal effectiveness to create stability in my relationships."<br>"My boundaries were violated growing up, but I use my FAST skills to insist on boundaries now." | Keira begins to identify safe and unsafe relationships through mindfulness and values. By choosing consistent, reciprocal connections, she rebuilds her template for belonging. |

Across all systems and domains, interpersonal effectiveness transforms dysregulation into connection. It teaches you that assertiveness and empathy can coexist and that relationships can be both safe and authentic. Integration begins in this balance, where you reclaim the power to relate without losing yourself.

## Special Considerations in Interpersonal Recovery

Interpersonal healing is both a psychological and physiological process. It's not only about how you speak or listen; it's about how your whole system responds to closeness, differences in opinions, and trust. Ultimately, it's about teaching your body, mind, and relationships to move together again.

Here are patterns that often emerge in trauma recovery as well as ways to restore regulation and authenticity in connection. Each of these strategies, whether calming the nervous system, reclaiming boundaries, or rebuilding trust, repairs a different thread of connection across the five systems and eleven domains. Over time, co-regulation replaces reactivity, authenticity replaces appeasement, and mutual respect replaces control or withdrawal. As your systems learn to respond to closeness with steadiness rather than fear, connection becomes not a threat to safety but its expression. Connection itself becomes the ground where integration takes root and where safety, truth, and belonging can coexist.

### 1. Co-Regulation and Nervous System Safety

Connection begins in biology before it becomes emotion or thought. When people interact, their nervous systems exchange subtle cues, such as tone, facial expression, rhythm, and posture, that signal either safety or threat. However, after trauma, the body may misread social cues. A raised eyebrow or firm tone can trigger alarm; a pause in conversation might feel like rejection. Relearning co-regulation starts with noticing these automatic responses and grounding in presence.

*Example:* During a group session, Maya feels her heart race when another member speaks sharply. She focuses on her breathing, softens her shoulders, and keeps her gaze open. As her body settles, she notices that the other person's tone was not anger, just passion. Her calm supports the group in settling too.

Practices such as breath awareness, gentle pacing of speech, safe eye contact, and mindful posture help the body rediscover that connection and safety can occur together. These actions stabilize the Body-Based System by calming the nervous system and refine the interoceptive domain by allowing inner sensations to register as information rather than alarm.

At the same time, they engage the Consciousness and Memory System, linking present experiences of calm connection with new emotional memories of safety. Over time, co-regulation becomes not only a biological process but a lived reminder that the body and relationships can work together to create steadiness, trust, and peace.

## 2. Recognizing and Releasing the Fawn Response

The fawn response develops when survival once depended on pleasing or appeasing others. It can appear as agreeing excessively, minimizing your needs, overapologizing, or trying to fix others' moods. While these patterns once prevented harm, they now prevent authenticity.

Healing begins with curiosity rather than shame. When you notice yourself nodding automatically or rushing to smooth tension, pause. Take a slow breath, and ask, "Am I agreeing because I mean it or because I am afraid not to?" A single mindful pause shifts your nervous system from automatic submission to conscious choice.

*Example:* Luis agrees to help a friend move even though he is exhausted. His therapist helps him rehearse saying, "I wish I could, but I need rest tonight." When he practices this, he feels anxiety rise and then pass. The friend responds kindly. Luis realizes boundaries do not always cause rejection.

Each act of authenticity weakens the grip of the fawn response, teaching your body and mind that connection does not require self-erasure. It strengthens the Action and Connection System, in particular the relational domain, by transforming compliance into genuine engagement, and it realigns the Mind and Meaning System with honesty, fairness, and self-respect.

As the Body-Based System releases its habit of scanning for others' approval, the Consciousness and Memory System records new experiences of safety in truthful self-expression. Over time, the nervous system learns that authenticity, not appeasement, is what sustains real connection, and effective relational responses align accordingly.

## 3. Recognizing and Releasing the Shutdown Response

The shutdown response develops when survival once depended on withdrawing, collapsing, or going still in the face of threat. Unlike the fawn response, which seeks safety through pleasing and maintaining connection, the shutdown response can appear as emotional numbing, going quiet under stress, freezing when confronted, or automatically giving in to avoid harm; in some forms this is referred to as "submit."

These reactions once protected you when resistance was impossible but can now keep you trapped in helplessness or self-doubt.

Healing begins with reawakening agency, not by pushing or forcing action but by bringing mindful awareness to the body's instinct to collapse. When you notice yourself going silent or shrinking inward, take a slow, steady breath and orient to the present, perhaps by feeling the ground beneath you, looking around, and reminding yourself, "I am safe now." Even small acts of presence begin to reconnect movement, voice, and will.

*Example:* During a conflict at work, Tasha feels her chest tighten and her mind go blank. Instead of withdrawing, she takes a breath, grounds her feet, and says, "I need a moment to think before I respond." The tension eases slightly, and she stays engaged in the discussion after a necessary pause. Later, she recognizes that pausing, rather than disappearing, helped her remain safe and connected.

Each act of mindful engagement loosens the hold of the shutdown response, teaching the nervous system that protection can come through awareness rather than collapse. It strengthens the Body-Based System by reintroducing gentle activation and restoring energy where shutdown once ruled. It also supports the Action and Connection System by helping you assert yourself and rebuild trust in your ability to act.

As the Consciousness and Memory System records new experiences of safety in standing your ground, the Mind and Meaning System begins to link strength with calm instead of fear. Over time, your body learns that stillness no longer has to mean submission and that safety can coexist with voice, choice, and vitality.

## 4. Power, Consent, and Choice

Trauma often involves experiences where choice was taken away. Reclaiming agency in relationships means distinguishing *assertiveness*, the balanced expression of needs, from control or submission. Assertiveness includes respect for both you and the other person. It emerges when you feel safe within yourself—not when you dominate the other person or simply comply with their requests.

Before difficult conversations, scan your body for cues: Are your shoulders tense? Is your voice sharp or quiet? Take a breath or a brief pause to settle before speaking. If you feel pressured, remember that consent includes the right to delay, decline, or renegotiate.

*Example:* During a heated family discussion, Amir senses his pulse quicken and an urge to shout. He places a hand on his chest, breathes, and says, "I want to keep talking, but I need a short break to calm down." This statement models respect for both parties and preserves safety.

Practicing conscious choice restores coherence across multiple systems. It strengthens the Mind and Meaning System so your actions come from a place of clarity and self-respect rather than fear or control. It also rebalances the Action and Connection System, transforming interactions from power struggles into mutual understanding.

As the Body-Based System settles through mindful pauses and grounding, the Consciousness and Memory System records new experiences of safety in choice and communication. Over time, your nervous system learns that power can be shared, consent honored, and assertiveness expressed without threat or withdrawal.

## 5. Attachment Repatterning and Relational Repair

Attachment wounds form when early caregivers or later relationships were inconsistent, rejecting, or unsafe. These experiences shape your expectations: closeness equals danger; distance equals safety. Recovery involves gently teaching your system new possibilities through safe, predictable contact.

This repatterning begins with small, consistent interactions, such as returning a text, showing up when you say you will, or staying present during safe conflict rather than fleeing. Equally important is learning repair: the ability to acknowledge misattunement and reconnect.

*Example:* After snapping at her partner, Janelle's instinct is to shut down in shame. Instead, she takes time to breathe, returns to the conversation, and says, "I noticed I got defensive earlier. I care about us and want to start again." Her partner relaxes, and after a few minutes, warmth returns between them. Janelle's body learns that repair can follow rupture.

These experiences strengthen the Developmental Integration System by restoring a sense of continuity in your relationships—helping you feel safe and able to trust that connections can be reliable. They also restore regulation within the Action and Connection System by demonstrating that closeness and individuality can coexist. As the Body-Based System calms through repeated experiences of safe reconnection, the Consciousness and Memory System forms new relational templates where repair replaces rupture. Over time, your nervous system learns that relationships can hold both conflict and care and that returning, not retreating, is what creates lasting security.

## 6. Recognizing State Shifts During Connection

Interpersonal moments can activate old survival responses. A raised voice might trigger fight; criticism might provoke flight; feeling unseen might lead to freeze or collapse. Recognizing these *state shifts* early on allows you to intervene before your body fully reenters threat mode.

Signs of a shift include shallow breathing, sudden numbness, intense emotion, or difficulty focusing. The antidote is gentle awareness: notice what's happening, name it, and ground yourself using your senses. Touch something solid, plant your feet and gently sway, or focus on color or texture to reorient to the present.

*Example:* While receiving feedback at work, Cassie feels dizzy and detached. She quietly presses her feet into the floor and names three objects she sees. Her awareness returns, and she hears the feedback accurately instead of through the filter of past criticism.

This practice links the Body-Based System with the Consciousness and Memory System, allowing your body sensations, awareness, and memory to communicate rather than collide. It also engages the Mind and Meaning System so that you interpret present experiences accurately instead of through the lens of past threat.

As your body learns to remain grounded while emotions and memories arise, your nervous system begins to associate connection with stability rather than danger, building resilience, confidence, and trust in your capacity to stay regulated within relationships.

### 7. Healthy Interdependence

Many survivors equate independence with safety. Dependence once meant vulnerability, and vulnerability led to pain. Yet true recovery requires *interdependence*, which is a balanced flow of giving and receiving support.

Healthy interdependence means sharing regulation without losing autonomy. It allows closeness without collapse and boundaries without isolation. Small steps like accepting help with a task, sharing a struggle, or offering comfort strengthen your capacity to stay connected under stress.

*Example:* During group therapy, Devon hesitates to ask for feedback on a personal goal. When he finally does, he feels warmth rather than judgment. The experience surprises him: Connection can feel empowering, not dangerous.

This balance strengthens the Developmental Integration System by restoring trust in connection and teaching that safety can include both giving and receiving. It also engages the Action and Connection System, where collaboration and mutual support transform old patterns of isolation into shared regulation.

As the Mind and Meaning System integrates new beliefs of worthiness and belonging, the Body-Based System learns that closeness no longer signals danger. Over time, your nervous system associates interdependence with strength, resilience, and genuine connection.

## Three Core Areas of Interpersonal Effectiveness

Healthy communication after trauma requires rebuilding balance in three areas that represent the foundation of this module: self-respect effectiveness, relationship effectiveness, and goal effectiveness. Each area addresses a relational challenge that trauma survivors often face, laying the foundation for healthy relationships grounded in values. Let's look at the three areas.

### 1. Self-Respect Effectiveness (FAST)

Trauma often undermines your sense of self-worth, leaving behind guilt, shame, and chronic self-blame. You may find yourself overapologizing, avoiding conflict, or compromising your values for others. To counter this, FAST teaches you how to maintain fairness, honesty, and self-respect in communication.

Practicing FAST engages the meaning and belief domain so you act according to your values. It also strengthens the relational and developmental domains, reinforcing self-trust and maturity in interactions.

The core question of FAST is "How do I want to feel about myself after this interaction?"

## 2. Relationship Effectiveness (GIVE)

When trauma damages relational safety, people often swing between extremes by overaccommodating to avoid rejection or building emotional walls to stay safe. GIVE teaches how to express authenticity, interest, and care in relationships without losing yourself.

This skill speaks directly to the relational domain, yet the most dynamic regulation comes in the nervous system and interoceptive domains. GIVE creates this regulation through reciprocal cues of calm engagement—eye contact, open and relaxed postures, and validation. In short, GIVE is a vehicle for co-regulation. As you offer and receive co-regulating cues, you begin to sense the difference between tension and ease, fear and openness, disconnection and calm. It also strengthens the developmental domain by restoring your social confidence and promoting secure attachment behaviors.

The core question of GIVE is "How do I want others to feel about me after this interaction?"

## 3. Goal Effectiveness (DEAR MAN)

Trauma survivors often struggle to identify, prioritize, and communicate their needs. You might minimize what you want or need to avoid conflict, or you might overstate your needs out of fear of being ignored. You also might struggle to say no or set other boundaries. To address these concerns, DEAR MAN teaches you how to assertively make requests, say no, and negotiate respectfully but confidently.

This skill activates the cognitive and meaning and belief domains to clarify your thinking and align your communication with values. It also engages the Action and Connection System so you act intentionally rather than reactively in relationships.

The core question of DEAR MAN is "What do I want or need from this interaction?"

## Balancing the Three Skills

Healthy communication means finding balance among all three skill sets so one area doesn't dominate at the expense of the others. For instance, you don't want to sacrifice self-respect for the sake of relationships or damage relationships in the pursuit of your goals.

Interpersonal effectiveness teaches you to be mindful of the interplay between FAST, GIVE, and DEAR MAN by continuing to return to and seek answers for the core questions in any given interaction. In that way, the use of these skills represents more than mere communication: It becomes the practice of becoming whole in your connection with others—with each interaction bringing your mind, body, and relationships into alignment with your values and your recovery.

# SKILL Self-Respect Effectiveness: FAST

Trauma leaves deep fractures in how you see and treat yourself. Many survivors carry patterns of shame, self-blame, and emotional suppression that once served as protective strategies but now limit their ability to speak, feel, and act authentically. Over time, these survival patterns erode one of the core foundations needed for recovery: your self-respect.

The FAST skill rebuilds that foundation by teaching how to honor your values so you can be in relationships in ways that strengthen integrity and self-worth. It is not about demanding respect from others. Rather, it is about remembering or discovering how to respect yourself. Each act of fairness, restraint, alignment, and truth is a small act of reclamation of what trauma once took.

The acronym FAST stands for: Be Fair, No Unnecessary Apologies, Stick to Your Values, and Be Truthful.

## Be Fair to Yourself and Others

Trauma often teaches you harsh self-judgment and perfectionism. You may hold yourself to impossible standards or take the blame to maintain peace. Being fair means extending compassion to yourself while remaining just and compassionate with others.

*Example:* A client in group therapy calls themselves "weak" after feeling anxious when sharing their story. Practicing fairness, they remind themselves, "My nervous system is reacting to old danger, not current weakness, and I would never call someone in the same situation weak." This reframe turns shame into understanding and self-compassion.

Fairness helps the Mind and Meaning System regain balance among emotion, thought, and meaning, grounding your self-evaluation in compassion rather than criticism.

## No Unnecessary Apologies

Survivors often overapologize out of fear of conflict, rejection, or judgment. This learned pattern communicates that your presence or needs are burdensome. FAST teaches discernment here; you should certainly apologize when you make an actual mistake and repair is needed, but not for being human, setting boundaries, having needs, or even existing.

*Example:* A client declines an invitation because they feel emotionally drained. Instead of saying, "I'm sorry for being difficult," they reframe the response to "Thank you for understanding. I'm taking care of myself tonight."

Choosing *not* to engage in unneeded apologies supports regulation in the Action and Connection System so you can engage with others from a place of calm confidence rather than submission or defensiveness.

## Stick to Your Values

Trauma blurs your personal values, replacing intentional choices with survival-driven patterns. In some instances, you may never have had the opportunity to consider your *own* values. Sticking to your values gives you the opportunity to discover what matters to you, and the practice of being faithful to your values anchors you in integrity and reduces confusion, guilt, and regret.

*Example:* After years of people-pleasing to stay safe, a client began identifying their core values of honesty, self-respect, and compassion. When their boss asked them to work another extra weekend, the client paused and said, "I can't this time." Though anxious at first, the client later felt grounded and proud. Each time they honored (instead of feared) their values, they strengthened their integrity and reduced confusion and guilt.

Acting from values strengthens the Mind and Meaning System, realigning thought and purpose with the behavioral domain so your actions feel self-directed and authentic.

## Be Truthful

Many survivors learn to hide their emotions or soften the truth to stay safe. Over time, this can make it difficult to be authentic and trust yourself (or be trusted by others). Being truthful means aligning your words and actions with your real experience, speaking with compassion rather than bluntness. Being truthful restores your integrity and your connection with yourself and your relationships.

*Example:* A client raised in a family where "everything was fine" begins to tell their therapist, "I'm actually scared and not doing well right now." Speaking truth replaces invisibility with recognition and integrates emotional and cognitive awareness.

Truthfulness strengthens the Mind and Meaning System and supports the Consciousness and Memory System by helping you face and express experiences that you once hid or minimized. Through honest reflection and communication, your thoughts, emotions, and memories begin to align, transforming fragmented or suppressed experiences into an integrated and coherent story. This process restores a sense of wholeness and self-trust that trauma may have disrupted.

Handout

# FAST Values List

Values guide how we want to live and who we want to be. Clarifying your values strengthens your self-respect, increases emotional stability, and supports posttraumatic growth. Use this list to identify what matters most to you by *circling* your five to ten top values. Then, use these values in the following *FAST Values Worksheet*.

| | | |
|---|---|---|
| Acceptance | Creativity | Safety |
| Accountability | Curiosity | Self-compassion |
| Adventure | Forgiveness | Self-discipline |
| Altruism | Freedom | Self-expression |
| Authenticity | Generosity | Self-respect |
| Balance | Gratitude | Sensitivity |
| Belonging | Growth | Service |
| Boundaries | Harmony | Sincerity |
| Calm | Healing | Spirituality |
| Care | Honesty | Stability |
| Challenge | Honor | Strength |
| Change | Hope | Support |
| Clarity | Humility | Tact |
| Commitment | Humor | Temperance |
| Communication | Integrity | Tolerance |
| Community | Patience | Trust |
| Compassion | Perseverance | Understanding |
| Connection | Playfulness | Vitality |
| Consistency | Power | Warmth |
| Contentment | Presence | Well-being |
| Contribution | Purpose | Wisdom |
| Cooperation | Respect | Other: ________________ |
| Courage | Responsibility | Other: ________________ |

# FAST Values

This worksheet connects your values to your behaviors. This increases alignment between who you want to be and how you live, and it reduces trauma-related distress by facilitating integrity-based action.

## 1. List Your Core Values

Identify three to five values from your values list that are most important to you right now.

______________________________

______________________________

______________________________

## 2. Describe How Each Value Can Be Expressed in Daily Life

Think about small, specific behaviors or decisions that reflect each value. Aligning your behavior with your values is how you live them. For example, if your value is "kindness," you might express it by checking in on a friend or being patient with yourself when struggling.

______________________________

______________________________

______________________________

## 3. Develop a Plan to Align Actions with Values

What steps can you take to close the gap between your values and your behaviors, even in small ways? For example, if you value independence yet tend to isolate, a plan might be to practice asking for support once this week while maintaining staying in control of your decisions.

______________________________

______________________________

______________________________

 

Worksheet

# FAST Values Conflicts

Trauma recovery often awakens values that feel at odds with one another. You may value self-protection while also longing for connection, or value honesty while wanting to protect others. These inner tensions are not signs of failure; they are natural signals that your systems are trying to find new balance.

This worksheet explores those tensions and helps you discover values-based paths that honor both safety and growth. Each reflection invites integration across the Mind and Meaning, the Action and Connection, and the Developmental Integration Systems, restoring coherence between what you feel, believe, and do.

As you explore these values conflicts, notice the sensations, emotions, and beliefs that arise. Each reflection is an act of integration, linking safety with openness, truth with compassion, and independence with connection. By recognizing and balancing your values, you strengthen coherence across all systems and reclaim the ability to live with integrity, authenticity, and self-respect.

## Scenario 1: Safety vs. Connection

**Conflict:** Staying home to avoid triggers versus attending a gathering to rebuild relationships.

How can you honor your need for safety while allowing for connection? Could you attend for a short time, bring a support person, or suggest a smaller, calmer setting?

____________________________________________________________

____________________________________________________________

This supports regulation in the Body-Based System by honoring your nervous system's need for safety, while gently engaging the Action and Connection System to reintroduce relational contact at a tolerable pace.

## Scenario 2: Honesty vs. Compassion

**Conflict:** Being truthful about your own struggles versus protecting a friend from vicarious emotional distress.

How can you be honest while also reassuring the other person that they don't need to solve your problems? Could you share your experiences gently, making it clear that the other person does not need to "fix" anything?

---

---

This strengthens the Mind and Meaning System, balancing emotional authenticity with compassionate communication in the relational domain. It helps align honesty with care rather than conflict.

## Scenario 3: Independence vs. Seeking Help

**Conflict:** Managing symptoms alone versus reaching out for therapy or support.

How can you seek help while still honoring your value of independence? Would trying therapy on a trial basis allow you evaluate its role in your recovery?

---

---

This activates the Action and Connection System, supporting help seeking as an empowered choice rather than a loss of autonomy. It also nurtures the Developmental Integration System by revising old patterns of self-reliance into collaborative strength.

## Scenario 4: Justice vs. Forgiveness

**Conflict:** Wanting accountability versus choosing to let go of anger to support healing.

How can you hold space dialectically for both justice and forgiveness? Is it possible to pursue accountability without staying stuck in bitterness?

---

---

Exploring this dialectic engages the Mind and Meaning System, transforming rigid "either/or" beliefs into "both/and" understanding. It allows moral and emotional clarity to coexist within your healing process.

## Scenario 5: Boundaries vs. Connection

**Conflict:** Protecting yourself versus allowing others to get closer.

How can you maintain safety while slowly building trust? Are there ways to express your boundaries that still invite connection? What do those words sound like?

__________________________________________

__________________________________________

Balancing boundaries and connection is centered in the Action and Connection System, with contributions from both the Mind and Meaning and the Body-Based Systems.

## SKILL Relationship Effectiveness: GIVE

Trauma disrupts your sense of safety that allows relationships to feel secure. You may withdraw from others, be mistrustful or on edge, or try to create safety by people-pleasing or hiding your feelings. The GIVE skill offers a way to rebuild connection without losing yourself.

GIVE is not about perfect politeness or earning love. It is about reclaiming your right to connect safely. Each time you show up genuinely, express interest, validate others, or soften your approach, you teach your nervous system that safety and connection can coexist. You remind yourself that you can be present, real, and safe with others all at once. In that space, relationships shift from a source of threat to a source of healing.

The GIVE acronym stands for Be Genuine, Show Interest, Validate, and Use an Easy Manner.

### Be Genuine

Being genuine means showing up as your full, authentic self rather than masking your emotions, hiding your needs, or performing a role to avoid rejection. Many trauma survivors fear being "too much" or "not enough." Expressing yourself honestly, but in a balanced way, helps you build trust with yourself and others. Admittedly, being "real" can feel risky, so move at a pace that respects your safety with small, honest disclosures offered to people who have earned your trust.

*Example:* A client who usually hides their anxiety from friends says, "I'm feeling overwhelmed today, but I wanted to show up anyway." By sharing honestly, they strengthen authenticity and take a meaningful risk to be connect with others.

Practicing genuineness engages the Mind and Meaning System, aligning your thoughts, emotions, and values. It also soothes the Body-Based System by teaching your body that openness can coexist with safety.

### Show Interest

Trauma can lead you to numb your feelings or be overly preoccupied with safety, making it difficult to stay attuned with others. Showing genuine interest invites you to get curious, focus your attention on the present moment, and let others know that they matter. This kind of mindful connection shifts your nervous system from defense to social engagement.

*Example:* A client who feels disconnected at a gathering practices asking questions and listening fully, noticing people's facial expressions and tone. Over time, this strengthens their ability to stay regulated and present when interacting with others.

Showing interest strengthens the Action and Connection System by promoting active engagement and responsiveness in relationships. It also nurtures the Body-Based System, as warmth, eye contact, and presence all signal safety to the body. At the same time, it engages the Consciousness and Memory System, anchoring awareness in the present moment and linking current connection with new, positive emotional memories. Over time, these experiences repattern the nervous system's expectation of danger, showing that curiosity and connection can exist safely in relationships.

## Validate

Validation means recognizing another person's emotions, perspectives, and experiences nonjudgmentally, *even if you see or experience things differently*. Many, if not most, trauma survivors were invalidated and told they were overreacting or too sensitive—if their experience was acknowledged at all. Learning to validate others models empathy, enhances trust, and reinforces the same compassion you need for yourself.

*Example:* Instead of becoming defensive or withdrawing, a client responds to a friend's frustration by saying, "I can understand why that would be upsetting. I see where you're coming from, and it makes sense."

Validation strengthens the Mind and Meaning System by allowing both people to feel seen and understood. It also repairs the relational domain of the Action and Connection System by rebuilding the trust and attunement that trauma often fractures. At the same time, validation engages the Consciousness and Memory System, linking present experiences of being understood with new memories of safety and belonging. Each validating interaction teaches your nervous system that connection can coexist with differences, and that understanding (not agreement) is what creates safety in relationship.

## Use an Easy Manner

Trauma sensitizes the nervous system, making you more reactive and prone to a sharp tone, closed posture, or blunt expression, even when you mean no harm. An "easy manner" uses a gentle voice, relaxed body language, and appropriate humor to signal safety and openness. These small cues regulate both you and the person you're with. Of note, using an easy manner isn't about being submissive or meek. You can maintain an easy manner quite successfully while being assertive.

*Example:* During a difficult discussion, a person maintains an open posture, makes eye contact, and softens their tone before saying, "Let's take our time with this." This calm presence invites collaboration and co-regulation instead of conflict.

Practicing an easy manner calms your body through the Body-Based System and restores ease in the Action and Connection System by inviting others into a shared rhythm of trust and collaboration. It also engages the Consciousness and Memory System by pairing these experiences of calm connection with new memories of safety in communication. Over time, these gentle exchanges retrain your nervous system to associate relational engagement not with danger or control, but with steadiness, confidence, and mutual respect.

## SKILL Goal Effectiveness: DEAR MAN

Assertiveness can be one of the hardest capacities to reclaim after trauma. You may have learned that having needs, opinions, or limits was unsafe. As a result, you may silence yourself and be overly accommodating to others, or you may swing to the other extreme and assert your wants and needs in ways that feel reactive or risky. Over time, this erodes trust in your own voice and reinforces the belief that asking for something will lead to rejection, punishment, or loss.

DEAR MAN is not about control or victory; it is about reclaiming your right to be heard and respected. Each time you use these steps, you remind yourself and your nervous system that your wants, needs, and boundaries matter and that you can express them safely and with confidence.

The DEAR MAN acronym stands for Describe the Details, Express Your Opinion or Feelings, Assert or Say No, Reinforce the Other Person, Stay Mindful of Your Goals, Appear Confident, and Negotiate as Needed.

### Describe the Details

Begin by describing what happened or what's led to the need for assertiveness. Use clear, neutral terms. Trauma can make you downplay or exaggerate your experiences, so stating the facts calmly helps organize your thoughts and engages Reason Mind.

*Example:* "Yesterday you raised your voice and called me irresponsible and disrespectful names when I forgot to text you back."

Describing events in this manner strengthens the Mind and Meaning System by bringing together your thoughts, emotions, and words. It also steadies the Body-Based System by focusing your attention on concrete details, and it engages the Consciousness and Memory System by linking your awareness with accurate recall.

### Express Your Opinion or Feelings

If relevant, express your opinion and emotions about the situation. Doing so authentically can add emotional weight to your words, though it is not always indicated or helpful. Use Wise Mind to decide whether this step will support your DEAR MAN goals, and as with the first step, do this with composure.

*Example:* "I felt dismissed and hurt when you said that, especially when you called me names. It was unkind."

Expressing your feelings strengthens the emotional domain of the Mind and Meaning System by linking your inner experience with words and meaning. It also engages the Body-Based System, allowing your body to release tension as you name and understand your emotions. This helps your nervous system settle, transforming raw emotional energy into clarity and coherence.

## Assert or Say No

Do not assume that others will know what you want or need. This step is where you are clear in asking, saying no, or setting appropriate boundaries. Don't hint or tiptoe around it: Be direct.

*Example:* "I need you not to yell at me when you're upset. If you need space or a break, then please just say that. Know that being disrespectful and calling me names is not acceptable. Please treat me with respect."

Assertiveness strengthens the Action and Connection System by pairing clear communication with respect, allowing you to express your needs without aggression or withdrawal. It also supports the Developmental Integration System by helping you grow in maturity, maintain healthy boundaries, and act with integrity. Through practice, your nervous system learns that directness and safety can exist together, transforming fear of conflict into confidence and stability.

## Reinforce the Other Person

Reinforcing cooperation helps the other person understand how meeting your request benefits both of you. This is not manipulation. Instead, it's a way to create shared motivation and reduce defensiveness. Note that some circumstances call for pointing out potentially negative consequences, yet on the whole, think about how to reward rather than punish others.

*Example:* "When we talk calmly, I feel more open and safe, and I'm more likely to listen and respond well. It improves the relationship for both of us."

Reinforcing the other person builds the capacity for give-and-take in the Action and Connection System, showing that cooperation and respect strengthen both of you. It also promotes co-regulation and shared safety through positive feedback. Over time, this practice teaches your nervous system that connection deepens through mutual understanding and appreciation rather than control or conflict.

## Stay Mindful of Your Goals

Trauma can make it difficult to focus when emotions rise. It is important to stay focused on your DEAR MAN goal, even when the other person reacts strongly or tries to change the subject. If you get distracted, mindfully return to your goals. Note that this also involves setting a boundary within the communication. In some instances, you may need to be a "broken record" by repeating your assertion over and over.

*Example:* If the other person tries to change the subject or deflect, say, "Let's stay focused on what I'm asking. We can talk about that other issue later."

Staying mindful of your goals engages the cognitive domain within the Mind and Meaning System, helping you stay focused and contain your emotions. It also activates the Consciousness and Memory System by keeping you grounded in the present moment so that old emotional patterns don't hijack the current communication. Over time, this practice teaches your nervous system to stay steady and intentional, maintaining clarity and boundaries even in moments of intensity.

## Appear Confident

Confidence is both a feeling and a behavior. Even if you don't feel confident, adopting a steady posture, tone of voice, and pace can signal safety to your nervous system and others'. Over time, your body learns that calm self-expression is safe. If confidence is hard, act "as if"—behave as though you are confident.

*Example:* Stand tall, maintain gentle eye contact, and speak evenly with appropriate tone and volume when making a request.

Appearing confident stabilizes the Body-Based System by promoting vagal regulation and grounding your body in steadiness and self-trust. It also engages the nervous system domain by showing you that calm, assertive expression is safe and effective. Over time, your posture, breath, and voice become associated with internal confidence, helping you embody confidence even before it feels fully natural.

## Negotiate as Needed

Be flexible and open to problem-solving if the situation requires it. Negotiation transforms assertion into collaboration. It prevents rigidity and models mutual respect. The goal is not to "give in" but to remain creative in finding solutions that honor both sides without abandoning your wants and needs. In some situations where negotiation stalls, "turn the tables" by asking the other person what they think would work.

*Example:* "If you need the TV on, could you use headphones at night? That way, I can sleep and you can still unwind."

Negotiation enhances the Action and Connection System by balancing self-advocacy with empathy and collaboration. It also engages the Mind and Meaning System, supporting flexible thinking and shared problem-solving. Through this process, your nervous system learns that compromise does not require a loss of power but the creation of mutual respect and stability within connection.

# DEAR MAN Factors to Consider

Using DEAR MAN effectively means more than following a script. It requires you to be aware of your timing, tone, and emotional state, as well as the relational context. When you use DEAR MAN with these factors in mind, you go beyond making a simple request to practicing regulation across your systems and domains.

Each of the following considerations tailors DEAR MAN to your lived experience, honoring your nervous system's needs while expressing yourself with integrity and calm.

## 1. Embrace Wise Mind

Recall from chapter 10 that Wise Mind is the balanced state between Emotion Mind and Reason Mind. Trauma often pushes people toward extremes, either feeling flooded by emotion or detached from it by being overly logical. Wise Mind allows both emotion and reason to coexist, supporting grounded, thoughtful communication.

*Example:* Before initiating a boundary-setting conversation, pause to breathe, feel your feet on the floor, and reconnect with your intention. Regulate your body and remind yourself of your goals.

## 2. Consider Your Level of Intensity

Trauma can distort your perception of intensity. You may silence your voice completely or express yourself with unexpected force, especially when your nervous system senses threat. Being aware of tone, volume, facial expression, and posture prevents escalation and promotes understanding.

*Example:* Rehearse with a therapist or observe yourself in a mirror to find your steady, assertive voice.

## 3. Prioritize GIVE

Trauma often trains you to expect rejection, criticism, or dismissal. Opening with GIVE sets a tone that invites others to stay open, which can disarm those fears by reducing defensiveness and modeling mutual respect.

*Example:* Begin a conversation with "I really value our relationship, and that's why I want to talk about something important."

## 4. Consider Timing

Trauma responses can cause you to delay conversations out of fear or rush into them out of urgency. Aim for "good-enough" timing rather than perfect timing. This balances caution with courage.

*Example:* Ask, "Is now a good time to talk?" or set a specific time so both of you can approach the conversation prepared.

## 5. Target the Right Audience

Assertiveness is most effective when it's directed toward someone with the capacity and willingness to respond. Trauma can make this difficult to discern, causing you to seek help from people who aren't available or avoid those who actually have the ability to assist. Choosing the right audience makes your efforts more effective.

*Example:* If you need time off, speak to your supervisor, not a coworker who lacks decision-making power.

## 6. Be Persistent

Assertiveness is a practice, not a one-time event. Trauma can make you feel hopeless or afraid to try again, making one failed attempt feel like the end. Calm and persistent efforts reinforce your right to be heard and help others take your needs seriously.

*Example:* Use the "broken record" approach to reinforce your position: "I hear you, but I still need to talk about this."

## 7. Consider the Context

Context shapes every interaction. Trauma can make it hard to gauge emotional safety, causing you to underestimate danger or overestimate threat. Consider the relationship, the setting, and your readiness before initiating a conversation. Preparation can transform anxiety into agency.

*Example:* Before discussing a sensitive issue with a partner, practice grounding skills, rehearse with your therapist, or choose a time when both of you are less activated, emotionally or otherwise.

Worksheet

## Integrative Interpersonal Effectiveness

This worksheet helps you prepare for and reflect on important conversations. It integrates all three sets of interpersonal skills to clarify your needs, strengthen trust in yourself and others, and achieve more effective outcomes. It also invites you to think about other skills that promote regulation in interpersonal interactions.

### Step 1: Clarify the Interaction

What is the situation you're preparing for or reflecting on?

____________________________________________

____________________________________________

What is your primary interpersonal goal? (Check all that apply.)

- ❒ Protect self-respect
- ❒ Repair, maintain, or improve a relationship
- ❒ Ask for something
- ❒ Say no/set a boundary
- ❒ Advocate for yourself or others
- ❒ Prevent harm or protect safety

Describe your goal here.

____________________________________________

____________________________________________

### Step 2: Identify Your Core Values (FAST)

- Fair: How will you be fair to yourself and others?

  ________________________________________

- Apologies (only when needed): Are you tempted to apologize when you don't need to?

  ________________________________________

- Stick to Values: What are one to three values you want to embody in this interaction? Examples might include honesty, respect, compassion, courage, or boundaries.

  ________________________________________

- Truthful: How will you express your truth with respect and care?

How do you want to feel about yourself afterward?

## Step 3: Strengthen the Relationship (GIVE)

- Genuine: How can you be authentic and transparent?
- Interested: How can you stay present and engaged?
- Validate: What in their experience can you acknowledge?
- Easy Manner: What tone or body language will foster safety?

How do you want the other person to feel about you?

## Step 4: Communicate Your Needs (DEAR MAN)

- Describe: What are the facts and details regarding the situation?
- Express: What opinions or feelings will strengthen your assertiveness?
- Assert: What are you specifically asking for or saying no to?

- Reinforce: How can you reward the other person for cooperating with your request?

________________________________________

- Mindful: What will help you stay focused on your goals?

________________________________________

- Appear Confident: What can you do to increase your confidence?

________________________________________

- Negotiate: What flexibility do you have in terms of negotiation?

________________________________________

What do you want or need from this situation?

________________________________________

________________________________________

## Step 5: Additional Skills

What skills from other modules do you need to be regulated in this interaction?

________________________________________

________________________________________

## Step 6: Postinteraction Reflection

Values (FAST): How well did you stay aligned? ❐ Fully ❐ Somewhat ❐ Not at all

________________________________________

________________________________________

Relationship (GIVE): Did you strengthen trust or connection? Why or why not?

________________________________________

________________________________________

Goals (DEAR MAN): Were your wants, needs, or boundaries respected? Did you meet your goals?

What other skills did you use and how did they help?

What will you carry forward from this experience?

Each interpersonal exchange offers a chance to practice presence, integrity, and growth. By working through this worksheet, you bring awareness to the systems that shape connection: the mind that clarifies, the body that regulates, and the heart that relates. Using FAST, GIVE, and DEAR MAN together enables you to communicate with both courage and compassion while staying grounded in your values.

 

## Interpersonal Effectiveness and Chronic Invalidation: Reclaiming the Right to Be Seen and Belong

For many trauma survivors, relational invalidation is not simply a painful memory; it is a defining part of the trauma. When your needs were dismissed, your boundaries ignored, or your voice silenced, your system learned that relationships were unsafe and connection came at a cost. Over time, you may have adapted by pleasing others to avoid conflict, staying silent to prevent rejection, or withdrawing to protect yourself. These survival strategies made sense then, yet they often leave you feeling unseen, unheard, and disconnected from your own values now.

Whereas relational invalidation fractures trust and distorts your sense of connection, interpersonal effectiveness skills begin the process of repair. They offer tools to ask for what you need, honor your limits, and navigate conflict with clarity and respect. Through practice, these skills rebuild the belief that you are allowed to show up in relationships guided by your values, whether those values are honesty, fairness, compassion, mutual respect, or something else.

Interpersonal effectiveness restores what invalidation eroded. It invites confidence where there was self-doubt, assertiveness where there was silence, and connection where there was isolation. Each time you communicate with honesty, balance, and self-respect, you strengthen your capacity to participate in relationships without abandoning what matters most to you. You learn that values can anchor your choices, shape your boundaries, and hold your place in relationships even when emotions run high.

Moreover, interpersonal effectiveness becomes an act of self-recognition. It honors your experience, renews your voice, and reconnects you with relationships that support healing. The Mind and Meaning System relearns that your needs and values are valid; the Body-Based System discovers that connection can feel safe; the Consciousness and Memory System integrates past relational injuries without reliving them; the Action and Connection System practices new patterns of communication and closeness; and the Developmental Integration System grows into a grounded, self-led identity capable of both giving and receiving care.

Each time you communicate clearly, set a boundary aligned with your values, or stay present in a vulnerable moment, you teach your system a new relational truth. Over time, you reclaim the essential freedom to show up fully, to connect without losing yourself, and to build relationships rooted in mutual respect, authenticity, and belonging.

# Appendix

## Master Skills List by Module and Classification

### Dialectics

*Finding balance between extremes in thoughts and behaviors.*

#### "Both/And" Thinking

Holding two (or more) seemingly opposing truths at once to find middle ground thoughts and actions.

**Classification:** Top-down as it requires reframing and expanding rigid "either/or" beliefs to build flexibility. (Note bottom-up ways to practice in the module too—for example, practicing stillness and movement, as well as holding and letting go.)

## Mindfulness

*Choosing to pay attention to the present moment, nonjudgmentally.*

### Wise Mind

Integrating emotional awareness and reasoned thinking.

**Classification:** Mixed as it combines bottom-up embodied awareness with top-down reasoning.

### Core Mindfulness Skills

The "What" to do and "How" to do it to get to Wise Mind.

**What Skills**

- **Observe:** Noticing present experiences without adding or taking away.

  **Classification:** Mixed as it involves both external observation (top-down) and sensory awareness (bottom-up).

- **Describe:** Using neutral language to label experiences and feelings.

  **Classification:** Top-down as it organizes experience via language and executive function.

- **Participate:** Fully engaging in the current experience with full attention.

  **Classification:** Mixed as it combines intentional choice (top-down) with immersive experience (bottom-up).

**How Skills**

- **One-Mindfully:** Focusing on one task or experience at a time.

  **Classification:** Mixed as it combines top-down attention direction with bottom-up sensory anchoring.

- **Nonjudgmentally:** Seeing things as they are without labeling as good or bad.

  **Classification:** Top-down as it reframes inner commentary from judgmental to descriptive.

- **Effectively:** Doing what works best in the present situation.

  **Classification:** Top-down as it relies on problem-solving and intentional choice.

### Teflon Mind

The mindful ability to let thoughts, emotions, and sensations pass through your awareness without sticking, clinging, or pulling you off balance.

**Classification:** Top-down as it requires awareness and a choice to release that which could be uncomfortable or painful.

## Distress Tolerance

*Surviving crisis and stress without making it worse.*

### ACCEPTS

A collection of seven distraction methods that redirect attention from crisis to stability:

1. **Activities:** Do something engaging that occupies you (e.g., cleaning, exercising, hobbies).

   **Classification:** Mixed as it combines cognitive choice with options that can be either top-down or bottom-up.

2. **Contributing:** Help or support someone else to shift focus outward.

   **Classification:** Mixed as it involves intentional empathy and altruism (top-down) and relational engagement that has both top-down and bottom-up aspects.

3. **Comparisons:** Recall times when you coped, times when your struggles were harder, or the fact that others struggle too.

   **Classification:** Top-down as it reframes perspective through cognitive appraisal.

4. **Emotions (Opposite):** Create different emotions by watching, reading, listening to, or doing something that evokes a contrasting feeling.

   **Classification:** Mixed as it uses emotional activation (bottom-up) guided by cognitive intent (top-down).

5. **Pushing Away:** Temporarily set aside distressing thoughts until you are more regulated.

   **Classification:** Top-down as it uses intentional compartmentalization to prevent overwhelm.

6. **Thoughts:** Replace distressing thoughts with other engaging thoughts (counting, reciting, puzzles).

   **Classification:** Top-down as it shifts focus through mental control.

7. **Sensations:** Engage strong physical sensations (hold something cold, listen to loud music) to interrupt emotional intensity.

   **Classification:** Bottom-up as it directly activates sensory pathways to regulate arousal.

### IMPROVE

A set of seven strategies for making a difficult moment more bearable or meaningful:

1. **Imagery:** Visualize calming, safe, or empowering scenes.

   **Classification:** Top-down as it uses mental imagery to guide your emotions and sensations (though it "lands" bottom-up).

2. **Meaning:** Reframe the experience to find purpose or growth.

   **Classification:** Top-down as it relies on cognitive reframing and belief systems.

3. **Prayer:** Connect to a sense of spirituality, values, or higher purpose.

   **Classification:** Mixed as it integrates belief-based cognition (top-down) with surrender and calm physiology (bottom-up).

4. **Relaxation:** Engage the body in calming actions such as breathing, stretching, or progressive muscle relaxation.

   **Classification:** Bottom-up as it directly regulates the nervous system.

5. **One Thing in the Moment:** Focus attention on one task at a time (e.g., noticing colors, tasting food, writing one email).

   **Classification:** Mixed as it combines mindful attention (top-down) with embodied awareness (bottom-up).

6. **Vacation:** Take a short mental or physical break from the stressor.

   **Classification:** Mixed as it involves cognitive permission to rest and may involve either top-down or bottom-up actions.

7. **Encouragement:** Use gentle, compassionate self-talk ("I can handle this one step at a time").

   **Classification:** Top-down as it activates the prefrontal cortex through verbal self-regulation.

## Self-Soothe with the Five Senses

Using sensory experiences (sight, sound, touch, taste, smell) to calm the nervous system.

**Classification:** Bottom-up as it directly engages sensory pathways to downregulate arousal.

## Pros and Cons

Evaluating the benefits and drawbacks of different options before acting.

**Classification:** Top-down as it is a structured cognitive appraisal that enhances impulse control and forethought.

## Bridge Burning and Barrier Building

Choosing to remove or limit access to the means of acting on harmful urges.
**Classification:** Top-down as it relies on strategic planning and choice.

## Urge Surfing (Ride the Wave)

Mindfully riding out an intense craving, impulse, or emotional urge without acting on it until it naturally rises, peaks, and passes.

**Classification:** Mixed as it combines moment-to-moment sensing of the body with mindful cognitive awareness to ride out urges without acting on them.

## TIPP

Rapid physiological interventions for extreme emotional arousal:

1. **Temperature:** Use cold water or ice on the face or neck to trigger the dive reflex and slow heart rate.

   **Classification:** Bottom-up as it engages parasympathetic activation.

2. **Intense Exercise:** Engage in brief bursts of vigorous movement to release stress hormones and restore equilibrium.

   **Classification:** Bottom-up as it uses physical exertion to metabolize adrenaline.

3. **Paced Breathing:** Practice slow, even breathing to regulate the nervous system.

   **Classification:** Bottom-up as it calms the vagus nerve and restores rhythm.

4. **Paired Muscle Relaxation:** Tense and release muscle groups to lower physical tension.

   **Classification:** Bottom-up as it signals safety through body relaxation.

## STOP

A brief crisis skill that interrupts automatic reactions by helping you pause, step back, observe internal and external cues, and then proceed mindfully.

**Classification:** Mixed as it uses top-down cognitive awareness to interrupt behavior while simultaneously allowing bottom-up physiological arousal to settle through the pause.

## Grounding Techniques

Practical strategies that anchor your attention in the present moment by engaging your senses, body, or surroundings to reduce overwhelm and restore stability.

**Classification:** Mixed as it combines primarily bottom-up strategies with a few top-down ones (e.g., Observing and Describing an environment, counting objects in a room).

## Radical Acceptance

Acknowledging and allowing reality as it is, without denial or resistance.

**Classification:** Top-down as it is cognitive willingness and reframing toward acceptance.

### Turning the Mind

Choosing again and again to accept what is, redirecting focus to willingness.

**Classification:** Top-down as it is an intentional cognitive commitment to acceptance.

### Willingness

Meet others and the situation where they are rather than where you wish they were.

**Classification:** Top-down as it involves an intentional shift in attitude that relies on cognitive choice.

## Emotion Regulation

*Understanding emotions, reducing vulnerability, and increasing positive experiences.*

### Mindfulness of Current Emotion

Fully noticing, naming, and experiencing an emotion as it arises without judging, avoiding, or acting on it.

**Classification:** Mixed as it combines awareness and cognition with body-based experiencing.

### Check the Facts

Distinguish between your thoughts and assumptions versus the actual reality of a situation.

**Classification:** Top-down as it involves cognitive reframing to correct emotional interpretations.

### PLEASED

Practicing self-care behaviors (Physical Health, List Resources/Barriers, Eat a Balanced Diet, Avoid Substances, Sleep Enough, Exercise, and Daily Habits).

**Classification:** Bottom-up as it stabilizes physiological foundations of emotion.

### Build Mastery

Taking small, achievable actions that foster competence and self-efficacy.

**Classification:** Top-down as it involves planning, goal setting, and recognizing your progress.

### Build Positive Experiences

Scheduling and engaging in pleasurable, value-based activities.

**Classification:** Mixed as it combines cognitive planning with embodied enjoyment.

### Opposite Action

Acting opposite to ineffective emotion-driven urges and behaviors (e.g., approach when you want to avoid).

**Classification:** Mixed as it requires intentional behavioral override of emotion-based impulses (top-down) alongside changes to posture, breath, movement, and facial expression to shift physiology (bottom-up).

## Interpersonal Effectiveness

*Building self-respect, maintaining relationships, and meeting goals.*

### FAST

Fair, No Unnecessary Apologies, Stick to Values, and Truthful.

**Classification:** Top-down as it represents values-driven and integrity-based decision-making.

### GIVE

Genuine, Interested, Validate, and Easy Manner.

**Classification:** Mixed as it combines cognitive empathy with embodied safety cues.

### DEAR MAN

Describe, Express, Assert, Reinforce, Mindful, Appear Confident, and Negotiate.

**Classification:** Top-down as it represents strategic communication and boundary-setting using cognitive planning and self-control.

## Related and Overlapping Areas of Dysregulation

While DTRM describes eleven primary domains of dysregulation across five interdependent systems, trauma research continues to identify additional areas of dysregulation that intersect with or extend beyond these core dimensions. The following categories, though not presented as stand-alone domains in DTRM, are clinically significant phenomena that can be meaningfully located within the model's existing structure.

Together, these additional constructs expand the conceptual terrain of dysregulation while reinforcing the integrative intent of DTRM. Rather than adding separate categories, DTRM subsumes these related phenomena within its unified systems framework, allowing clinicians to locate them precisely within the interacting mind-body-developmental network of trauma response and recovery.

### Existential or Transpersonal Dysregulation

Some trauma survivors experience profound disruptions in faith, morality, or sense of connection to something larger than themselves. These crises, which are sometimes framed as a *spiritual injury* or *loss of existential coherence*, often manifest as despair, nihilism, or a search for meaning after trauma.

Within DTRM, these experiences are captured under meaning and belief dysregulation, which already encompasses worldview and identity-based meaning making. However, the existential or transpersonal dimension extends beyond self-referential beliefs ("I'm broken") into broader questions such as "Why live?" or "Where was God?" Future iterations of DTRM may designate this as an explicit spiritual/existential subdomain to better encompass posttraumatic growth, moral repair, and restoration of purpose.

### Moral Injury or Ethical Dysregulation

In populations such as veterans, first responders, and survivors of moral betrayal, trauma may appear as a violation of conscience or a perceived transgression against deeply held values. This moral injury involves guilt, shame, and disorientation within one's ethical framework.

In DTRM, these processes are integrated within meaning and belief dysregulation, which addresses trauma-shaped distortions of morality and self-concept. Nonetheless, because moral injury encompasses social, cognitive, and spiritual dimensions, it could be conceptualized as a named subdomain in future refinements of the model.

## Social/Systemic Dysregulation

Beyond the intrapsychic and interpersonal, trauma also operates at the systemic level—through racism, poverty, colonization, gender-based violence, and institutional invalidation. These forces sustain chronic dysregulation by reinforcing feelings of danger, powerlessness, and shame.

DTRM locates this dynamic within its biosocial foundation, conceptualizing trauma as arising from the interplay between individual vulnerability and invalidating environments. While not a discrete domain, systemic invalidation functions as a transdomain influence that shapes and maintains dysregulation across all five systems.

## Identity Dysregulation

Chronic or developmental trauma can leave people feeling fragmented, with a sense of self that feels diffuse or unstable. Survivors may oscillate between different self-states or struggle with a consistent sense of "who I am."

In DTRM, this reflects both developmental dysregulation (identity diffusion rooted in early trauma) and dissociative dysregulation (fragmentation of awareness). DTRM treats these identity disturbances as cross-domain outcomes that reflect disrupted integration across both the Developmental Integration System and Consciousness and Memory System.

## Attachment System Dysregulation

Attachment is a core neurobiological regulation system that helps us seek closeness, regulate our emotions, and feel safe. Trauma that occurs in attachment relationships disrupts this system at its foundation.

Within DTRM, attachment dysregulation is distributed across the relational and developmental domains, where it manifests as impaired trust, boundary confusion, and relational fear. Some clinicians may choose to reference *attachment dysregulation* explicitly when the central treatment goal is to help the client relearn safety and connection through co-regulation and relational repair.

## Temporal Dysregulation

Many trauma survivors live in "trauma time," where the past feels present and the future remains inaccessible. This loss of temporal sequencing reflects a disruption in the brain's capacity to situate experiences in chronological order.

DTRM embeds this construct within the memory domain of the Consciousness and Memory System, which addresses the fragmentation and loss of temporal coherence that give rise to flashbacks and reexperiencing. Naming *temporal dysregulation* within this domain can help clarify the mechanism by which unintegrated memory keeps survivors trapped in repetitive emotional time loops.

## Metacognitive Dysregulation

Trauma impairs not only thought content but also survivors' ability to think about their own thinking (i.e., metacognition). This deficit explains why cognitive insight alone rarely produces change in trauma recovery.

DTRM conceptualizes this function within the cognitive domain, while recognizing its developmental roots in early attachment and reflective caregiving. Skills such as mindfulness, Wise Mind, and dialectical thinking explicitly target this metacognitive function, strengthening clients' ability to observe their internal experience without judgment and reestablish executive control.

# Therapist Dysregulation Self-Assessment

Therapists, like clients, regulate themselves through five interrelated systems. When stress, exposure, or vicarious trauma accumulate, you might notice dysregulation surfacing across these domains, narrowing your perspective, empathy, and presence.

Use this self-assessment to stay aware of your own dysregulation cues and ensure that you are remaining a co-regulating presence for your client. Rate each domain on a scale from 0 to 5, where 0 = "no dysregulation" and 5 = "severe dysregulation interfering with effectiveness."

## I. Mind and Meaning System

| Domain | Therapist Manifestation | Reflective Prompts | Rating (0–5) |
|---|---|---|---|
| **Emotional** | Emotional fatigue, irritability, or empathic overwhelm that clouds attunement or compassion. | "What emotions am I carrying into session?"<br>"Am I matching my client's affect or absorbing it?" | |
| **Cognitive** | Overthinking, judgment, or racing thoughts; difficulty seeing multiple perspectives. | "Am I thinking flexibly or stuck in right/wrong thinking?"<br>"Do I assume I know the outcome?" | |
| **Meaning and belief** | Self-critical narratives about your competence, worth, or control (e.g., "If I were good, my clients wouldn't relapse"). | "What beliefs do I have about myself or the work right now?" | |

## II. Body-Based System

| Domain | Therapist Manifestation | Reflective Prompts | Rating (0–5) |
|---|---|---|---|
| **Nervous system** | Autonomic dysregulation like fight-flight urgency, freeze, or shutdown that affects your tone, pacing, and capacity to co-regulate. | "Am I keyed up, rushed, or flat?"<br>"Is my pace in sync with the client's?" | |
| **Somatic** | Physical tension, pain, or fatigue signaling unprocessed stress. | "Where do I feel tightness or collapse?"<br>"What is my body communicating?" | |
| **Interoceptive** | Ignoring or misreading internal cues (e.g., hunger, fatigue, thirst, irritability). | "Have I checked in with my body today?"<br>"Do I override exhaustion to stay productive?" | |

## III. Consciousness and Memory System

| Domain | Therapist Manifestation | Reflective Prompts | Rating (0–5) |
|---|---|---|---|
| **Dissociative** | Numbing, spacing out, or detaching in sessions; "performing therapy" while being emotionally absent. | "Do I feel distant or mechanical?"<br>"Am I avoiding my own emotional response?" | |
| **Memory** | Difficulty recalling session details or overidentifying with client stories due to your own personal history. | "Do certain stories blur with my own?"<br>"Am I remembering or reliving?" | |

## IV. Action and Connection System

| Domain | Therapist Manifestation | Reflective Prompts | Rating (0–5) |
|---|---|---|---|
| **Behavioral** | Avoidance, overfunctioning, drifting boundaries, or reactive decision-making. | "Am I procrastinating, rescuing, or overworking?"<br>"Where am I saying yes when I mean no?" | |
| **Relational** | Countertransference, overidentification with the client, or withdrawal from team/community support. | "Am I relating as a partner or in a caretaker/savior role?"<br>"How open am I to feedback and repair?" | |

## V. Developmental Integration System

| Domain | Therapist Manifestation | Reflective Prompts | Rating (0–5) |
|---|---|---|---|
| **Developmental** | Replay of early attachment patterns like people-pleasing, defiance, perfectionism, or fear of failure. | "When do I feel like a child, parent, or rebel rather than a clinician?"<br>"What early lessons about worth or duty might be shaping my reactions?" | |

### Interpretation and Use

- **3 or higher:** Any score ≥3 signals a need to use regulation skills or seek consultation.
- **Look for clusters:** Patterns across systems can mirror the challenges your clients are facing or the demands of your work environment.
- **Consultation:** Discuss any elevated domains in supervision or peer consultation to promote co-regulation and effective responding.

### Self-Regulation Miniprotocol (RISE for Self)

If any of your scores are ≥3:

1. **Recognize:** Note which domains are activated.
2. **Identify:** Link your activation to context or triggers (e.g., client theme, workload, systemic pressures).
3. **Skills:** Choose bottom-up and top-down regulation strategies.
4. **Evaluate:** Rerate each domain; notice any shifts in your body and perspective.
5. **Share:** Bring insights to supervision or consultation to model transparency and skill use.

Remember that clinician regulation is client safety. In addition, staying aware of your own regulation across systems transforms supervision into a space for co-regulation and sustains the integrity of the DTRM model.

# Trauma Neurobiology Glossary

Trauma does not damage a single part of the brain. It alters communication among various brain regions that shape how we perceive safety, process threat, store memory, and recover from distress. Understanding trauma through this lens helps demystify trauma responses like hyperarousal, dissociation, or emotional numbing.

Fortunately, the same neural circuits that once adapted for survival also remain capable of healing and change. Through mindfulness, grounding, connection, and other regulation practices, the brain can learn new patterns that support safety, presence, and integration.

This glossary provides an overview of key brain regions and circuits involved in trauma. Each entry includes a brief description of the structure's role in healthy functioning, how trauma may alter its activity or connectivity, and a real-world example to illustrate its effects in daily life. Use this glossary from both a scientific and compassionate lens: as a way to see trauma symptoms not as personal failures but as adaptive brain-body responses that can be reshaped through awareness, skill, and connection.

| Brain Region/ Network | Role | Trauma Impact | Example |
|---|---|---|---|
| **Amygdala** | Detects threat, supports fear learning, and drives arousal. | Tends to be hyperreactive and more tightly linked to salience networks, amplifying startle responses and "alarm" signals. | A shopper hears a cart bang and their heart jumps; they scan for exits before realizing it's harmless. |
| **Anterior Cingulate Cortex (ACC)** | Engages in conflict monitoring, error detection, and emotion regulation. | Dorsal ACC overmonitors for threat, while the rostral/ ventral ACC is less effective at downregulating distress. | During a tense meeting, tiny noises feel painfully salient, and it's hard to stay on task. |
| **Central Executive/ Frontoparietal Network** | Supports working memory, attentional control, and goal-directed behavior. | Communicates less effectively with the DMN and salience networks under stress, reducing cognitive control when it's needed most. | You're trying to complete a form at the doctor's office, but your mind keeps slipping back to a recent trigger. |
| **Cerebellum** | Coordinates timing, prediction, cognitive-emotional balance, and autonomic tuning. | Smaller cerebellar volume among those with PTSD affects coordination, emotion, and cognition. | Under stress, your speech, emotion, and posture feel jerky or "out of sync." |
| **Default Mode Network (DMN)** | Handles self-referential processing, autobiographical memory, and narrative integration. | Altered connectivity and reductions in DMN strength can lead to rumination, dissociation, and intrusive recall. | You drift into a trauma scene while doing a routine task, losing track of time and your surroundings. |
| **Hippocampo-Prefrontal-Amygdala Circuit** | Updates threat memories and facilitates safety learning. | Disrupted signaling makes it difficult to update conditioned fear patterns. | Despite many safe fireworks shows, your body still "predicts" danger on July 4. |

| Brain Region/ Network | Role | Trauma Impact | Example |
|---|---|---|---|
| **Hippocampus** | Supports contextual memory, sequences events, and distinguishes "then" from "now." | Often shows reduced volume and altered function, contributing to fragmented, intrusive memories and context misattribution. | The smell of diesel on a calm street evokes a vivid scene from a convoy years ago. |
| **Insula** | Tracks internal bodily states and engages in salience mapping. | Often hyperconnected with the amygdala and ACC, making bodily sensations feel intense, ambiguous, or alarming. | A flutter of gastrointestinal discomfort spirals into "Something is wrong with me." |
| **Locus Coeruleus** | Primary norepinephrine source that regulates arousal, vigilance, and stress reactivity. | Often overactive in PTSD, leading to hypervigilance and sleep disruption. | Even mild noises at night jolt you fully awake, heart racing. |
| **Medial Prefrontal Cortex** | Regulates limbic responses to support threat appraisal and safety learning (extinction). | Underactivity and disrupted connectivity with limbic system impair your ability to pump the "brake" on threat responses. | Even though you logically know that fireworks are scheduled, your body still lurches because the "brake" doesn't engage fast enough. |
| **Periaqueductal Gray** | Coordinates defensive responses (fight, flight, freeze, and collapse) and modulates pain. | Altered connectivity after trauma is tied to sustained threat states and immobility reactions. | Upon hearing angry shouting nearby, your body locks and your breathing becomes shallow. |
| **Salience Network** | Flags biologically relevant cues and shifts resources between the DMN and central executive network. | Becomes biased toward threat, quickly pulling attention to reminders of the trauma. | A door slams, and your attention is pulled away from a conversation and instantly snaps into scanning mode. |
| **Thalamo-Cortical Visual Circuits** | Handles basic visual processing and orientation. | Trauma exposure heightens reactivity to simple visual stimuli, priming hyperorientation to movement. | Someone rushes past you in your peripheral motion, triggering a disproportionate jolt of alarm. |
| **Thalamus** | Relays sensory information and filters input to the cortex. | Changes in nuclei volume after trauma make sensory filters feel "too open." | Motion in a crowd feels overwhelming, as if too much sensory input is getting through at once. |
| **Ventral Striatum** | Supports motivation, pleasure, and reward anticipation. | Reduced reactivity can contribute to anhedonia and difficulty initiating tasks. | Hobbies that once felt satisfying now feel flat; it's hard to get going. |

## Trauma-Focused Outcome Measures

This table includes a selection of trauma-focused outcome measures that may be used to assess symptom severity, monitor progress, and evaluate treatment effectiveness. Consistent with evidence-based practice, clinicians are encouraged to collect and use outcome data to inform clinical decision-making, guide treatment planning, and evaluate the impact of interventions over time. Routine measurement supports accountability, enhances precision in care, and strengthens the overall quality of treatment.

| Category | Measure | Description |
|---|---|---|
| **PTSD and Complex Trauma (C-PTSD)** | PTSD Checklist for *DSM-5* (PCL-5; Weathers et al., 2013) | • 20-item self-report; measures *DSM-5* PTSD symptoms.<br>• Free, brief, widely validated. |
| | Clinician-Administered PTSD Scale (CAPS-5; Weathers et al., 2018) | • Structured interview for C-PTSD.<br>• Requires training; allows for diagnostic depth. |
| | International Trauma Questionnaire (ITQ; Cloitre et al., 2018) | • Measures PTSD and C-PTSD per ICD-11.<br>• Well suited for clients with developmental or chronic trauma. |
| | Structured Interview for Disorders of Extreme Stress (SIDES; Pelcovitz et al., 1997) | • Evaluates features of C-PTSD (e.g., affect, somatic, dissociation).<br>• Used clinically and in research on complex trauma. |
| **Dissociation and Complex Symptomatology** | Dissociative Experiences Scale-II (DES-II; Carlson & Putnam, 1993) | • 28-item scale for measuring dissociative symptoms.<br>• Free and widely validated. |
| **Emotional Dysregulation and DBT Skill Tracking** | Difficulties in Emotion Regulation Scale (DERS; Gratz & Roemer, 2004) | • Assesses six facets of emotional dysregulation (e.g., nonacceptance, clarity, impulse control).<br>• Strong psychometric properties.<br>• Recommended for DBT-informed care. |
| | Emotion Regulation Skills Questionnaire (ERSQ; Grant et al., 2018) | • Tracks DBT-style skill acquisition (e.g., acceptance, modulation, understanding of emotion).<br>• Designed for treatment outcome monitoring in DBT and related therapies. |
| **Functioning and Life Impact** | World Health Organization Disability Assessment Schedule (WHO-DAS 2.0; Üstün et al., 2010) | • Measures functioning across six domains: cognition, mobility, self-care, etc.<br>• Recommended by *DSM-5* as a global functioning indicator. |
| | Recovery Assessment Scale—Revised (RAS-R; Corrigan et al., 2004) | • Measures hope, empowerment, life goals, and recovery orientation.<br>• Excellent for tracking subjective recovery. |

| Category | Measure | Description |
|---|---|---|
| **Attachment, Interpersonal, and Relational Health** | Experiences in Close Relationships—Revised (ECR-R; Fraley et al., 2000) | • Assesses adult attachment patterns (anxiety/avoidance).<br>• Useful in DTRM phase 3 for relational healing. |
| | Inventory of Interpersonal Problems (IIP-32; Barkham et al., 1996) | • Identifies patterns in interpersonal conflict and difficulty. |
| **Alliance and Client-Perceived Progress** | Session Rating Scale (SRS; Duncan et al., 2003) | • 4-item visual analog scale completed at the end of each session.<br>• Measures therapeutic alliance across four domains: relationship, goals, approach, and overall.<br>• Prevents dropout and enhances alliance. |
| | Outcome Rating Scale (ORS; Duncan et al., 2004; Miller et al., 2003) | • 4-item visual analog scale completed at the beginning of each session.<br>• Measures individual, relational, social, and overall well-being.<br>• Excellent for tracking weekly outcomes and guiding care.<br>• Supported by research and widely adopted in feedback-informed treatment (FIT) models. |

Handout

# DTRM Group Expectations

To create a safe, respectful, and effective treatment environment, all clients participating in DTRM in a group format are expected to follow these guidelines:

- **Be willing to engage.** Actively participate in your recovery. Come prepared, ask questions, contribute to discussions, and complete skills practice, the RISE Worksheet, the Diary Card, and Behavior and Solution Analysis. Follow recommendations and collaborate with peers and therapists.
- **Attend consistently.** We expect 100 percent attendance at group. If you need to miss a session, speak with your therapist beforehand. Attendance below 90 percent will result in an attendance contract. Continued absences may lead to discharge.
- **Keep things confidential.** What's shared in the program stays in the program. Respect the privacy of your peers. Breaking confidentiality will result in discharge.
- **Limit level of detail.** This program does *not* involve reliving or detailing traumatic events. Instead, you're encouraged to share general symptoms or triggers. For example, it's appropriate to say, "I'm having intrusive thoughts about being abused," but not to describe the abuse in detail. This helps keep everyone safe and focused on skills.
- **Show respect for all.** Treat your peers and therapists with respect. This includes using kind language, listening actively, and contributing to a safe and inclusive environment.
- **Take medication as prescribed.** If you're on medication, take it as directed. Misuse or sharing of medications will result in discharge from the program.
- **No self-injury or substance use on premises.** Group must be a safe space. Engaging in self-injury or using alcohol or drugs during sessions or on-site will result in discharge.
- **Address substance use.** If you're using substances, this will be addressed through Behavior and Solution Analysis and treatment goals. If substance use is primary, you may be referred to chemical health treatment.
- **Report progress and concerns.** Let us know about any changes in your mental health, medication side effects, or concerns about your treatment. This helps us tailor your care.
- **Plan for discharge.** As you near the end of the program, we'll help you prepare for the next steps that might include connecting you with mental health, substance use, and community resources to support your continued recovery.

Thank you for following these expectations. They exist to create the kind of environment where real healing is possible for you and for everyone else in the room.

Handout

# How to Use Skills Coaching

Skills coaching is a focused, problem-solving approach that helps you apply skills between sessions when difficult situations arise. The goal is to support you in using skills in real time to stay on track with your treatment. These guidelines explain what skills coaching is, what it isn't, and how to use it effectively:

- **Therapist availability:** Coaching depends on your therapist's availability, which may vary depending on their schedule and other responsibilities. Your therapist will make every effort to offer predictable coaching times.
- **Understand and follow boundaries:** You must be familiar with and respect your therapist's boundaries for skills coaching.
- **Brief sessions:** Coaching is brief and to the point, typically lasting no more than five minutes.
- **Prebehavior coaching only:** You must reach out for coaching *before* engaging in a problem behavior, not after.
- **Post–problem behavior rule:** Skills coaching cannot be used within twelve hours of a problem behavior. Before coaching can resume, you must complete a Behavior and Solution Analysis for that behavior.
- **Scheduled coaching:** Coaching may be scheduled ahead of time, especially if you know a challenging situation is coming up.
- **Focus on problem-solving:** Coaching is not a therapy session. It is not for venting, socializing, or discussing problems in general. The focus is on applying specific skills to solve a specific problem.

**Remember:** Skills coaching is most effective when used *proactively*, not reactively. The goal is to support skill use in the moment, helping you avoid behaviors that interfere with your recovery. Let your therapist know if you have questions about using skills coaching.

Worksheet

# Skills Coaching

This worksheet clarifies coaching expectations and highlights your coaching needs. To maximize the effectiveness of coaching, first read through the following the expectations, then use the prompts to reflect on your current challenges and plan your skill use.

**Coaching expectations:**

- I will focus on skill use. I understand that coaching is not a therapy session, is not focused on venting, and is not for socialization.
- I agree to seek coaching before I act on a problem behavior and that coaching is not available immediately following a problem behavior.
- I will respect time limitations (e.g., from the therapist or the environment) and other boundaries set by my therapist.
- I'm willing to be coached and practice the suggested skills.

Describe your problem or difficulty.

____________________________________________________________

____________________________________________________________

Describe the skills you have tried.

____________________________________________________________

____________________________________________________________

Brainstorm what skills might be useful to try.

____________________________________________________________

____________________________________________________________

Describe what skills or supports you can use if your therapist is not immediately available.

____________________________________________________________

____________________________________________________________

Worksheet

# Behavior and Solution Analysis: Short Form

Name: ____________________ Date: __________

This worksheet will help you avoid your problem behavior and meet your wants and needs effectively with skills.

What was the problem behavior? Be specific.

______________________________

______________________________

What led to the problem behavior? Give specifics of what made you vulnerable and other factors (e.g., emotions, thoughts, behaviors, sensations, situations) that came before the problem behavior.

______________________________

______________________________

What did you gain or expect to gain by making the choice you did? How did you think it might help or benefit you?

______________________________

______________________________

What were the negative consequences of your problem behavior for you and others?

______________________________

______________________________

What skills can you use to meet your wants and needs effectively next time (in the short term and long term)?

| **Short-term plan:** | **Long-term plan:** |
| --- | --- |
| ______________ | ______________ |
| ______________ | ______________ |
| ______________ | ______________ |

Worksheet

# Behavior and Solution Analysis: Long Form

Name:________________________________________ Date:________________

This worksheet will help you avoid your problem behavior and meet your wants and needs effectively with skills.

## Step 1: Describe the Problem Behavior

What did you do?

____________________________________________________________

____________________________________________________________

How did you do it?

____________________________________________________________

____________________________________________________________

Where did you do it?

____________________________________________________________

____________________________________________________________

When did you do it?

____________________________________________________________

____________________________________________________________

Who else was involved?

____________________________________________________________

____________________________________________________________

List skills to use at this step.

____________________________________________________________

____________________________________________________________

### Step 2: Identify What Was Happening Before the Problem Behavior

What event set off the problem behavior?

______________________________________________

______________________________________________

What were the events leading up to the event that set off the problem behavior?

______________________________________________

______________________________________________

Which of the events leading up to the problem behavior were the most important?

______________________________________________

______________________________________________

What were you feeling prior to and during the problem behavior?

______________________________________________

______________________________________________

What were you thinking prior to and during the problem behavior?

______________________________________________

______________________________________________

What wants or needs were you trying to meet with the problem behavior?

______________________________________________

______________________________________________

At what point did you decide to engage in the problem behavior?

______________________________________________

______________________________________________

List skills to use at this step.

______________________________________________

______________________________________________

## Step 3: Identify the Consequences of the Problem Behavior

How have you benefited from the problem behavior (in the short term and long term)?

______________________________________________

______________________________________________

How have you and others been hurt by the problem behavior (in the short term and long term)?

______________________________________________

______________________________________________

Following the problem behavior, what changes happened with:

Your emotions: ______________________________________________

______________________________________________

Your thoughts: ______________________________________________

______________________________________________

Your physical sensations: ______________________________________________

______________________________________________

Your behaviors: ______________________________________________

______________________________________________

The events around you: ______________________________________________

______________________________________________

The way others treat you: ______________________________________________

List skills to use at this step.

______________________________________________

______________________________________________

 

## Step 4: Review and Summary of Steps 1–3

What DBT skills could you use next time when similar events take place?

______________________________________________________________________________

______________________________________________________________________________

What is the earliest point at which you could use skills?

______________________________________________________________________________

______________________________________________________________________________

What consequences (or potential consequences) to the problem behavior will help you control or avoid that behavior in the future?

______________________________________________________________________________

______________________________________________________________________________

How can you remove access (i.e., burn the bridge) to the problem behavior?

______________________________________________________________________________

______________________________________________________________________________

What can you do to get your wants or needs met effectively that will not hurt you, others, or your treatment?

______________________________________________________________________________

______________________________________________________________________________

## Step 5: List Additional Feedback From Your Therapist or Group

______________________________________________________________________________

______________________________________________________________________________

______________________________________________________________________________

______________________________________________________________________________

 

Handout

# Body-Based Opposite Action Skills: A Guide to Bottom-Up Practices That Restore Regulation

These body-based practices shift emotional states by regulating the nervous system directly. Each technique works through the Body-Based System, using posture, breath, movement, and sensory awareness to interrupt survival responses and support grounded presence. The following are definitions of some core interventions used in this teaching.

## Safe Posture Practice

Adopt an upright, open posture that gently lifts the chest, lengthens the spine, and relaxes the shoulders. This stance signals safety to the nervous system and counters fear- or shame-based collapse.

## Slow, Deep Exhale Breathing

Pace your breathing by emphasizing longer exhales than inhales. Longer exhales stimulate the parasympathetic nervous system and reduce arousal.

## Grounded Stance

Stand with your feet firmly planted, your knees relaxed, and your weight evenly distributed. This stabilizes the body and promotes a sense of physical security.

## Gentle Orienting

Slowly turn your head and look around the environment without urgency. This signals to your nervous system to exit hypervigilance, engaging the social engagement system and confirming present safety.

## Relaxed Jaw and Tongue Release

Soften your jaw, unclench your teeth, and rest your tongue on the floor of your mouth. This reduces sympathetic activation and eases tension throughout the face and neck.

## Eye Gaze Softening or Widening

Soften your eye focus or gently widen your peripheral vision. This moves the nervous system out of threat mode (narrowed attention) toward relaxed awareness.

### Grounding Touch

Place a hand on your chest, abdomen, or another comforting area. This offers a calming anchor through warmth, pressure, and steady contact.

### Steady, Balanced Walking

Walk at a comfortable, consistent pace to discharge activation or increase engagement. Movement regulates both hyperarousal and shutdown. For added sensory benefits, take it outdoors.

### Cooling-Based Reset

Use cool water, fresh air, or a cold compress to shift your physiological state. Cooling activates the dive reflex and reduces sympathetic arousal.

### Power-Down Movement

Intentionally slow down your gestures, walking speed, and muscle contractions. This interrupts anxious urgency or anger-driven momentum.

### Full-Body Stretch

Lengthen your muscles through gentle stretching to expand your posture, increase circulation, and counter collapse or tension.

### Warmth-Based Soothing

Apply warmth through blankets, baths, warm beverages, or heating pads to promote comfort and signal safety to the body.

### Gentle Movement (Yoga, Stretching, Tai Chi)

Engage in slow, mindful movement practices that integrate breath and body awareness, building grounding and reducing tension.

### Rhythmic Walking or Movement

Engage in repetitive, predictable movement (like walking, swaying, or rocking) that supports regulation through rhythmic input to the nervous system.

### Bilateral Movement or Tapping

Alternate left-right movements or tapping to support grounding and reengagement when dissociation or shutdown appears.

 

### Rhythmic Rocking or Swaying

Use gentle forward-back or side-to-side motion that provides vestibular soothing and helps shift out of freeze or collapse.

### Voice Modulation

Intentionally lower your volume or soften the tone of your voice. Calmer vocalizations cue the body away from fight responses.

### Nervous System Reset ("Shake It Out")

Briefly shake your arms, legs, or whole body to release accumulated tension or mobilize energy during shutdown states.

### Sensory Grounding

Use sight, sound, touch, smell, and taste to anchor your attention in the present. This supports reconnection when dissociation or numbness is present.

### Expansion Instead of Contraction

Open your chest and lengthen your spine, allowing your shoulders to roll back instead of inward. This expansive posture counters nervous system collapse and increases your capacity for engagement.

### Temperature Shift

Intentionally introduce a change in temperature—for example, by splashing cool water on your face or holding a warm wrap—to disrupt autonomic arousal and move into a more balanced state.

### Willing Hands

Rest your hands open on your lap or at your sides rather than holding them clenched or tense. This posture signals safety to your nervous system and reduces limbic reactivity.

### Half-Smile

Soften your facial muscles into a gentle, accepting expression by gently lifting the corners of your mouth. This subtle movement reduces sympathetic arousal and shifts your body into a more open and connected state.

# Bibliography

For your convenience, purchasers can download and print selected resources from this book at **pesipubs.com/integrativeDBT**


American Psychiatric Association. (2022). *Diagnostic and statistical manual of mental disorders* (5th ed., text rev.). https://doi.org/10.1176/appi.books.9780890425787

American Psychological Association. (2006). Evidence-based practice in psychology. *American Psychologist, 61*(4), 271–285. https://doi.org/10.1037/0003-066X.61.4.271

Barkham, M., Hardy, G. E., & Startup, M. (1996). The IIP-32: A short version of the Inventory of Interpersonal Problems. *British Journal of Clinical Psychology, 35*(1), 21–35. https://doi.org/10.1111/j.2044-8260.1996.tb01159.x

Batten, S. V., & Hayes, S. C. (2005). Acceptance and commitment therapy in the treatment of comorbid substance abuse and post-traumatic stress disorder: A case study. *Clinical Case Studies, 4*(3), 246–262. https://doi.org/10.1177/1534650103259689

Blechert, J., Michael, T., Grossman, P., Lajtman, M., & Wilhelm, F. H. (2007). Autonomic and respiratory characteristics of posttraumatic stress disorder and panic disorder. *Psychosomatic Medicine, 69*(9), 935–943. https://doi.org/10.1097/PSY.0b013e31815a8f6b

Bowen, S., Chawla, N., Collins, S. E., Witkiewitz, K., Hsu, S., Grow, J., Clifasefi, S., Garner, M., Douglass, A., Larimer, M. E., & Marlatt, A. (2009). Mindfulness-based relapse prevention for substance use disorders: A pilot efficacy trial. *Substance Use & Addiction Journal, 30*(4), 294–305. https://doi.org/10.1080/08897070903250084

Bowlby, J. (1988). *A secure base: Parent-child attachment and healthy human development.* Basic Books.

Brewin, C. R., Gregory, J. D., Lipton, M., & Burgess, N. (2010). Intrusive images in psychological disorders: Characteristics, neural mechanisms, and treatment implications. *Psychological Review, 117*(1), 210–232. https://doi.org/10.1037/a0018113

Carlson, E. B., & Putnam, F. W. (1993). An update on the Dissociative Experiences Scale. *Dissociation: Progress in the Dissociative Disorders, 6*(1), 16–27.

Chappelle, W., Goodman, T., Reardon, L., & Prince, L. (2019). Combat and operational risk factors for post-traumatic stress disorder symptom criteria among United States air force remotely piloted aircraft "Drone" warfighters. *Journal of Anxiety Disorders, 62,* 86–93. https://doi.org/10.1016/j.janxdis.2019.01.003

Classen, C. C., Butler, L. D., Koopman, C., Miller, D., DiMiceli, S., GieseDavis, J., Fobair, P., Carlson, R. W., Kraemer, H. C., & Spiegel, D. (2011). Supportive-expressive group therapy and distress in patients with metastatic breast cancer: A randomized clinical intervention trial. *Archives of General Psychiatry, 58*(5), 494–501. https://doi.org/10.1001/archpsyc.58.5.494

Cloitre, M., Courtois, C. A., Charuvastra, A., Carapezza, R., Stolbach, B. C., & Green, B. L. (2011). Treatment of complex PTSD: Results of the ISTSS expert clinician survey on best practices. *Journal of Traumatic Stress, 24*(6), 615–627. https://doi.org/10.1002/jts.20697

Cloitre, M., Shevlin, M., Brewin, C. R., Bisson, J. I., Roberts, N. P., Maercker, A., Karatzias, T., & Hyland, P. (2018). The International Trauma Questionnaire: Development of a self-report measure of ICD-11 PTSD and complex PTSD. *Acta Psychiatrica Scandinavica, 138*(6), 536–546. https://doi.org/10.1111/acps.12956

Corrigan, P. W., Salzer, M., Ralph, R. O., Sangster, Y., & Keck, L. (2004). Examining the factor structure of the Recovery Assessment Scale. *Schizophrenia Bulletin, 30*(4), 1035–1041. https://doi.org/10.1093/oxfordjournals.schbul.a007118

Courtois, C. A., & Ford, J. D. (Eds.). (2009). *Treating complex traumatic stress disorders: An evidence-based guide*. Guilford Press.

Dana, D. (2018). *The polyvagal theory in therapy: Engaging the rhythm of regulation*. W. W. Norton.

Dorahy, M. J., Brand, B. L., Şar, V., Krüger, C., Stavropoulos, P., Martínez-Taboas, A., Lewis-Fernández, R., & Middleton, W. (2014). Dissociative identity disorder: An empirical overview. *Australian & New Zealand Journal of Psychiatry, 48*(5), 402–417. https://doi.org/10.1177/0004867414527523

Duncan, B. L., Miller, S. D., & Sparks, J. A. (2004). *The heroic client: A revolutionary way to improve effectiveness through client-directed, outcome-informed therapy* (2nd ed.). Jossey-Bass.

Duncan, B. L., Miller, S. D., Sparks, J. A., Claud, D. A., Reynolds, L. R., Brown, J., & Johnson, L. D. (2003). The Session Rating Scale: Preliminary psychometric properties of a "working alliance" measure. *Journal of Brief Therapy, 3*(1), 3–12.

Duncan, B. L., Solovey, A. D., & Rusk, G. S. (1992). *Changing the rules: A client-directed approach to therapy*. Guilford Press.

Ehlers, A., & Clark, D. M. (2000). A cognitive model of posttraumatic stress disorder. *Behaviour Research and Therapy, 38*(4), 319–345. https://doi.org/10.1016/S0005-7967(99)00123-0

Felitti, V. J., Anda, R. F., Nordenberg, D., Williamson, D. F., Spitz, A. M., Edwards, V., Koss, M. P., & Marks, J. S. (1998). Relationship of childhood abuse and household dysfunction to many of the leading causes of death in adults: The Adverse Childhood Experiences (ACE) Study. *American Journal of Preventive Medicine, 14*(4), 245–258. https://doi.org/10.1016/S0749-3797(98)00017-8

Fisher, J. (2017). *Healing the fragmented selves of trauma survivors: Overcoming internal self-alienation*. Routledge.

Foa, E. B., Gillihan, S. J., & Bryant, R. A. (2016). Challenges and successes in dissemination of evidence-based treatments for posttraumatic stress: Lessons learned from prolonged exposure therapy for PTSD. *Psychological Science in the Public Interest, 14*(2), 65–111. https://doi.org/10.1177/1529100612468841

Ford, J. D., Chang, R., Levine, J., & Zhang, W. (2013). Randomized clinical trial comparing affect regulation and supportive group therapies for victimization-related PTSD with incarcerated women. *Behavior Therapy, 44*(2), 262–276. https://doi.org/10.1016/j.beth.2012.10.003

Ford, J. D., & Courtois, C. A. (Eds.). (2020). *Treating complex traumatic stress disorders in adults: Scientific foundations and therapeutic models* (2nd ed.). Guilford Press.

Ford, J. D., Courtois, C. A., Steele, K., Van der Hart, O., & Nijenhuis, E. R. (2005). Treatment of complex posttraumatic self-dysregulation. *Journal of Traumatic Stress, 18*(5), 437–447. https://doi.org/10.1002/jts.20051

Fraley, R. C., Waller, N. G., & Brennan, K. A. (2000). An item-response theory analysis of self-report measures of adult attachment. *Journal of Personality and Social Psychology, 78*(2), 350–365. https://doi.org/10.1037/0022-3514.78.2.350

Grant, M., Salsman, N. L., & Berking, M. (2018). *Emotion Regulation Skills Questionnaire (ERSQ, SEK-27)* [Database record]. APA PsycTests. https://doi.org/10.1037/t70998-000

Gratz, K. L., & Roemer, L. (2004). Multidimensional assessment of emotion regulation and dysregulation: Development, factor structure, and initial validation of the Difficulties in Emotion Regulation Scale. *Journal of Psychopathology and Behavioral Assessment, 26*(1), 41–54. https://doi.org/10.1023/B:JOBA.0000007455.08539.94

Harned, M. S., Korslund, K. E., & Linehan, M. M. (2012). A pilot randomized controlled trial of DBT with and without the DBT prolonged exposure protocol for suicidal and self-injuring women with borderline personality disorder and PTSD. *Behaviour Research and Therapy, 50*(7–8), 381–386. https://doi.org/10.1016/j.brat.2014.01.008

Herman, J. L. (1992). *Trauma and recovery: The aftermath of violence—From domestic abuse to political terror*. Basic Books.

International Society for the Study of Trauma and Dissociation. (2011). Guidelines for treating dissociative identity disorder in adults (3rd rev.). *Journal of Trauma & Dissociation*, *12*(2), 115–187. http://dx.doi.org/10.1080/15299732.2011.537247

Janoff-Bulman, R. (1992). *Shattered assumptions: Towards a new psychology of trauma*. Free Press.

Lanius, R. A., Frewen, P. A., Vermetten, E., & Yehuda, R. (2020). *Restoring large-scale brain networks in PTSD and related disorders: A neurobiological framework for treatment*. Cambridge University Press.

Levine, P. A. (1997). *Waking the tiger: Healing trauma—The innate capacity to transform overwhelming experiences*. North Atlantic Books.

Linehan, M. M. (1993a). *Cognitive-behavioral treatment of borderline personality disorder*. Guilford Press.

Linehan, M. M. (1993b). *Skills training manual for treating borderline personality disorder*. Guilford Press.

Linehan, M. M. (2015). *DBT skills training manual* (2nd ed.). Guilford Press.

Mehling, W. E., Price, C., Daubenmier, J. J., Acree, M., Bartmess, E., & Stewart, A. (2011). The Multidimensional Assessment of Interoceptive Awareness (MAIA). *PLOS ONE*, *7*(11), e48230. https://doi.org/10.1371/journal.pone.0048230

Miller, S. D., Duncan, B. L., Brown, J., Sparks, J. A., & Claud, D. A. (2003). The Outcome Rating Scale: A preliminary study of the reliability, validity, and feasibility of a brief visual analog measure. *Journal of Brief Therapy*, *5*(1), 5–16.

Najavits, L. M. (2002). *Seeking safety: A treatment manual for PTSD and substance abuse*. Guilford Press.

Neacsiu, A. D., Rizvi, S. L., & Linehan, M. M. (2010). Dialectical behavior therapy skills use as a mediator and outcome of treatment for borderline personality disorder. *Behaviour Research and Therapy*, *48*(9), 832–839. https://doi.org/10.1016/j.brat.2010.05.017

Norcross, J. C., & Goldfried, M. R. (Eds.). (2005). *Handbook of psychotherapy integration* (2nd ed.). Oxford University Press. https://doi.org/10.1093/med:psych/9780195165791.001.0001

Ogden, P., & Fisher, J. (2015). *Sensorimotor psychotherapy: Interventions for trauma and attachment*. W. W. Norton.

Payne, P., Levine, P. A., & Crane-Godreau, M. A. (2015). Somatic experiencing: Using interoception and proprioception as core elements of trauma therapy. *Frontiers in Psychology*, *6*, 93. https://doi.org/10.3389/fpsyg.2015.00093

Pearlman, L. A., & Saakvitne, K. W. (1995). *Trauma and the therapist: Countertransference and vicarious traumatization in psychotherapy with incest survivors*. W. W. Norton.

Pederson, L. D. (2015). *Dialectical behavior therapy: A contemporary guide for practitioners*. Wiley-Blackwell.

Pelcovitz, D., van der Kolk, B. A., Roth, S., Mandel, F., Kaplan, S., & Resick, P. (1997). Development of a criteria set and a structured interview for disorders of extreme stress (SIDES). *Journal of Traumatic Stress*, *10*(1), 3–16. https://doi.org/10.1002/jts.2490100103

Perry, B. D., & Szalavitz, M. (2017). *The boy who was raised as a dog: And other stories from a child psychiatrist's notebook—What traumatized children can teach us about loss, love, and healing* (3rd ed.). Basic Books.

Porges, S. W. (2011). *The polyvagal theory: Neurophysiological foundations of emotions, attachment, communication, and self-regulation*. W. W. Norton.

Porges, S. W. (2017). *The pocket guide to the polyvagal theory: The transformative power of feeling safe*. W. W. Norton.

Price, C. J., & Hooven, C. (2018). Interoceptive awareness skills for emotion regulation: Theory and approach of mindful awareness in body-oriented therapy (MABT). *Frontiers in Psychology*, *9*, 798. https://doi.org/10.3389/fpsyg.2018.00798

Rosenthal, M. Z., Gratz, K. L., Kosson, D. S., Cheavens, J. S., Lejuez, C. W., & Lynch, T. R. (2008). Borderline personality disorder and emotional responding: A review of the research literature. *Clinical Psychology Review*, *28*(1), 75–91. https://doi.org/10.1016/j.cpr.2007.04.001

Saakvitne, K. W., Gamble, S. J., Pearlman, L. A., & Lev, B. T. (2011). *Risking connection: A training curriculum for working with survivors of childhood abuse*. Sidran Institute.

Schnurr, P. P., Friedman, M. J., Engel, C. C., Foa, E. B., Shea, M. T., Chow, B. K., Resick, P. A., Thurston, V., Orsillo, S. M., Haug, R., Turner, C., & Bernardy, N. C. (2003). Cognitive behavioral therapy for posttraumatic stress disorder in women: A randomized controlled trial. *JAMA, 297*(8), 820–830. https://doi.org/10.1001/jama.297.8.820

Schore, A. N. (2001). The effects of early relational trauma on right brain development, affect regulation, and infant mental health. *Infant Mental Health Journal, 22*(1–2), 201–269. https://doi.org/10.1002/1097-0355(200101/04)22:1<201::AID-IMHJ8>3.0.CO;2-9

Schwartz, R. C. (2001). *Internal family systems therapy*. Guilford Press.

Shapiro, F. (2001). *Eye movement desensitization and reprocessing: Basic principles, protocols, and procedures* (2nd ed.). Guilford Press.

Shin, L. M., Rauch, S. L., & Pitman, R. K. (2006). Amygdala, medial prefrontal cortex, and hippocampal function in PTSD. *Annals of the New York Academy of Sciences, 1071*(1), 67–79. https://doi.org/10.1196/annals.1364.007

Siegel, D. J. (2007). *The mindful brain: Reflection and attunement in the cultivation of well-being*. W. W. Norton.

Steele, K., Boon, S., & van der Hart, O. (2017). *Treating trauma-related dissociation: A practical, integrative approach*. W. W. Norton.

Tronick, E. (2007). *The neurobehavioral and social-emotional development of infants and children*. W. W. Norton.

Üstün, T. B., Kostanjsek, N., Chatterji, S., & Rehm, J. (Eds.). (2010). *Measuring health and disability: Manual for WHO Disability Assessment Schedule (WHODAS 2.0)*. World Health Organization. https://iris.who.int/server/api/core/bitstreams/13c8676c-bdd5-41e9-beae-30343a96d4f0/content

Valentine, S. E., Bankoff, S. M., Poulin, R. M., Reidler, E. B., & Pantalone, D. W. (2015). The use of dialectical behavior therapy skills training as standalone treatment: A systematic review of the treatment outcome literature. *Journal of Clinical Psychology, 71*(1), 1–20. https://doi.org/10.1002/jclp.22114

van der Kolk, B. A. (2014). *The body keeps the score: Brain, mind, and body in the healing of trauma*. Viking.

van der Kolk, B. A., Roth, S., Pelcovitz, D., Sunday, S., & Spinazzola, J. (2005). Disorders of extreme stress: The empirical foundation of a complex adaptation to trauma. *Journal of Traumatic Stress, 18*(5), 389–399. https://doi.org/10.1002/jts.20047

Wagner, A. W., Rizvi, S. L., & Harned, M. S. (2007). Applications of dialectical behavior therapy to posttraumatic stress disorder and related problems. In M. J. Friedman, T. M. Keane, & P. A. Resick (Eds.), *Handbook of PTSD: Science and practice* (pp. 428–446). Guilford Press.

Wampold, B. E. (2010). The research evidence for the common factors model: A historically situated perspective. In B. L. Duncan, S. D. Miller, B. E. Wampold, & M. A. Hubble (Eds.), *The heart and soul of change: Delivering what works* (2nd ed., pp. 49–81). American Psychological Association.

Weathers, F. W., Blake, D. D., Schnurr, P. P., Kaloupek, D. G., Marx, B. P., & Keane, T. M. (2018). *The Clinician-Administered PTSD Scale for DSM-5 (CAPS-5)*. National Center for PTSD. https://www.ptsd.va.gov/professional/assessment/adult-int/caps.asp

Weathers, F. W., Litz, B. T., Keane, T. M., Palmieri, P. A., Marx, B. P., & Schnurr, P. P. (2013). *The PTSD Checklist for DSM-5 (PCL-5)*. National Center for PTSD. https://www.ptsd.va.gov/professional/assessment/adult-sr/ptsd-checklist.asp

# Acknowledgments

A project of this size and depth may look like the work of one person, but this manual stands on the shoulders of a community of colleagues, collaborators, friends, and family. I am deeply grateful for every person who helped bring DTRM to life.

My publishing team, Kate Sample and Kayla Church, kept this project moving with steady support. After reviewing an early draft, Kayla and my editor Jenessa Jackson saw that the work could grow well beyond a trauma-focused DBT skills curriculum. Their invitation to think more broadly, and their belief in the model's potential, set DTRM on the path to becoming a comprehensive clinical orientation.

My deepest thanks go to Jenessa, whose insight, clarity, and editorial craftsmanship elevated every chapter. She has the rare ability to preserve the heart of an idea while refining its form, and her developmental edits, structural guidance, thoughtful questions, and meticulous attention to detail consistently sharpened both the writing and the model itself. Jenessa could see the emerging shape of DTRM before I fully articulated it, and her partnership was pivotal in bringing this manual to its final form.

I am also grateful to Carrie Broadwell-Tkach for her careful editorial work. In addition to precise copyediting, she offered thoughtful developmental suggestions that strengthened clarity, organization, and flow throughout the manuscript, meaningfully improving it.

I am endlessly grateful to the entire PESI team, from publishing to training, for their support, professionalism, and good humor. Jon Olstad, my business manager, and the many people behind the scenes who coordinate logistics, marketing, and trainings have not only promoted my work but made the journey enjoyable. Traveling and teaching with the PESI crew blends hard work with camaraderie, inside jokes, and the kind of laughter that turns long days into lasting memories.

My sincere appreciation goes to Tamera Klein, formerly of the Bureau of Prisons. Our collaboration on the BOP's DBT trauma manual years ago set me on the path that would eventually lead to DTRM. That early partnership planted the seed for this model long before I knew where it would lead, and I remain grateful for her vision and trust.

I also want to acknowledge Mike Connor and Mike Olson, whose leadership, partnership, and support across many years opened doors and created opportunities that allowed this work to grow.

At Mental Health Systems, Inc. (MHS), my business partner Mark Carlson has been in the trenches with me from the earliest days, designing programs, troubleshooting challenges, and building a shared vision for clinical excellence that has endured through the ebbs and flows of clinical practice.

Also, at MHS, I am beyond appreciative of our dedicated therapists, and especially our RISE team who put DTRM into action on the practice level. They validated that precise mapping and targeted skills improve the lives of those living with trauma.

To my family—Cortney, Sophie, and Sawyer—you are the heart of everything I do. Cortney has been a grounding force and an inspired sounding board, offering thoughtful feedback, perspective, and encouragement throughout the development of this model. Sophie and Sawyer bring joy, meaning, and pride to my life. And to our Dalmatian Yadi, who faithfully curled up under my desk through the long hours of writing: Your dogged loyalty was the quiet, steady presence every writer hopes for.

Finally, to the clients and seminar attendees who have shared their courage, struggles, and insights with me over the years: Thank you. You have shaped my understanding of trauma and healing more than any textbook ever could. Your resilience, honesty, and willingness to let me walk beside you are woven into every chapter. DTRM exists because of your stories and your strength.

Thank you to each of you who helped make this work possible. It has been an honor to learn from, collaborate with, and be supported by this remarkable community.